# Memories of a Ranch Wife

**By Lottie Evans Woods**

June 23, 2015

**Memories of a Ranch Wife © 2016**
**by Lottie Evans Woods**

First Print Edition
ISBN-13: 978-1530482795
ISBN-10: 1530482798

# TABLE OF CONTENTS

# Foreword

My mother, Lottie Evans Woods, is a remarkable woman. After having lived the first 88 years of her life on ranches, in 2005 she and my father, Blackie Woods, sold their ranch near Van Horn, Texas, and moved to a retirement home in Lubbock. Three weeks after that move, her husband of 69 years went to be with the Lord. She had given up her car and moved from the quietude of their beloved ranch to live in a busy, noisy city in an apartment that was perhaps one-fourth the size of the home she had lived in for some 28 years. She handled all of these changes with class and grace, and without complaint.

Although there were many activities available to residents of this retirement home, the only thing there that was of much interest to her was a small creative writing group that met there weekly. Each member of the group would write a short story each week, then would read his story aloud at the next meeting. Each time she wrote one of these short stories, I would type it for her on the computer. Since it was just a story for the writing group, she wrote about whatever came to mind that week that she thought would be of interest to her group. I am not sure at what point it was decided that this would become a book. It posed some organization and editing challenges because of the random order of the stories, but I am sure it will be of great interest to anyone who knew Lottie and Blackie, as well as readers who are interested in history.

—Judy Woods Roach

# Memories

*E V Ranch 1894*

**How do you record a lifetime of memories?** Why are some things remembered, while others, possibly equally important, are lost? I don't know, but here goes:

My childhood to adulthood was lived in a box canyon in the mountains. This was where my grandparents, George Wesley and Kate Isobel Means Evans, had settled and built their first house in 1886 after arriving in the Davis Mountains in 1884. This was where my father, Paul Means Evans, grew from birth to adulthood, and as the seventh son stayed to operate the ranch and care for his parents. This is where my parents, Paul Means and Susan Wertie Powell

Vans brought me, Lottie Virginia, after I was born in El Paso,Texas. Two years later, my sister, Frances Elaine, was born, and less than two more years my brother, Paul Means Evans Jr., so close in age that we were almost like triplets.

We lived in a plastered adobe house a short distance from my grandparents' home.  A creek ran down this canyon right in front of our home.  This canyon was the low point of the ranch.  You had to ride up a mountain to reach the pastures where the cattle grazed. This narrow box canyon was formed by a narrow canyon from the north watershed which lay between the mountain on the north and the mountain on the east.  This was Panther Canyon.  A smaller canyon lay between the mountain on the south and the mountain on the east.  We called it Right Hand.  These two canyons merged at the foot of the mountain on the east, making a "Y" shape, with the tail of the "Y" running in front of our house.

*E V Ranch*

To us this was just "The Creek."  It was dry most of the year, but when it rained on those watersheds, it became a raging torrent, sweeping away everything in its path—limbs, rocks, even trees.  No living animal caught in it could have survived.  You could hear the roar of it approaching as it swept rocks and gravel as it came. One time it washed a big rock the size of a car and deposited it in the middle of where our road crossed the creek. It was such a thrill when it rained to hear the grating roar of the water coming down the canyon.

A canyon bisecting the mountain on the north we called Short Canyon because its watershed arose just at the top of the mountain. When it ran we could see the water pouring off a waterfall near the top, visible from our house. They were comparatively short watersheds, so the creek never ran water for very long unless it continued to rain for several days. When it ran down to just pools of clear water, the little spiders and water bugs were there as if they had never been disturbed. How they survived that raging torrent, I don't know.

The sand and gravel would be washed clean and smooth. It made a great place to play in the shade under the walnut and desert willow trees. As children, we made our "ranches" on this nice clean sand. Thin rocks standing on edge outlined our pastures as fences. Small many-colored rocks or the little round walnuts were our cattle. Sometimes when the walnuts were in their green husks we used them and they would stain our hands brown. We smoothed roads in the sand with rocks shaped like cars. Flat rocks made our houses. I don't recall that we actually played with these ranches. Seems the construction of them was our main interest. We did keep improving and enlarging them.

When the Creek had run down to a gentle stream was our favorite time to play in it. Such fun to wade in the stream and paddle around in the pools of water! Farther up the canyon above our house there were lovely pools in solid rock. Once I remember we were playing in these pools, going farther and farther up the canyon. Then we saw Dad coming. He was very upset because he had been watching the clouds and it was raining on the north watershed—the canyon we were in. He was concerned for our safety. When a wall of water came down that canyon, it came very rapidly because of the degree of very steep fall. We could have been caught unaware and swept away to our deaths. From then on, we learned to watch the clouds.

Farther up Panther Canyon there were big cisterns that were always full of water. This area was called Dead Man, for a skeleton that was found there in early years. There were three waterfalls on this canyon below those cisterns. I could climb two of them, but one was too tall and steep. It didn't have many footholds. Believe me, I tried climbing it, but I could never get to the top. I had to climb around it. My youngest son, who grew to adulthood on this ranch, could climb that waterfall with the advantage of his six foot-plus height and young man's strength. He inherited my compulsion to always climb higher to reach the top. These cisterns at Dead Man were a great place to have a picnic or just swim and catch tadpoles. The water was warm to about a 6-inch depth; beneath that, it was very cold.

The mountains were our continual playground. There were places where the big rocks surrounded a space that was like walls around a room. These were our playhouses. We were possibly 500 feet up the mountain in plain sight of our mother at our house. The mountain immediately south of our house was only about 30 feet from our back door to where it started steeply upward. Climbing these mountains was as natural as walking. I liked to start on one rock and leap from rock to rock to the first ledge about 500 feet up the mountain. These mountains were very rocky.

I have always liked to climb—trees, mountains, even windmills, though windmills are scary. I preferred something solid like a mountain. Mother said that as a toddler I climbed everything in the house except the big upright piano. It was always a challenge to me to see what was a little higher up. Then what a thrill when I reached the top to see the vista from there!

*Lottie at one year old*

**I remember a rodeo in Valentine when I was quite young,** for my dad participated in the goat roping. I don't recall that they had calf roping. They roped short-haired Mexican goats. Goats are hard to rope. They do not run straight like calves when turned out of the chute. They may suddenly veer to one side or the other, stop, or even turn back very unpredictably. These cowboys did not practice roping continually as ropers do now. They just used the skills they had acquired in their usual ranch work, but they were accomplished ropers.

There was a community meal at the schoolhouse. I guess it was a 4th of July celebration. I remember it was hot weather, and I welcomed the cold lemonade.  The cowboys must have ridden their horses from whatever ranch to Valentine.  Horse trailers were not even dreamed of then.  It was a 30 mile ride for my dad—a one day ride.  He probably brought two or three horses besides the one he rode.  That is the only rodeo I recall in my childhood.  In later years they had rodeos and horse races at Marfa.

I was my daddy's girl.  I tagged along after him every time I could.  When we were going on a trip, he practically rebuilt the car to make sure everything was working right.  I was right there hanging over his shoulder, fascinated by how the motor and other parts worked.  I might have become a lady mechanic, but I couldn't stand the feel and smell of the grease on my hands.    When he was soldering something, I was right there.  When he had to melt Babbitt, an alloy of tin, copper and antimony, an antifriction mixture to replace a bearing on a windmill, I was right there in the way.

I was fascinated by the tools in the shop, and entranced with the forge.  I liked to watch Dad hammer the white-hot metal into a part to fix something or make something.  My interest in tools helped later in life, for I knew what tools were needed to work on windmills when we had to pull a pump.  My dad was good at working with metal.  When he lost one of his spurs, he forged an exact duplicate except for the silver inlay, which he did not have the equipment and materials to do.  My son, Tim, has that pair of spurs.

# The Shotgun

*William Musgrove Evans with 10 gauge double barrel shotgun*

**There was a double barreled shotgun** in the workshop at EV Ranch that had been there ever since I could remember. It was minus the hammers and could no longer be shot; otherwise it was intact and in good shape. My dad told of a time when he was seven years old and his brother Ell B, two years older, took this gun that was longer than they were tall and went quail hunting to the corrals at the windmills. Quail were plentiful in that area. These Blue quail watered and fed in these corrals. With both barrels loaded, Ell B, who was a precocious and daring boy, rested the gun on one of the horizontal logs enclosing the corral and pulled both triggers simultaneously. The impact of the gun's kick knocked him backward, rolling him down the creek bank where he raised up and immediately asked, "How many did I get?" I think after that Grandmother Evans saw that the hammers were removed from the gun.

There was a large photograph, 18" x 24", in a store room at EVs of a man with black hair and beard holding this gun. I did not know who the man was until I was asked to be the photo chairman for Means and Evans Camp for Bloys Association Centennial celebration 1989-1990. A cousin sent me some pictures and mementoes that had belonged to her father, Will Evans, my father's oldest brother. Among these was a tintype of this bearded man holding this double barreled shotgun, doubtless the gun he had used when he fought for Texas Independence before 1836. This tintype was of my great grandfather, William Musgrove Evans. William was thirteen years old when he had started one afternoon after the milk cows, and kept going to where he could hear the sounds of battle at San Jacinto. The other soldiers would not let him go to the front lines, but he had his part in the war for Texas independence.

I surmised that William M. had given this gun to his son, George Wesley Evans, before George and Kate migrated to west Texas in the early summer of 1884. Guns were scarce and much-prized possessions then. William Musgrove died November 1884. I had kept this gun because I regarded it as a valuable family relic even before I knew its history. Our son-in-law, Bobby Hart, had a friend in El Paso who knew how to refinish and "blue" the barrel of this 10 gauge shotgun. I let Bobby take it to El Paso. Quite some time passed when the gun was not foremost in my thoughts. Then Chance bought a new home and new furniture. She planned to sell her present furniture, so she put an ad in the paper. The main buyers for furniture and household goods in El Paso are Mexicans from Juarez. A couple from Juarez bought her living room set. To get the couch through a door, it had to be turned on its edge. When the cushions were removed to turn the couch over, there was my 10 gauge shotgun, wedged against the back of the couch. Bobby had forgotten about it. My gun narrowly missed being taken to Mexico, and I would have never known what happened to this priceless family treasure that must be about two hundred years old. My son Tim now has this gun displayed over the fireplace mantel of the living room of their new home.

**My mother was a captivating person.** She delighted in special occasions and parties. She remembered family and friends on their birthdays by sending cards. Birthdays were very special to her. Holidays and our birthdays were celebrated with parties. I recall one birthday party for me when I was 5 or 6 years old. All the decorations were butterflies—butterflies on streamers from the central light fixture, to the butterfly-decorated tablecloth, plates and napkins. To me it looked like fairyland. I was thrilled. She had planned far ahead, for anything like that had to be ordered from somewhere distant. There was nothing like that available in the small town where we shopped for basic supplies at the general store, the Valentine Trading Company. A long time had to be allowed to prepare for a special occasion because we didn't go to town for mail and supplies but about every two weeks, or sometimes longer intervals.

Mother loved flowers and had a special knack for growing them—a knack made up of lots of hard work and attention to the requirements of the different plants. Bearded iris and dahlias were her specialty. When our yard became filled with her plants, she dug flower beds outside the yard fence. To protect them from the rabbits and the milk cow, Dad obligingly moved the yard fence to enclose these new flowers. This enlargement process was repeated several times as

Mother's flower garden continued to expand.

Mother ordered what were supposed to be flowering pomegranate shrubs. Under her care they produced big, rosy, edible pomegranates. They were delicious. In the early 1970's when I again lived at EV Ranch, I won Best of Show at Culberson County Fair with three of those beautiful and big-as-grapefruit rosy pomegranates.

There was a bench across the creek from where we lived where in the spring the wild flowers were almost like a garden. There were bluebells, rock daisies, black-eyed Susans, Indian paintbrushes, and many others that we never knew the names of. We had a great time picking armfuls of these flowers to take to Mother, who dutifully put them in vases, jars, and even cans.

**My grandfather, George Wesley Evans, never learned to drive a car**, although about 1908 he bought one of the first cars in this area. At about age 60, why should he attempt to drive one of these new contraptions when he had sons eager to exhibit their expertise in driving a car? After my mother, Wertie Powell, married Paul, Mother was the designated driver when the sons and ranch hands were horseback working cattle or fixing windmills away from headquarters. Mother learned to drive a car after she married and never felt competent as a driver. She drove as though the car were an antagonist to be coped with. Grandfather called her "Barney" after Barney Olefield, a famous race car driver of that time. Grandfather wore a big gold pocket watch on a heavy gold chain on which was mounted a grizzly bear's claw with a gold fastener. When Mother started the car, which had to be cranked, Grandfather looked at his watch, and when they arrived, he looked at it again. This did nothing for Mother's confidence or composure, though he never criticized her in any way. She was able to drive, and he was not.

In another incident with a car, Mother was not driving. The hired man, Mr. Clyde, was driving when about half-way of the thirty miles from the EV Ranch to Valentine, our shopping center, this topless car slowly turned over onto the driver's side. Mother, little sister Frances, and I (Lottie) fell over onto the hired man. Mother had held my brother, Paul, who was a baby, so that he would not fall or be hurt. Evidently the tie rod broke. Mr. Clyde had to walk the 9 or 10 miles to the nearest ranch for help. We were all riding in the front seat because the back seat was filled with a whole dressed and wrapped beef and hog that were to be shipped to El Paso. Every year my Dad butchered and shipped a beef and a hog to Grandfather Evans at Christmastime. Dad cut the beef and hog into a number of big roasts. Grandfather and Dad went to the Chief of Police and got him to take them to the needy people, where they distributed those roasts. When finished, Grandfather said, "Now I can enjoy Christmas."

Mother needed to go from EV Ranch to Van Horn, about 35 miles. On the road were several cattle guards, but one gate—a big heavy plank gate at the top of a steep little hill. When you are driving alone and come to a gate, you must stop the car, get out and open the gate, and make sure it is propped so it won't close before you can drive through. You drive through, stop and get out to close the gate, get back in the car, and go on your way. At this little hill you had to maintain enough momentum to go up the hill but stop before you got to the gate. When Mother got to the hill, she had enough momentum, but when she tried to stop she had no brakes. Her momentum carried her right through the closed gate. When she returned home, she had to tell Dad about the gate. When questioned about it later, she said, "I always have wanted to run through that gate."

My mother was very fond of perfumes and things that smelled good. I first remember a scented sachet-type powder called Djer Kiss that she used. I later found a bottle that had contained Djer Kiss, complete with the metal sliding top. The glass bottle had been turned by the sunlight to a deep amethyst as time passed. What a treasure in my collection of sun-purpled glassware.

The next scented product she used was Evening in Paris perfume. This came in a flattened cobalt blue flask-type bottle with glass stopper. I liked the way this perfume smelled. My dad was very sensitive to odors. He did not like the aroma of Evening in Paris perfume. I was surprised to find that Evening in Paris perfume is still available today.

Mother tried several perfumes, trying to find one she liked that Dad liked too. Finally they settled on White Shoulders. Dad liked it and Mother used it lavishly. Her clothing, her bedroom, and even her purses smelled of White Shoulders. Our sons, Beary and Tim, stayed with their grandparents at times during the summer. Tim particularly remembers that while driving to church Mother would offer him chewing gum which she carried in her purse. White Shoulders has a very permeating scent. The chewing gum tasted just like White Shoulders perfume smelled. He did not want to refuse her offer of chewing gum, but he still remembers how terrible it tasted.

Only one time that I know of Mother did not share her flowers. A visiting woman kept asking where Mother got a rare and expensive variety of iris. Mother knew the woman was hinting to be given some bulbs. Finally, to hush her hinting, Mother said, "I bought them." But most of the time, Mother loved sharing the beautiful flowers she grew. She started taking them to the church in Van Horn when she and Dad started attending. The Baptist pastor, Bro. Marsh, would come to EV Ranch on Sunday afternoon and hold a Bible study for those who lived there—nine or ten people When Blackie and I moved with our three children and my sister, Frances and husband Charles also moved, there were only Mother and Dad at EV's. They decided to attend church in Van Horn each Sunday. It was no farther for them to go than it had been for Bro. Marsh to come to them.

Saturday evening Mother would gather flowers and immerse them in water. Some flowers had to be gathered Sunday morning. The flowers were loaded into their Ford car and taken to Van Horn early enough for Mother to arrange them in vases before Sunday school. Mother taught a class of young girls in Sunday school. To have time to make the arrangements of flowers as she had studied and practiced, she had to be at the church very early. It took over an hour to drive from EV's to Van Horn. While Mother arranged flowers, Dad folded the bulletins that were run off on the mimeograph. As he folded each bulletin, he said to me, "Some people think these come already folded."

Family was very important to Dad. To foster good family relations he would have "Round-ups" of family and friends. Word would be spread of the date of the Round-up and family and friends would come from far and wide. Dad enjoyed hosting and feeding people. He felt that you had not really visited him unless he served you coffee and cake or cobbler.

For the Round-up he prepared an entrée and coffee on the campfire outside. Mother made iced tea, salads and desserts. Guests brought casseroles and desserts. There was always an abundance of food, visiting and picture-taking. Mother would be busy everywhere to make sure all went well. Someone commented on Mother's activity. Dad responded, "Just wait until tomorrow. She will be just like a bowl of wilted lettuce."

*Paul Evans grilling steak*

As Dad's health deteriorated Mother persuaded him to go to a doctor in El Paso.  This doctor checked him over and advised him to quit smoking.  Since his younger days Dad had smoked roll-your-own Bull Durham.  The time of getting out a cigarette paper, pouring a small amount of Bull Durham tobacco out of the little cotton sack into this thin paper, held just so in the fingers, rolling the paper around the tobacco, sealing it with a lick of the tongue and twisting the ends just right was not conducive to chain smoking.  But as Dad began to feel physically ill after he moved to Van Horn, he bought "ready-made" cigarettes.  The worse his health became, the more he smoked. This doctor didn't tell Dad, but he told my brother, Paul Jr., that Dad had about 3 months to live; his heart was damaged and one lung was gone.  Dad went home, quit smoking, and lived 13 more productive years. He was Chairman of the Board of Deacons for First Baptist Church of Van Horn, Chairman of the Executive Committee of Bloys Campmeeting Association, and Chairman for the Baptist Big Bend District. He was also Worthy Patron for the Eastern Star for many years. He chewed lots of Juicy Fruit gum in those years, but he never smoked another cigarette.

Church and his attendance there were an essential joy to him. On Sunday morning he put on his suit and went to Sunday school and Church. He did this even when the emphysema got so bad he would have to stop to rest at least three times—every ten feet—between the front door and his car.

Dad had driven Ford cars from that first Model T when I was 4 years old, through a Model A, then the V8's. His Ford Ranchero had a lot of age on it, so when his youngest brother, Graves, bought a new car he gave Dad his Chrysler New Yorker. Dad had always liked to drive fast. In those Fords, you were very conscious of your speed. At sixty or sixty-five the roar and rattle and keeping the car on the road made you very aware of your speed. Not so with this Chrysler. Dad sailed along at ninety or more so smoothly that he must not have realized his excess speed, but he liked it. When highways were two-lane, he maintained that fast drivers didn't cause wrecks—they would go on and get out of the way. It was the slow drivers poking along in the way that caused wrecks. Dad never got to fly in an airplane. I think he would have liked it. Mother traveled by plane several times after she was widowed.

Dad's health continued to worsen. He was diagnosed with cancer of the bladder. They gave him some radiation treatments which made him even sicker. He stopped going for radiation. He knew it was futile—that his time was limited. He told us, "I have looked across a river and it wasn't the Rio Grande." He had a phobia about hospitals. He did not want to die in a hospital. My brother, Paul, brought Dad from the hospital to his home in El Paso.

The house at EV Ranch had just been remodeled. For this venture we moved everything out of the house and lived in a trailer house during the remodeling. My children were all planning to come to EV's for Thanksgiving and deer hunting season. I had been staying in El Paso helping with Dad, but I had to get moved back into the house before they came. At our home at the EV Ranch the Monday before Thanksgiving about 3 p.m. as I was carrying some articles from the place they had been stored, the whole canyon became diffused with the most glorious light. I was very conscious of Dad's presence. I knew that he had left this earthly life and that his spirit was in this canyon where he had spent most of his life and loved it so dearly. This heavenly light did not last long, but for that time I was very close to Dad. Later when we compared the time of his death, I had known it before Mother and Myrtle in the next room from him.

**My parents liked to go on picnics.** Anything could call for a picnic. If Dad had to work on a windmill or clean out a spring, they made a picnic of it. But there really didn't have to be a reason. One place we liked to go was another but smaller canyon, called the Salome' place, for an old Mexican man who lived there and worked for the Evans'._This place was about 2 miles from our home. There was a windmill and a rock and concrete tank 30 feet across that we could swim in. In fact, that is where I finally overcame my fear of drowning and learned to swim. I would swim very close to the wall of the tank, so close that I could grasp the wall if I got scared, until I gained confidence enough to swim across the tank. Here, years later, I taught my grandchildren, Kippy and Kim Hart, to swim by putting the crotch of a pair of Levi's under their bodies while I held the legs and supported them until they got the hang of it and no longer needed the Levi's.

For these picnics we would take thick-sliced bacon to fasten on pronged green limbs to cook over the campfire. What a delightful aroma that made! We were hungry after swimming. There was a little wooden house—a shack, really—where a Mexican couple had lived. The inside walls were papered with pages from Godey's Ladies Magazines. Louisa had used flour and water to paste to the walls the pages from the magazines my Grandmother Evans had given her. It was attractive and helped to insulate the little hut from the wind that came through the cracks.

As a teenager, I would saddle my horse and ride the 3 miles or so to a reservoir that had been made by building a concrete and rock dam across a narrow canyon which had filled with water when it rained. That water was cold! Parts of it were shaded by the high bluffs on either side so that the sun never shined on it to warm it. After this reservoir filled with washed-in sand and gravel so that it no longer held water, I was alarmed at the chances I had taken. Huge boulders had been submerged in the water where I had dived and swam. If I had dived into one of those boulders, it surely might have killed me. I am not sure my parents always knew where I was going. My guardian angel was really kept busy.

**My dad, Paul Evans, told me of a harrowing experience** he had when he was a young man. He had gone horseback with a crew of four Mexican ranch hands to the other Evans ranch about 30 miles over in the Davis Mountains. There was a two-room house made of pine logs for them to stay in. They arrived, cooked supper on the wood stove, and then went to bed. As was his custom, Dad removed his boots, socks and outer clothes. He had a bed in the room with the cook stove; the Mexican men slept in the other room.

Dad was awakened by the choking smell of the room full of pine smoke. The house was burning. He crawled to where the wash basin and towel were, wrapped the towel around his head and face, crawled out of the burning room, and went to wake the other men. They were sleeping soundly in their clothes. They all got out of the fire alive, but all of Dad's clothes and his boots were burned. They had to ride the 30-mile distance back to the EV Ranch the next day, Dad in only his BVD's, the men's undergarment of that time, with burns on his body. Thankfully, their saddles were not burned. I can only imagine Dad's mother's concern when she saw him riding down the mountain in such condition.

**Our house was built when I was two years old** and my sister Frances was a baby. Before that time my parents had lived in the big house with Dad's parents, George and Kate Evans, their only daughter, Gracie Kate, and youngest son, Amos Graves, then twelve years old.

On January 1, 1917, Gracie Kate married William Hart Cowden in a double wedding ceremony with her cousin, Cole Alfred Means, who married Ruby Bean. This double wedding ceremony was held at EV Ranch with many relatives and friends attending. The wedding dinner was held in the twenty-two foot square dining room. The oak pedestal dining table placed diagonally seated twenty-two persons. I have that table, but not all the leaves that extended it.

Mother and Dad were glad to be at last in a home of their own. Mother had a picture of me, age 2½ years, pushing my doll buggy to move into the new house, though I really don't remember that occasion. I do remember not long after that going to the Moon Ranch where there were large cottonwood trees and Bermuda grass around a dirt tank of water. Dad sawed limbs 4 to 5 inches in diameter off the trees, took them to our home, and planted them in the deep holes he had dug. They rooted and made big shade trees in our yard.

In the 1920's a screened porch was added across the entire north side of the house, so it made a cool place to sit and even to sleep on summer nights. At that time Dad had an olla made to cool our drinking water. This olla was made of a rare porous rock that let the water very gradually seep through the pores of the rock and cool by the process of evaporation. The olla was made by an old Mexican man in Fort Davis skilled in the almost-lost art. This olla is 18 inches deep with an inside diameter of 13 inches at the top with a flange 15 inches square so it could be set into a wooden frame. The capacity is about 4 gallons. It was filled in the evenings with water from a pipe with a faucet so it would cool through the night. My son, Tim, has this olla and has welded a beautiful wrought iron frame for it.

My mother and dad were so young. Mother was 18 on May 9. Dad reached 21 years June 15, and they married June 21, 1916. This was a very dry year; rain was delayed, so their honeymoon was spent driving to the Little Well and Salome' Place for Dad to keep the gasoline engines running to pump water for the cattle. It was also necessary to check the gravity flow pipelines in the flat area of the ranch to avoid any water being wasted by leaks in the pipe or a float pan on a trough malfunctioning.

Dad taught Mother to cook after they married and had their own home. Dad had six older brothers who had all learned to cook, keep house, and do laundry, as Dad had also learned. Biscuits were Dad's specialty. He called bought bread "wasp nests" or "gun wadding" and never ate it. To make biscuits he put a pile of flour on the bread board, made a well in the center, added lard and sour milk, soda and salt, and mixed this into the flour with his hand to make a soft dough, rolled the dough out and cut it into rounds, and baked them in a very hot oven. They turned out just right every time. He never used a measuring cup or spoon. In later years his specialty was fruit cobbler. Helen Norman, wife of a pastor in Van Horn, asked Dad for the recipe for his peach cobbler. This recipe had never been written down, but Dad did his best for Helen, and this was the result:

### Peach Cobbler Recipe

"Use enough peaches to make as much pie as you will need. You can tell how much you need by the number of people you are going to feed.

Drain off the juice of the fruit into a pan the size you will need for the right amount of pie. If you don't have peaches, plums will do. Sometimes I make it out of apricots. They are good too. If you do not have enough of one kind of fruit, mix them all together. That makes it better.

Put a hunk of butter, or more, into the juice. Put enough flour in a pan to make the right amount of pie crust. You make pie crust just like you make biscuits, only you put in more grease. Make the crust dough stiff enough to roll out real thin. Take a saucer and cut the dough into round pieces. Put your fruit on the dough and fold over like you are making fried pies, and drop into the juice and butter warmed enough to melt the butter.

Add enough sugar and nutmeg to make it taste good. Cook it until it is the right color brown.

Serve with good, thick cow cream.

If you follow these directions CAREFULLY, you will never have a failure."

—*by Paul M. Evans*

# Education

**When it was time for me to start school,** my parents arranged for me to stay with Dad's cousin, M. O. (Bug) and his wife Marylee Means, who lived on the Moon Ranch, 8 miles away. They jointly hired a young woman, Evelyn Estes, from Midland, Texas, as governess. The plan was for me to stay with the Means' at Moon Ranch through the weeks of the fall semester; then their only child, Cole Cowden Means, would stay with us for the spring semester. The governess would also stay with us.

Coley was six months to the day older than I was. We had a great time climbing the mountain which their house was built against. The rim rocks above the house made great forts to watch for and fight Indians. Fridays were really looked forward to, as my parents came to take me home for the weekend. I experienced my first homesickness at this time. For some reason this plan didn't work out. After the fall semester Marylee bought a house in Valentine for the spring semester. Perhaps she couldn't bear to be away from her only child? *Quien sabe?*

So I stayed with my great aunt Rhoda Means Evans and her daughter, Chance, at their home in Valentine. They petted and bragged on me, and I adored them. Rhoda was my Grandmother Evans' oldest sister who, after she was widowed, married my Grandfather Evans' father, also widowed. After being married four years, they had this one child who Aunt Rhoda said was her last chance to have a child. She was past 45 years of age. The baby was named Chance Ann Kate Evans. It was supposed to bring good luck if your initials spelled a word. Because of the complicated relationship we just called her Aunt Chance. She didn't marry, so after Aunt Rhoda died she lived with my Grandmother Evans who was then a widow.

Aunt Chance used to pose this riddle: "My mother had five children and my father had five children, and together they just had nine."

My beloved Grandfather Evans died of pneumonia in 1925 January 13 at age 75. I had pneumonia shortly after that. I was so ill that I was out of it for I never knew how long. I remember being carried from the room where I usually stayed to another room. Later I learned that was because my brother was brought in from the ranch and was sicker than I was. He was three years old and was so ill with pneumonia and such high fever that later his blonde hair looked dead. He was unconscious several days, but the doctor kept him alive on whiskey. The registered nurse would give him little sips of whiskey until he regained consciousness enough to take food. This was during Prohibition and long before antibiotics.

I finished the first grade in Valentine. When I learned to read, it opened up a whole new world. Mother had always read to us, but now I could read for myself. For the next school year my parents hired a governess who lived with us. The reason for hiring these governesses was because our ranch was 30 miles from the nearest school. Thirty miles in the cars of those days was not what you would do every day. My father had been taught by governesses.

Mother had received the Calvert School Course from Maryland. Her sister-in-law, Beulah Evans, who lived on an isolated ranch in New Mexico, had used this to teach her children. This course of study was very advanced. I wrote themes in second and third grade on Ancient History, which I didn't believe was true until we studied about Egypt and the Pharaohs, which I had learned about from the Bible and knew was true. Perhaps my skepticism was caused by

Mother admonishing me that the Greek mythology I had studied the first semester was not true.

I completed the second and third grades that year. We were not especially fond of this third grade governess. She was an old maid farm girl from Clyde, east of Abilene. She talked very differently than people in West Texas. She also had a nasal sound to her voice. We thought it was because she talked through her long nose. Our classes recessed at noon for the wonderful food my mother cooked, and were to resume from 1 to 3 p.m.

My dad and his brother Rube had bought 250 angora goats. I guess the old Mexican herder and his aged wife went with the deal. This old couple camped at water and he herded the goats to good pasture. Dad would take supplies, flour, beans and tobacco to their camp. One day at noon this old herder brought the goats down the canyon, through the corrals, the orchard, and the yards. Maybe he needed tobacco. Anyway, I decided he needed some help, as the goats were scattered. He certainly did not have any need for our help. He carried a slingshot, and with it he could place a rock right in front of the nose of any goat that started to stray. His aim was accurate to at least 200 yards—perhaps farther. My brother and sister, at my leading, started after the goats, unmindful of the time, until we saw Dad coming in the car. We knew we were in trouble, for we should have been in school. We didn't really intend to play hooky—it just happened. But we didn't do that ever again.

I was the one who thought up these plans that got us into trouble. Frances and Paul were always good. They never thought of doing anything they shouldn't, but they followed my leadership even when it got us into trouble.

We only went to school seven months of the year. With individual instruction you learn so much more for the time spent. Since our school was over early in April, it was decided to send me to stay with my mother's sister, Alice, and her husband, Ell Evans, my father's brother, to be sure I was keeping up with the public schools. I was away and gone ahead of the third graders in Cisco, Texas.

I was enchanted with the profusion of wild flowers that bloomed along the way I walked to school. They were so different from the flowers where I lived.   On a picnic to Lake Cisco we went swimming.  Now, I couldn't swim, but there was a place roped off for those like me.  As I was playing in this area I began to slip into the deeper part out of the ropes.  Evidently the lake bottom began to slope steeply.  I was going down for the third time when someone pulled me out.  This experience gave me a great fear of water which only with great determination did I later overcome enough to learn to swim.

Before returning home I wanted to buy something to take to my family.  Mother always brought us presents when she had been away from us.  I had a little money, so my Aunt Alice took me to a store where I picked out a present for each one except Dad.  Then I found the perfect gift for him—a phonograph record of Jimmy Rogers' songs.  I knew Dad loved music, and particularly the popular music of Jimmy Rogers. But alas!  The record cost 79 cents, and after paying for the other three gifts I had only 47 cents.  Even after much persuasion to pick out a gift I could pay for, I was adamant that nothing else would do.  After consulting with the store owner, my aunt told me he would let me have the record for 47 cents.  What a nice man!  Only after I grew up enough to have some sense did I realize my aunt had paid the difference.

I had ridden to Cisco with Dad's brother, Rube and his wife, Mary Kate.  I was to ride the train home.  My cousin, Kitty Carpenter, was to board the train in Mineral Wells; that evening I was to board the same train in Cisco.  We were to share a berth that night.  I had

24

ridden trains, but this upper berth was a new experience for both of us. We thought of several things that necessitated our climbing down from the berth, then up and down several times. I am sure those in the lower berth did not enjoy their trip. We finally settled down to sleep. Sometime in the night I waked, climbed down from the berth, and looked out a window. It was fairly moonlight and I was sure I recognized the terrain west of Kent and that we had gone past our destination. I climbed up and waked Kitty with the terrifying news. The terrain from Midland to El Paso along the Texas and Pacific railroad looks very much the same. I never did know where we were, but it was far to the east of Kent. I guess the porter got us back to bed, for we slept and then were awakened in time to depart the train at Kent where my parents met us.

**Perhaps the most momentous event of the year 1931 was the earthquake** we experienced the first week in August. About 3 a.m. we were awakened by our beds vigorously shaking. We arose, turned on lights, and agreed, "That must have been an earthquake, ha, ha." We went back to bed and to sleep when just before good daylight **The Earthquake** hit. We all ran outside to a fearsome spectacle. Rocks were rolling and sliding off the mountains, bouncing and hitting other rocks, making sparks with a very metallic odor and much dust, and the terrible grating, grinding noise of the earthquake itself.

Thankfully, no one was hurt. As the tremors subsided, we returned to the house. A huge chunk of rough stucco plaster had fallen onto the beds where my sister and brother had been sleeping in the screened-in sleeping porch that had been added onto the house. Had they been in their beds when it fell, it surely would have killed them. The walls of our adobe house were cracked so that they had to be braced and re-plastered.

The center of this 6+ on the Richter scale earthquake was Valentine, where no one was killed or injured.  The adobe walls of many houses were too badly broken to be repaired.   The houses had to be abandoned.  Lesser quakes continued for more than a year, as if that mountainous part of the earth was having a hard time settling down. You could hear these quakes coming—a fearful, terrible, grating roar—a warning that the quake was inevitable.   There was no stopping it.   The tremors gradually lessened in intensity and frequency.

# Mountain Lion Cubs

While I had been in Cisco my dad had, with his dogs, caught a mountain lion that was killing a neighbor's cattle. This lion had just given birth to three kittens. Not wanting the little orphans to starve, my dad brought them home. Like all cats, they did not have their eyes open. Mother used Paul's outgrown bottles and nipples to feed them cow's milk, and they thrived! When I returned they were about three weeks old and hardly larger than a

*Lottie and sister Frances with lion kittens*

domestic cat of the same age. They were spotted in a camouflage pattern. These lion kittens were our playmates. We held them like babies, dressed them in doll clothes and took them swimming in the creek. They could really swim well—they didn't have to be taught, but they didn't seem to enjoy it. When they got old enough to chew the nipples off the bottles, Dad would kill rabbits for them to eat. Then he would bring in a wounded rabbit for them to kill, which they did with no coaching. They had a natural killer instinct even at that young age.

27

We kept them until they were about six months old. Cliff Caldwell, who had bought the Nunn Ranch from the Evans', bought the female and one male to put in the Abilene zoo. The other male was very friendly with the governess of that year and stayed in her room a lot. When school was over, she took him home with her to Brownwood, Texas. We heard that any young men who called on her were startled to see a large live lion draped on the back of her couch.

During our long summer vacations we continued to play cowboys, riding lecheguilla stalks as horses. They made really good horses. They were easy to twist out of the center of the lecheguilla plant. Lecheguilla is a small species of the century plant and, like the century plant, dies after it blooms. These stalks were many different colors—some solid white, some with brown spots, some with mauve stripes. Others were a beautiful chestnut brown. This made it easy to name each of our horses. The stalks were smooth with no stickers. Sometimes we had a string for a bridle, but most of the time we just held the head end of the lecheguilla stalk in our hand. We had better control that way. We traveled many, many miles on those horses.

For my seventh grade I stayed with my dad's brother Will and his wife Allye Evans in Marfa. They had a red-headed daughter, Madie Fern, two years older than I was. We had always, as cousins, been very close. They lived on the far eastern edge of Marfa, which was a good mile or more to the school. That walk was not bad until cold weather arrived. It can get really cold in Marfa. At about one mile in altitude and in a low swag between open hills, it registers some of the lowest temperatures in the Trans-Pecos area. In a really cold spell, Aunt Allye would take us to school in the car if she could get it started.

My geography teacher gave me a lasting interest in geography and maps, which served me well later with the Census. She had us study a map and then draw it from memory. I liked that. My penmanship teacher—yes, they did at one time have such—gave an award to the student whose writing (penmanship) improved the most during the year. She told me I had the best chance to win it. I just went to school in Marfa the fall semester, but there was no way I could have won that award, though I faithfully practiced the round overlapping circles and vertical strokes of proper penmanship.

I finished 7th grade at home with the governess, Blanche McDonald. She thought my dad was a hero because he caught mountain lions with his dogs. She called him "Daniel" for Daniel Boone. Dad had some shirts with this latest invention, the zipper, opening the shirt front, and she would zip and unzip it. I think Mother was jealous of Blanche, though she had no reason to be on Dad's part. Mother was Dad's great, undying, and only love.

Blanche showed me how to "marcel" (set in waves) my unruly hair. Marcel hair sets were the style at that time. As a young child I always got some very short haircuts from the town barber. There were no beauty shops. This barber would try to cut my hair in the current little girl style, parted in the center and bobbed on the sides with bangs in front. My little sister, Frances, with her soft straight hair, looked adorable that way. When this barber combed one side of my hair down and cut it, then combed the other side down, the first side had recoiled to a shorter length; and to match it the second side got cut even shorter, until I guess he quit while I still had some hair. Bangs didn't behave for me either.

For my eighth grade and freshman year in school we moved to Valentine. Mother was expecting a much-wanted baby and was not up to the extra work entailed by having a governess. Dad rented a house in Valentine, but, Horrors! It did not have indoor plumbing. This seemed to be the accepted norm for those unprogressive people in that little town which had an ample supply of water. This was

29

hard for me to accept. We had always had a full bathroom. I survived that year, but I did not learn to like it. The ranchers all had bathrooms in their houses right after or before 1900. My great uncle John Means in his bathrooms had toilets with water tanks at ceiling (10 foot) height, and when you pulled the cord to flush, they flushed with a terrific whoosh!

**The year in Valentine was a time of mixed experiences**. Thirteen is a hard age for everyone concerned. My independent spirit pushed against the boundaries. I think a good example of thirteen is illustrated by some friends' teenage daughter who for Christmas wanted a fur coat and combat boots. Mixed emotions of thirteen.

The dresses that Mother made for me did not satisfy my idea of what I wanted to wear. Mother sewed dresses for us only of necessity. She did not enjoy sewing, so it was a very hard task for her. I knew how to operate the treadle Singer sewing machine. I just needed to learn to read and follow patterns. These were pretty well self-explanatory. I bought this fabric and started sewing. The first garment I attempted was a pair of lounging pajamas with full wide legs and a bolero top— not at all practical, but they fit my idea of glamour. After that I made almost all my dresses. A purchased (store-bought) dress was a rare luxury. At thirteen I had attained my full height of 5 feet 3 ¼ inches. Although I so wished to be tall, I never grew any taller. Mother was 5 feet 5 inches, which I thought was a good height. Girls did not grow to the heights they do now.

We had dances in the big auditorium of the schoolhouse in Valentine. It had a hardwood floor, and with some cornmeal sprinkled on it, it was wonderful for dancing. The music was furnished by a man playing the fiddle, my dad playing guitar, and a woman who played piano. A man was learning to play guitar to take Dad's place. Dad loved to dance and was an excellent dancer, so he took a lot of time off from playing to dance. Everyone in the town and from surrounding ranches came to the dances—grandparents, babies, children—everyone. These dances were social affairs, usually with a covered dish supper beforehand. We danced square dances, polkas, schottisches, put-your-little-foot, two-steps, and waltzes. Such fun! The dance usually ended soon after midnight because the woman who played piano for dancing also played piano for Sunday school and church Sunday morning, though she was of a very different faith from the rest of us. This church was non-denominational—open to everyone. The Catholics had a church across the railroad tracks.

Sometimes the ranchers would have all-night dances. My parents hosted several of these through the years. We had a barn with a center concrete section fifty feet long and ten feet wide to dance on. Every family and all the cowboys in the area were invited. Everyone came for a good time of clean fun. No alcoholic beverages were ever brought to one of our dances at EV Ranch; everyone respected Dad's position on this. At first Dad would hire our faithful cook, Elisandro Valdez, to prepare a chuck wagon supper. My grandmother, Kate Evans, had taught Elisandro to cook when he was a young man. Dad would engage a local band of Mexican musicians. Theirs is the best music I ever danced to, with their big guitars, violins, and that special horn they play. Such wonderful harmony and tempo! As the depression and drought worsened and none of us had any money, guests would bring casseroles and desserts, so we had an abundance to eat at these all-night dances. Fiddles and guitars played by local people furnished our music.

We needed these fun times, for times were hard in the early 1930's. In 1931 it rained unusual amounts in September and October. I remember clear water running in all the low flat areas. Then it did not rain at all through the years 1932—1934. Those were the dust bowl years. The dust storms from the northeast were terrible. You could see them coming like a brown wall from horizon to horizon moving toward you, coating everything with this gritty red-brown dirt. It became very hard to breathe during these dust storms. They penetrated even into the houses. After these dust storms when the rains came we had many undesirable invader weeds, such as tumble weeds, bitter weeds, and others, evidently blown by the dust storms. We had not had these before that time.

Because of the nationwide depression, there was no good market for cattle. Then because of the drought they became too thin and weak to be marketable. The US government started a program that was supposed to help the ranchers. When the government proposes to help you, "Watch Out." Their plan to help ranchers and improve market conditions was to kill a percent of a rancher's cows or sheep. Now, there is no chance of a calf to sell from a dead cow. For each cow killed the government would pay $4.00. These cows were to be killed and buried or burned. The plan was carried out through the County Agent in each county. These men were honorable and understanding, so for the most part only the weakest and poorest cows were killed.

Since we had no refrigeration—only a water-cooled "milk tray" to keep food, we learned to can meat. We were already canning fruit and what vegetables we could grow in the garden. These we canned in glass jars. To can the meat required longer and hotter processing in cans. We had a device to seal the cans when they were filled with the raw meat. It clamped to the edge of a table. You put the filled can in it with the lid clamped in place, turned the handle of this device and as it rotated, the edge of the lid rolled over the flange on the can, making an air-tight seal. The cans were then put in a big pressure cooker and processed at 15 pounds pressure.

To label the cans you wrote with a lead pencil on the top of the cans the name of the contents. When processed, this label became permanent, but not very noticeable. This meat was very good— much better than any canned meat product available today. Mother shipped some of this canned meat to her sister Alice. Alice's husband Ell Evans was a wildcatter in the oil business, and the oil business was hard-hit by the depression. They did not notice the penciled label—it did not show plainly. They had great fun guessing before opening a can what kind of meat they would have for lunch.

**In early 1931 Dad bought a Model A Ford** car enclosed with glass windows—a great improvement over the open Model T. When he told Mother about the new car he was getting, she asked what kind it was. He told her it was a Ford. She said, "Take it back. I don't want another Ford." He had a hard time convincing her this Ford was different. He had bought it while she was in the hospital after giving birth to a beautiful baby girl. Mary Sue was born February 9, 1931. This car was especially to take Mother and the new baby in comfort from El Paso to Valentine in cold February weather. Mary Sue was our adorable doll. I had never been around a baby before, so this was a very different experience, and one of intimate joy.

I learned to drive this Model A Ford and got my first driver's license when I was thirteen. That was when driver's licenses were first required in Texas. Everyone who sent in their information got a driver's license. There was no driver's test. When you learned to drive over the country roads of just two ruts, you learned where your wheels were. As long as you kept your wheels in those ruts, it was smooth going; but if you steered to one side or the other, you got some terrific jolts as the wheels bumped out of the ruts and then bumped back where you should have kept them.

When the Evans' had the Nunn Ranch, we had to drive north to Highway 80, then east to Kent and on south up Dobie House Canyon to get to the Nunn Ranch by car. The winding Dobie House creek ran clear water all year. The road up the canyon crossed this creek thirteen times. As children we begged our parents to stop and let us wade in this beautiful water. Of course, they did stop at least once a trip. At the mouth of the canyon the Reynolds Long X Ranch had an orchard and a vineyard that were watered by a big spring. Here we would stop to eat our lunch, and in season, to enjoy some of the fruit that the gardener gave us.

At the head of the canyon we had to climb a steep hill. We had Model T Fords and Dad would turn the car around and back up the steepest parts. I didn't know why until much later. I learned it was because the Model T had a gravity flow from the gasoline tank to the carburetor which didn't flow when the front of the car was headed uphill, higher than the gasoline tank. These Model Ts were not very powerful. Many times we would have to push the car to help Dad up the places he could go, or "scotch" the wheels with a rock placed behind each wheel so the car would not roll backward. Traveling in these Model Ts was not a spectator sport.

On our trips to El Paso, 150 miles away, to visit our Evans and Powell grandparents, we would leave the ranch early in the morning and eat our lunch at Findlay, a railroad station west of Sierra Blanca. One time I remember eating our lunch under the railroad overpass just west of Van Horn. Perhaps we got a late start or had some kind of trouble on the way. Flat tires were frequent occurrences. Then Dad would have to jack the wheel up, remove the wheel, take the tire off and patch the inner tube, which was not much bigger around than a bicycle inner tube. When the tire and inner tube were put back on the wheel, Dad had to pump it up with a hand pump. Before Highway 80 was built, the cars would get stuck in the sand at Plateau. The men cut soapweed daggers and laid them across the ruts that were the road. This gave the cars traction to keep from sticking in the sand. This was long before my time. There was a road of sorts as I remember.

It was an all day trip to El Paso. We usually would arrive close to El Paso about dark. We were amused at the Mexican peddlers' rickety carts with their wobbly wheels. These peddlers with their wobbly-wheeled carts pulled by one old horse would come to the houses in my Grandmother Powell's neighborhood selling, meat, vegetables, fruits and flowers. I don't recall she ever bought meat, but she had certain peddlers she bought vegetables and fruits from. Downtown on the street corners Mexican women peddled sweet peas, beautiful, large sweet peas of all colors in newspaper cornucopias. We listened for the Good Humor man and got our nickels ready when we heard his lilting tunes. Ice cream was a rare treat for us.

My Grandmother Powell was a spunky, delightful person—an ideal grandmother. She planned special treats for us. One great adventure was taking us riding on the streetcar. She knew and was friends with all the conductors. The streetcar rails ended at the side of her house on what was then the outskirts of El Paso—the end of the line. The conductor stopped, lowered the contact pole from the overhead electric wire, went through the car turning the hinged backs of the seats so the passengers always sat facing forward, raised the contact pole at that end of the streetcar, and only then opened the door where we were impatiently waiting to board this big yellow conveyance. We dropped our money in the slot and chose our seats for the trip. Then we were off—clang, clang—the warning to motorists that the streetcar did not stop at intersections unless there were people waiting at the corner to "catch" the streetcar. We watched out the windows as the houses became closer together and we reached downtown El Paso—the Plaza in the center of El Paso surrounded by tall buildings two to four stories high. The plaza in downtown El Paso had a large pond with several sluggish alligators—huge, ugly, scaly monsters. I always wondered, "Why alligators in El Paso?" It was quite an attraction, for there were always people watching the alligators that rarely moved.

Sometimes we would depart the streetcar downtown and go to

Kress's, the five and dime store with all these wonderful treasures to choose from. Should I get this, or was something else more desirable? We had to look at everything to be sure. Grandmother never hurried us in our exploring all these wonderful things. She understood our delight at looking at these desirable items. I was fascinated with the glassware—the glassware that is now valued by collectors as Depression glass. Kress's had several sizes of cobalt blue violin-shaped vases that I lingered over. Either I didn't have enough money or chose something else, but I always wished I had bought a blue violin vase. Many years later I found one in a secondhand store and fulfilled my wish. When we had finally made our choices and paid for them, we crossed the street to the Plaza to await the next streetcar for the ride home, excited with the treasures we had chosen.

Memories of grandmother's cooking and kitchen? Not of my maternal grandmother Eula Virginia Mixon Powell, who always signed her name E.V. Powell. Her interests, which were many and diverse, were not in the kitchen. When we visited her in El Paso we had something to eat, but I don't remember any particular dish. My main memory of food at her home is the special pleasure of the ice cream she served my sister, brother and me in beautiful pressed glass berry bowls with matching saucers of cookies. She made it a festive party with the ice cream, which was such a rare treat for us. It was served at the dining room table, not in the kitchen. This added to the specialness of the occasion. Ice cream has never since tasted so good.

Her house was in an area higher than Fort Bliss army post and downtown El Paso. It made a good vantage point for watching the fireworks displays at Christmas and New Year's. We were allowed to stay up late to watch these. Our fireworks consisted mainly of sparklers—coated sticks which, when lighted, emitted fiery sparks that made fascinating patterns as we twirled them around. I don't remember firecrackers; I never liked anything that made sudden loud noises. My brother could have set off small firecrackers but we never had anything like the big dangerous explosives now available—not even Roman candles. We did not have the money for those even if our parents had consented to them.

My Grandmother Powell's kitchen was not a place of delectable aromas. She had a natural gas burning cook stove and the whole kitchen always smelled of that gas. It was not a gas leak. The substance added to the gas to make that odor is so volatile that it escapes where the gas cannot. It is not an appetizing scent. Grandmother Powell cooked with the gas turned on high—no long slow cooking for her; she cooked with gas. Sometimes her food was slightly scorched—her mind was often on more interesting things than cooking—but her apple pies were made very carefully. She washed the apples, peeled them, and boiled these peelings in a little water. After the apples were cored and sliced into the pie crusts, she added some of the liquid from these cooked peelings, along with sugar and spices. Her apple pies were always juicy and delicious.

**My maternal grandfather, Grandpa Jim Powell**, played the violin—the fiddle, he called it. In his younger days he probably played for their dances—"breakdowns" for square dances, as well as waltzes, two-steps, and schottisches at Fort Davis dances. One tune he played for us when we were young was the Indian Warrior. He could make his fiddle sound just like Indian war whoops. We always begged him to play the Indian song. Now in his retirement from ranching he would sit in a straight cane-bottomed chair in the center of the kitchen and play his fiddle with the kitchen door closed. Why the kitchen? Were the acoustics better in there? I don't know. Did these mini-concerts bring back memories of his ranching days, when Jim would organize and boss trail herds of 1,500 to 2,000 of his steers and sometimes a thousand or so of a neighboring rancher's steers to drive them to markets in the north, Oklahoma and Kansas?

Included were a hundred or two heifers. There was no market for heifers so they were killed for beef to have a continuous supply of fresh meat.

A *cusinero* (cook) had to be hired to drive the chuck wagon and prepare the meals for ten to fifteen cowboys. The chuck wagon was loaded with barrels of flour, a keg of sugar, sacks of frijoles and potatoes, and jugs of molasses—"lick," the cowboys called it. And in the safest place in the chuck wagon was loaded Jim's fiddle in its case.

Evenings after the steers had grazed their fill on lush gramma and crowfoot grasses and were bedded down for the night with no threat of a stampede, after supper Boss Jim Powell would retrieve his fiddle from its secure place in the chuck wagon and play for the cowboys in camp, but not for long. They needed to get some sleep before time for them to relieve those riding herd now, when the Big Dipper made half its swing around Polaris, the North Star, denoting midnight.

The herd would have been travelling along the Pecos River to Roswell, where they would swing toward the Texas Panhandle with its prairie grasses and playa lakes for water. When the market city was reached and the steers sold, Jim was paid in cash, probably gold pieces placed in his saddle bags and tied securely behind his saddle. These saddle bags went everywhere he did. They had no organized banking system at that time. Now Jim would visit the big general store to buy gifts for his family—pocket knives and vests or jackets for his two young sons and lengths of beautiful fabrics to be made into dresses for his wife and three daughters—fabrics such as were not available in Fort Davis.

The trip home was much faster with only the remuda to drive. The horses knew they were going home. The cook with the chuck wagon could travel faster; antelope were plentiful for fresh meat. When they reached home in Fort Davis, there was great rejoicing over the successful trail drive.

Were these thoughts and memories going through Jim Powell's mind as he sat in the kitchen and played his fiddle?

**Music was an important part of my early life**, as it continues to be. Mother sang in her clear soprano voice as she did her housework. She and Dad sang as he played guitar in the evenings after supper. My unfulfilled desire was to take voice lessons to learn how to sing as I could feel it inside. I think that wish will be granted when I reach heaven.

I had piano lessons when I was in the first grade and learned to read music. The widow who gave piano lessons seemed to be more interested in asking me about family affairs than in instructing me in music. Hence, I did not learn the basics of playing music. I could play pretty well by ear. We did not have a piano then, so my ability to play never developed. My appreciation and love of music has continued.

Old time dances to the music of fiddle, guitar, and sometimes piano were our recreation when I was a teenager. My dad taught me to dance waltzes, two steps, schottisches, polkas, and square dances. He was a talented dancer and guitar player. After Prohibition was repealed, some of the local men brought their liquor to dances. That spoiled the fun and eventually killed our dances.

There was a local woman who was an excellent dancer. Dad said she would even follow a misstep. Word got around town of her indiscretions. When Mother heard of it she said to Dad because she did not want his reputation to be endangered, "Don't you ever dance with that woman again."

"Yes, Ma'am," Dad replied, and he never did.

The man I married was tall and athletic and an excellent dancer. When he told me he felt it was too silly to dance unless he had several drinks of liquor, I said, "Then we won't go to dances." Since he had an alcoholic father, three alcoholic brothers, and a borderline sister, it was not worth the risk. I felt alcoholism was something I could not live with. He did not drink alcohol any other time. I gave up going to dances, but I have never relinquished the desire to dance to the rhythm of music.

**The magazines of my youth were filled with illustrations by Russian-born designer and artist Erte'.** They depicted unnaturally tall and slender women of the Art Nouveau style, always holding a cigarette. I decided to show the town kids how sophisticated I was by smoking cigarettes. What an oxymoron— thirteen and sophisticated!

I started smoking and liked it, though that first Lucky Strike made me a little giddy. I am sure I inhaled the smoke. I didn't think my parents knew I smoked, but it is no secret when anyone smokes— they smell so bad. Nothing was ever said to me about smoking, but I knew they did not want me to smoke. I smoked about 2 or 3 years, but never in my parents' presence.

During Bloys Campmeeting, a group of teens climbed a hill to where a quarry had been. When we reached the top, we lighted up. A feeling of revulsion came over me for what I was doing. I couldn't smoke in my parents' presence, and I was ashamed to smoke "behind their backs," as it were. I threw down the cigarette I had just lighted and without an explanation I quit the habit cold turkey— one of the best things I ever did. I am convinced that all it takes to quit smoking is to really want to do it. Now with all the helps— patches, pills, etc., there is really no excuse not to quit.

**My father was a very innovative person.** He devised many labor-saving and helpful aids to ranching. One thing he ideated was a way to get firewood to the houses in the canyon. Wood was our cooking and heating fuel; but the source of wood was the oak trees on Boracho Peak on the top of the mountain. To reach this area with a wagon and team entailed a fifteen mile trip around through the pastures. After the wagon was loaded with logs, there was the fifteen mile trip home—a long, hard day's work.

There is a gap in the rim rock of the mountain on the north side of Panther Canyon. Dad availed of this gap to firmly set a large post to which he fastened a cable that reached to the bottom of the mountain. There he had a sturdy metal plate braced to stop the logs. The logs were fastened to the cable with long fence staples. The log was given a shove and down the mountain it came with a high-pitched zinging noise. The cable was engineered with enough slack that the speed of the log was somewhat controlled. It did not hit this metal plate at the bottom at top speed. Some of the dry hollow logs would shatter when they hit. At times a log would stall where the cable sagged, and someone would have to climb the mountain and give it a shove to start it on its way. The time to attach and send the logs down the cable had to be spaced so the logs would not jam. This cable must have been 800 or 1000 feet long. It was exciting to see the logs zinging down the cable. Now it was easy to haul the logs across the creek to our wood pile. With one long wagon trip, several wagon loads of logs could be hauled to the rim rock and unloaded to send down the cable later.

To saw the logs to useable lengths, Dad had a table saw powered by a single horizontal piston engine. This engine was water-cooled and had a glass oil dispenser that let a controlled amount of oil drip onto the piston. The engine had a big flywheel on each side of the piston chamber. On one of these flywheels, a belt ran from it to the pulleys on the table saw.

41

Once we were playing at sawing wood. I was manning the table saw while my sister and brother were using their hands to turn the pulley that ran the saw. We were really sawing wood when, in pushing the log up to the saw, I got one of my fingers in the way. Blood began to gush! I ran screaming to the house. I thought I had sawed my finger off. It turned out I had just sawed down the side of one finger nail. I still had all my fingers, but I had lost my desire to saw wood. Dad wore heavy gauntlet gloves when he sawed the wood. He had a healthy respect for that wicked saw, a respect I learned to share. Bringing in baskets of "chips", the small pieces of wood used to start fires, was a task we hated. I'm not sure why—it wasn't really hard. It was our job each evening to bring in armloads of wood to fill the wood boxes for the kitchen stove and the fireplace. There were different lengths of wood for each one—shorter lengths and smaller pieces fit the firebox of the kitchen stove, while the fireplace needed longer and much larger logs.

**Ranchers were always in need of more good horses** when that was their main way of working cattle and travelling to other ranches. About 1930 my dad's younger brother, Graves Evans, had heard of the horses bred and raised on the Casey's KC Ranch. He drove to the east side of the Davis Mountains where the ranch was situated. On arriving he asked a cowboy where he would find the ranch owner. "Here she comes now," exclaimed the cowboy. Around the corner of the barn appeared this woman astride a bucking horse, riding and whipping him up one side and down the other every jump with her quirt. She got the horse under control, dismounted, and introduced herself. Yes, she did have horses for sale, but they were not broke. They had always run free out on the mountainside pasture. They had never felt a rope or a saddle. Graves looked the horses over and liked what he saw—well-bred, well-built horses weighing from 800 to 1200 pounds, four and five years old. He bought twenty head, sorrels and bays, handsome horse stock, but wild as the mule deer with which they shared the pasture. He brought some saddle horses from the EV Ranch to drive with these wild ones back to the EVs. Then the process of turning these creatures into usable horses began.

It is amazing how a 150 pound man with ropes and a snubbing post can subdue a 1200 pound horse. It takes a lot of patience and perseverance to teach a horse to respect ropes before he is introduced to a saddle. Some of these wild horses resisted all attempts to gentle them; some reared up and their necks were broken when they fell back. But most of them became usable, though not gentle mounts. They became good polo horses, for they had the speed and stamina necessary for the game.

In the 1930s my dad, Paul, his brothers, Graves and Rube, nephew, Truett Evans, and a neighbor, Robert Everett, formed a polo team. The Means brothers, Cole, M. O. (Bug), Huling and Sam had a polo team also. About a mile below the houses they used heavy crossties to drag and smooth an area for a polo field with goal posts at each end. They rode their good ranch horses with their western saddles. They did have regulation mallets and balls. They did not play cowboy polo, which uses a much larger ball.

Polo is the most exciting game I have ever seen. No other sport comes anywhere close for speed, timing, coordination and skill. The horses learn to watch the ball as closely as the men do. It is truly the sport of kings. About this time saw a cartoon where seven men, mallets, and horses were in a heap. One lone player was riding around, his mallet ready, saying, "The chance of a lifetime, and I can't find the damn ball."

When the Evans team played teams from Marfa's Fort DA Russell, Fort Bliss at El Paso, teams from Midland, San Angelo, and Lamesa, Texas, as well as a Mexican Army team from Mexico City, these horses were much admired and desired. At this time, West Texas was suffering not only from a nationwide Depression but a devastating drought. The offers to buy some of these horses were too good to resist. Money in this area was almost non-existent. Also, Graves Evans had bought a ranch in New Mexico, so their polo team fell apart. They sold some of these outstanding horses and received enough money to finish weathering the drought. It had been an interesting experience.

After learning to play riding their western saddles, they did get the flat English style saddles—no saddle horn or cantle. Their riding skills really came into play then—you ride with your knees—but their horses did not have to carry so much weight. There were some collisions and spills, but no one was seriously hurt. The worst injury occurred when playing the Means team at the Y6 Ranch. Someone swung at the ball too close to Dad's head and his ear was cut loose from his head for about ½ inch. There was a doctor in Valentine, some five miles away. Demands on his services were not very heavy, so he did not always keep regular office hours. This day he was found pitching horseshoes at the railroad roundhouse with the railroad men. He came back to his office and, without even washing his hands, sewed Dad's ear back in place. There was no infection and it healed right up. I guess it was good sterile horseshoe dust.

We were fortunate as children that we did not have any serious injuries. My brother, Paul, slipped trying to climb the wall of the tank at the Salome' place, and broke his arm above his wrist. It was a clean break and healed with no complications in the plaster cast he had to wear. We had numerous scraped knees and small cuts on our hands. Once some cousins and I were making doll clothes while sitting on a cot. Somehow I managed to sit on the scissors, which pierced my thigh. That was very painful and took a long time to heal. That gave me a great respect for scissors and to keep them in sight always.

**The year I was fifteen** I had numerous bouts of tonsillitis. A good friend of the family, Dr. Marshall, was at Bloys that year, and he offered to remove the tonsils in his office in Dallas for no charge. My Uncle Graves Evans had the same tonsil trouble and the same offer, except he went to a hospital for the surgery. We went to Dallas.

I stayed with my Aunt Alice Powell Evans' family. Dr. Marshall removed the tonsils with a local anesthetic. This was done in his office on the 22nd floor of the Medical Arts Building in Dallas. It was something I would not advise anyone to have with a local anesthetic. They told me later that they had a very hard time persuading me to get into the elevator after the surgery. Of the many surgeries I had later, this tonsillectomy was the most painful to recuperate from.

After a week of misery in Dallas, I rode the train to Monahans to start school a week late. When I had been in the junior classes about three weeks, the superintendent and the principal decided I could include enough senior courses to graduate that school year, a heavy course. This was a great boon to my parents, for I know it was a sacrifice for them to send me to school in Monahans and hire a governess for my brother and sister at the ranch. Depression and drought years were hard.

That school year I lived with my uncle and aunt, Bill and Freda Powell, both teachers. Every Saturday we thoroughly cleaned house. The sand in Monahans gets everywhere, so we wiped down all the furniture, which they had very attractively painted with enamel paint, and mopped all the linoleum-covered floors. I learned a lot about efficiency, management and discipline that year.

This was my introduction to a shower for bathing. I was sold on that method for bathing. My uncle had installed a pipe for the water to pour out from the wall—no shower head—but that lovely stream of water was very enjoyable to bathe in.  I told my dad about the shower and he rigged a similar arrangement over our bathtub.  He used a burner from an old gas cook stove for a shower head.  It worked amazingly well.  On ranches you improvise and use what you have to get the job done.

That year I had the measles.  Because of our isolated lifestyle we missed the contagious diseases of early childhood, though Mother said I had the mumps when I was nine months old.  After the doctor said I was no longer contagious, I went home to the ranch for a week.  That doctor was very mistaken, for my brother and sister had such terrible measles and chickenpox that Mother thought they might have had smallpox.  The doctor in Valentine assured her it was not smallpox.  It seems I had chickenpox too and thought the two or three little ulcers I had were part of measles.

Groups of us young people used to walk out east of Monahans to play in the sand dunes.  We had great fun sliding and rolling down those sand dunes.  This area is now a State Park.  Now when we drive that highway, I am surprised at how far it is from Monahans and at the distance we walked for fun.  There was an underground storage tank that had been built to hold a million barrels of oil.  There must have been a crack in it somewhere because it was never filled with oil.  We would go out to it and climb through the man hole down into the tank.  I didn't like that, but I certainly was not going to be chicken.  Amusement for young people was simpler then.

I did do one thrilling thing that year.  A pilot came there in a Ford tri-motor airplane.  He would take a person up for a ride for 25 cents.  I think my entire senior class of 10 students went for the ride.  I certainly was glad I had the 25 cents to be able to go up.  We circled the town of Monahans and a little of the adjoining country a couple of times and landed. What a thrill! I had flown in an airplane!

While in Monahans I missed the mountains. I felt as if I were in a giant overturned bowl that sat on the horizons with no mountains to hold up the sky. To go home on some occasions, I caught the bus on Friday right after school to ride to Kent. I eagerly watched to see the silhouette of Gomez Peak when we reached Pecos, 90 miles from home and the mountains. I rode the train back to Monahans Sunday evenings.

**Who ever heard of a small town high school chartering a train** to go to a football game? This oil boom town for years had had no church. An enterprising woman placed a jar for contributions at the filling station on Highway 80 with a sign that Monahans was the only town of its size in Texas without a church.

When I attended high school in Monahans, there were only ten seniors—nine girls and one boy. Four of these seniors came from Grandfalls and Imperial where there were no high schools. This enterprising woman's husband was the station agent in Monahans for the Texas & Pacific Railroad. There was a trunk line from Monahans to Jal, New Mexico, to pick up the tank cars of oil. This station agent arranged for two passenger cars to be added to the steam locomotive-pulled train to be available the day of the Monahans-Jal football game. The train departed Monahans soon after noon for the less than fifty-mile run to Jal and returned that night. The fare must have been about one dollar—no one could have afforded more than that in those Depression days. This chartered train made it possible for students to attend this important game, for students did not have their own cars then as they do now. Students and fans boarded this train early the afternoon of the game. Football games were played in the afternoons—there were no field lights. We were in high spirits. For some young people it was a first time to ride a train. For each passenger it was a special occasion. For me it was one of the first football games I had ever seen. I didn't know anything about the game. When the others yelled, so did I. I became as hoarse as any true fan.

The football field at Jal was hard-packed soil, not the soft sand that comprised the field at Monahans. Early in the game Monahans had the ball. The captain of our team was running toward the goal. The Jal team converged on him. He was downed. When the other boys rose to their feet, our team's captain was still on the ground. The crowd grew quiet—a player was hurt. The ambulance arrived. This injured player was rushed to the hospital. Word came to us that his leg was broken. So were our high spirits. The game was resumed despite the fact that our underclassmen were no match for the burly sons of oilfield workers. A weary and solemn crowd of fans boarded this chartered train to return to Monahans that night. Still, it was a once-in-a-lifetime experience. Probably none of those fans has ridden on a chartered train to another high school football game.

**My maternal grandmother who lived in El Paso made delicious apple pies**. Her son, W. T. (Bill), was really fond of Mama's pies. She would bake pies, take them on the street car to the railroad station downtown, and deliver them to the station agent there, who put them on the train to Monahans, where Uncle Bill eagerly waited for them. The station agent in Monahans was Aunt Freda's father, who had the contact with the agent in El Paso. When the train stopped in Monahans, Bill would be there to claim his pies. Life was simple and very personal then.

My Uncle Bill asked me not to call him "Uncle Bill" in school, so I dutifully called him Mr. Powell except one time in study hall I slipped and came out with "Uncle Bill." The students thought that was hilarious. At graduation time I had the grades to be Valedictorian, but since I had gone to school in Monahans only that one year, the school board decided to give that honor to my Aunt

Freda's younger sister, who had attended there from first grade. At that time I was so timid and shy that I was only relieved that I would not have to give a speech.

I had one very disillusioning experience that year. Aunt Freda's mother, an industrious, civic-minded woman, started a little café next to the school so the students could have a hot lunch. For $10 a month (20 meals) she furnished nourishing and delicious lunches. She would put them on a tab and you could pay at the end of the month. My science course was Foods & Nutrition—a snap because I already knew how to cook. The teacher assigned desk mates for us. My desk mate was a trashy dumb girl who was not even clean. The teacher wanted me to help this girl. My parents had sent me the money to pay my café tab. Lacking a pocket, I put it in my desk drawer when we went to the kitchen. When class was over, I reached to get my money. It was gone. I immediately told the teacher. She called the class back and announced the problem. She told them she would leave her desk drawer unlocked for the money to be put back during the noon hour. The few coins I had for spending money were put in her drawer, but not the $10 bill. I am positive that trashy girl took that money. She was the only one who knew I had it. That created a double hardship for my parents to replace that money. That experience added to my feeling of distrust for girls.

I did get a trip to Austin, Texas, through that Foods course. The teacher picked me to go to a state contest in Nutrition. Another girl went for sewing. The teacher and we two girls drove to Austin. I remember the swinging bridge over the river at Junction. This was made of boards swung from cables. As you drove across the boards they moved to give you the sensation of going uphill. They clattered loudly. It was an odd sensation. It was a one-way bridge, the width for only one car. In Austin we stayed in a hotel on Congress Avenue. I guess that was a first time for me for that. We went to the

Capitol Building and climbed to the very top of the dome and to the tower. We went out on the balcony. It was a memorable experience.

**The only eligible young men for dating** when I was in high school were the cowboys working on surrounding ranches. The three or four boys my age in school were still just kids not ready for dating, though we had a good time together in school activities. These cowboys were mainly young men from 16 to 22 years of age from the Central Texas area around San Angelo. Some of them had a pickup, or a buddy who did. They were a good bunch of boys just trying to get a start in life, but some of them were pretty rough-looking. If I ever had a date with one of these rough-looking boys, my Dad would say, "How would you like to look across the breakfast table at him for the rest of your life?"

I could have saved my parents a lot of needless anxiety and worry, for I never saw a man I even considered loving until I met my future husband. I liked these boys and enjoyed going places with them, but I knew I never felt anything like love for any of them. I had some cousins and girlfriends who professed to be "madly in love" with nearly every boy they dated. I thought that was the silliest thing I ever heard of. Maybe I was a little mercenary in some of my dating, but it was their invitation and the only way I had to go places. I dated every boy I ever wanted to.

Recreation in Valentine was nil. There was a movie theater in Marfa 50 miles away that showed movies in the evenings. Occasionally there would be a silent movie on the Mexican side of the tracks with captions in Spanish. These were exciting even if we were not always sure what was said. It was some place to go.

A man I dated and I went shooting prairie dogs nearly every Sunday afternoon. He worked in his brother's grocery store weekdays. Prairie dog shooting was a sport of quick reactions and much skill.

50

We used .22 rifles for this. We would drive to a large prairie dog town on the Y6 Ranch and wait for a prairie dog to stick his head up above his hole. You had to be ready and fast to get a shot. Usually from the time you pulled the trigger to the time the bullet got there he had ducked safely back into his hole. Sometimes a dog would run from his hole to another and give you a running shot. They were hard to hit. We used lots of .22 shells.

These prairie dogs are really rodents—very destructive, invasive and prolific rodents. They not only eat the grass and line their nests with it, but their main food is the grass roots, thereby killing the grass and destroying large areas of grass around their holes. They are big enough to eat a lot of grass roots.

When we were young at EV Ranch and the creek ran a moderate stream we would ride to the hay field where the water spread out. With our shovels we would ditch the water into the prairie dog holes and hopefully when he came out, kill him with our shovels. They are not so fast when they have had to swim out of their holes. But sometimes they had a back door where they could escape. On one such occasion, Paul had ditched water into a hole but the prairie dog hadn't come out. Paul knelt down to see why not and looked a big rattlesnake in the face. That put a damper on our sport. Rattlesnakes find these prairie dog holes a good place to live.

The government through the county agents instigated a program for killing prairie dogs with hydrogen disulphide gas. I was never present for this, so I am not sure how the gas was dispensed into the hole. After it was, the hole was covered and closed with dirt. It was a very effective program and a great help to the ranchers.

**My father and his brothers, Lee and G. W. Jr. (Dub)** who ranched in New Mexico, had a good friend who enjoyed hunting the bear and mountain lions which were plentiful on the New Mexico ranches and the mule deer on Dad's Texas ranch. This man, whom we knew as "Mr. Kirk," had the Ford car agency in El Paso. He had hunted with these Evans brothers and visited their families. He knew that all our families spent Christmas in El Paso where our Evans grandparents and my Powell grandparents lived.

One year before Christmas Mr. Kirk wanted to do something special for my cousin, Pansy Evans, and me. Pansy was two years older than I. I was 15 1/2. He arranged for two of his handsome young salesmen to escort us to a very fancy dinner and dance. This was before cell phones, or even telephone communication to the New Mexico ranches. Postal service was our only means of contact, and our reception and sending of mail was infrequent. Pansy's mother was the postmaster at Beaverhead Ranch, where mail was delivered once a week. We got our mail only when someone made the 30 mile trip to Valentine, our nearest post office. How all the details and arrangements for this occasion came together took a lot of doing by my mother and her sisters-in-law.

I had no formal gown, nor did Pansy, who lived on an isolated New Mexico mountain ranch and had no more use for a formal gown than I did. But our Aunt Lou C attended the Cattlemen's Convention in Albuquerque and had evening gowns that would fit Pansy and me. I marvel at how all this correspondence worked so well. Our Texas ranch was 350 miles from Pansy's parents, and Aunt Lou C lived on a ranch on what is now a Navajo Indian Reservation at least 200 miles farther away from there.

The date for this special occasion arrived. All the arrangements were complete. One young man came for Pansy at 2100 Grant Avenue; then they drove to 4231 Hastings Street, the home of my Powell grandparents, which was on what was then the very eastern edge of El Paso. I felt very grown up in Aunt Lou C's apricot slinky velvet gown when the young man in his tuxedo came for me. The affair was held in the ballroom of the Hotel Paso del Norte, the finest hotel between San Antonio, Texas, and Albuquerque, New Mexico. Here was my first taste of caviar, which I thought was highly overrated; and one sip of the cocktail convinced me that I didn't like it.

After the dinner we danced a while and then the young men suggested we go somewhere else. This place was about a block away. We went from the sidewalk down some stairs where one of the young men knocked on a door, and we were admitted to a room full of tables and chairs. This was during Prohibition but I think we could have had any drink we wished. We each had a small glass of tomato juice. Pansy and I were taken to our respective grandparents' homes at a reasonable hour by these polite young men. My family was interested in the events of the evening, but somehow I forgot to tell them about the visit to the speakeasy.

Through the years since then as I remember this occasion, I have wondered what incentive Mr. Kirk used to persuade those young men to escort two young ranch girls they had never seen to a formal ball. Also I have marveled at my parents' confidence in Mr. Kirk to consent to such an arrangement. Times were very different then; you could trust people.

**In 1933 I had met a young man at Bloys Campmeeting** who lived at Dinero, south of San Antonio. We corresponded during the following year. His parents came to Bloys in 1934; but this young man was working at a job he couldn't leave, so he wanted me to come to Dinero with his parents. I liked to go places, so I accepted the invitation. This was the last part of August. I was not prepared for the intense, unrelenting heat of south Texas, or the low altitude. This was long before air conditioning, and I had never been to such a low altitude. It was miserable for me.

He did much to make my visit interesting. We went through a bakery his family owned. He showed me where he had swum over the tops of tall trees when the river had flooded. It all looked like flat country to me—no mountains. They planned a trip to Corpus Christi and I was looking forward to cooling off in the Gulf. Was that a disappointment! How disillusioning when I stepped into that murky-looking water at about body temperature. I was used to water to swim in being cold.

In San Antonio we went to the Alamo and saw the name of my relative who perished there. We toured Brackenridge Park. I was entranced with an old Chinese man who played a small harp in a tea room. From San Antonio I rode the bus to Valentine and then home. He sent me 18 red roses for my 18th birthday, by Parcel Post. They were a little wilted when I received them many days later.

After I graduated from Monahans High School, there was no money for college; so I stayed with my brother Paul and sister Frances in a rented house in Valentine so that they could attend school. I had time, so I enrolled in courses I had not been able to take in Monahans because of my combined necessary courses for junior and senior years. I had the freedom to come for my courses and leave when they were over. I could go home and prepare lunch for Frances, Paul, and me. This way Mother and Mary Sue could be at the ranch with Dad.

Sometime in the spring of 1935, probably March, I was walking from school in a terrible dust storm. The dust was so thick and the wind so strong that it stung my face and legs and I could not see an arm's length ahead. I was fighting to even stand up. Suddenly rain began, great splashing drops of rain—rain that was plastering me with mud. By the time I reached the house I was coated with mud and shaking with the cold. The rain was so wonderfully welcome after the extreme drought we had been in.

# Memories of a Ranch Wife

We had a neighbor who was a very good friend of my dad. Dad had caught many cattle-killing mountain lions for John. His family lived in the house next to us in Valentine. His ranch had timber on it for a plentiful supply of wood for fuel. When he brought a pickup load of wood to town, he unloaded half of it at his house and the rest at our house. He was one of the fairest men, and as honest as any human could be. For spending money I cleaned his wife's house every Friday afternoon after she went to the ranch. I washed the dishes piled in the sink and washed the week's accumulated laundry. She had an electric washer with a wringer and tubs for rinse waters. I hung the clothes on the clothesline to dry while I cleaned the wood floors that had not been touched since I had cleaned them the week before.

They had four little girls, the youngest less than one year old. That poor baby's bed was the foulest thing I had even encountered. This was before waterproof panties. I could not imagine any mother letting her baby get in such condition. For all this I was paid 50 cents and the use of her washer to wash our clothes. I was glad to get it. There were not job opportunities in that little town of one drug store, one grocery store, and one general merchandise store, each operated by the owner.

At times I was having spells of intense pain in my side. The doctor in El Paso diagnosed it as appendicitis and recommended surgery. At that time, as now, if some organ didn't work right or gave trouble, the doctor's solution was to remove it. So I was relieved of my appendix. While I was convalescing, my Uncle Graves Evans, who was at EV Ranch on business, asked me to go to his New Mexico ranch with him. I welcomed the chance to see his wife, Gene, again. Graves was an interesting talker and traveling companion. He told about places we journeyed through and made trips with him very enjoyable.

For me to return home, he took me to the bus station and left me in (then) Hot Springs, later renamed Truth or Consequences. Because it was raining in the area, he needed to get home before the creeks ran. Because of this rain the bus had to wait for a creek to run down enough to be crossed. This caused my departure to be several hours delayed and my arrival in El Paso to be very late. I caught the last streetcar at midnight to my grandmother's home. The house was locked and the doorbell brought no response. My grandfather had his bedroom in the basement, so I supposed he could not hear the doorbell. This house had floor-to-ceiling windows that opened from the dining room and a bedroom onto the porch. I tried the window into the bedroom. It was locked. I then tried the window into the dining room. Thankfully, it opened.

After a good night's rest, I discovered that my grandfather was also gone; I was there alone. My grandmother was away from home so much in the summer that she had her telephone on discounted rates where you could call out but not receive incoming calls. I called my Uncle Rube's house in El Paso. Luckily, Aunt Mary's nephew, Charles, who worked for Burdick Windmill Company, was in town. He came for me, but all the nosy neighbor saw was the two of us coming out of my grandmother's house that morning. She reported some scandalous news when my grandmother returned home.

**Sometime in 1934 I was at a dance** at the Selman place on top of the mountain from EV Ranch. I looked across the room to see a tall, handsome young man that Angie Everett had introduced me to at a dance in Valentine. As we looked across the room at each other, something electric and magical happened between us. We danced, and he started coming to Valentine to see me. I don't even remember who had brought me to that dance. No other young man was interesting to me now.

To get to Valentine from east of Kent where he worked, you had to go by way of Van Horn, a distance of 95 miles. After working all day at Cowden's ranch, Blackie would drive that distance to see me. If we went to a dance, he might return to Cowden's just in time to get the milk bucket and milk the cow, and then work all day with no sleep. We had no telephone communication, so I didn't always know when he was coming. He came to Valentine one time when I had gone to a movie in Marfa with some other young man. My sister Frances entertained him, but he didn't stay until I returned. I was surprised that he ever came back, but he did.

For Bloys Campmeeting 1935 Blackie was there, much to my joy. Only later when I had some sense did I realize Aunt Grace and Uncle Bill's part in Blackie's being there. Gracie had talked to Blackie and found that he was not a Christian, so Uncle Bill had paid someone to stay at his ranch in Blackie's place and provided a tent for Blackie to stay in so he could attend Bloys. Blackie made his decision for Christ that week. Great is their reward in heaven!

One incident of that week: Blackie had bought an economy-sized tube of shaving cream to have for a long time of use. Billy Cowden, barely four years old, found that this tube of shaving cream would make interesting foamy squiggles. He was having a great time squeezing it around. Someone said to him, "You shouldn't do that." Billy replied, "Oh, Blackie doesn't care what I do." Billy and Blackie were great buddies. As Billy would say, "Blackie and I are double-tough." I am sure Blackie didn't say anything when he found that depleted tube, but that tube of shaving cream had cost him several days' pay.

For the school year 1935-36 I taught Paul and Frances. I was probably as qualified as some of the governesses we had had. At least what I taught them was still fresh in my mind, for I had so recently studied it. We always used textbooks from the local public schools. Since I lived at EV Ranch, it was only about 40 miles for

Blackie to come to see me.

# Ranch Life

Before the mobility that pickups afforded we took dinner at noon to the cowboys who would have the cattle gathered out in the pasture. After a pre-dawn breakfast Mother would begin preparing the food to be taken out to the round-up area. There was either roast beef or steak, potatoes, vegetables, always a pot of frijoles, and biscuits or hot rolls, and the makings for coffee. To carry these cooking pans safely, each was placed in the center of a large dish towel. The diagonal corners were brought together and each pair tied tightly over the lid. This assured safe transport without the lid sliding off. The tin plates fit nicely together with the camp cutlery, the tin cups, and the coffee pot with sugar and the can of coffee. All of this had to be loaded in the car so that nothing would tip over and spill while traversing the rough pasture road. With all of this and her three children, Mother would drive to the place Dad told her the herd would be. Dad would have a fire built to get the coffee started. Cattle work was either in the spring or fall of the year, so a fire and hot coffee were welcome. It felt so comforting to cup your cold hands around that hot tin cup of coffee. The children did not drink coffee at home—it was a special treat at round-up time.

Until Dad and his sister, Grace Cowden, had corrals built between their pastures, the cowboys would come to dinner in shifts. The first group ate hurriedly so they could relieve those holding the herd. With the corrals, everyone could eat at the same time after the cattle were penned. The corrals also made working the cattle easy on the cattle and the men. After lunch and any branding were finished the fires were completely extinguished. No fire was left burning or even smoldering. Then everything had to be readied for the trip home.

Working the cattle before the corrals were built entailed the cowboys holding the herd, while the owner or foreman cut out the cattle to be branded or shipped.  Dad said that was easy when they had longhorn-type cattle because each calf was colored with the same pied pattern as its mother.  With the red Hereford cattle you had to watch until the cow claimed her calf.  As these pairs were "cut" (separated) from the main herd, they were headed toward the cut, held by younger or more inexperienced workers.  But disgrace to them if they let any animal go back to the herd!

After the cut was made the remaining cattle were turned loose to graze.  I remember the bulls fighting.  All afternoon they would be pawing the dirt, bellowing a challenge, and butting heads with another bull, long after the cows had returned to their grazing grounds and were out of sight.  Meanwhile one or two ropers— according to the number of cattle and cowboys—roped the calves to be branded and dragged them to the flankers near the fire where the branding irons were heated.  After throwing the stiff legged calf to the ground, this pair of flankers held the calf, one man holding the folded front leg and the other a stretched-out hind leg.  A man vaccinated for Blackleg and another earmarked or neutered as necessary.  Still another man branded the calf before it was released.  This coordinated teamwork was efficient and fascinating to watch.  If they were shorthanded any duties except for the ropers and flankers could be combined.  During the Depression years we were always short-handed, but neighbors helped each other.

A family story about cutting cattle recalled that when my grandfather was up in years, he was cutting the cattle.  A nester who had only one cow saw her in the herd and began to try to drive her out.  He was disrupting the cattle so my grandfather told him to get out of the herd.  The nester heatedly said to Grandfather, "You go to hell."  One of the cowboys reprimanded the nester, "You should not talk to that old man like that.  He owns these cattle.  You should apologize."

The nester's apology: "I told you to go to hell, old man, but you don't have to if you don't want to."

**On a ranch, to have fresh milk it was necessary to keep milk cows,** usually Jerseys. The men milked the cow every evening. The bucket of milk was brought to the house from the milk pen and strained through a very fine mesh into crocks. These were put into the milk tray to cool and for the cream to rise to the top. Mother's milk tray was a metal rack with three shelf spaces. The sides were enclosed with an absorbent cotton flannel cloth that extended from the water in the galvanized top tray to the deeper water in the concrete trough the rack sat in. Clothes pins held the cloth to the rim of the top tray. A process of osmosis and evaporation kept the milk fairly cool. Dad fixed a water pipe and faucet that could be adjusted to a constant drip to keep the top tray full of water.

Before a meal, the cream that had risen to the top of the milk was skimmed off and kept separate. We drank the milk that remained. It was richer and better-tasting than modern skim milk. Some of the cream we used on cereal or desserts. This cream was very rich, thicker than modern whipping cream. The accumulated cream was used to be churned into butter. We had a glass one-gallon Daisy churn with paddles turned by gears attached to a handle. This Daisy churn made making butter easy.

My mother-in-law, Eva Woods, used a two gallon crock about 24 inches tall and fitted with a wooden dasher that you splashed up and down through a hole in the top to make butter. Later, she had a Daisy churn. When this churning or splashing separated the butter particles from the milk, you slowly and carefully gathered it into a ball. We removed this ball of butter with a wooden paddle and worked the milk out with this paddle in a large bowl. We added water in this bowl and washed the remaining milk out so the butter would keep and be sweet. The milk left from churning we called buttermilk even though the butter had been removed.

Some crocks of milk were left for the natural enzymes to turn it sour. This made a soft solid that was slightly acid. For some reason it always tasted cooler than sweet milk—the acid in it, I guess. If you whipped this solidified milk it made a product similar to yogurt, but it was not slimy like yogurt. We called the semi-solid milk clabber.

My mother-in-law had a cream separator, for she sold cream to a creamery. This separator worked by centrifugal force. Right after bringing the milk to the house, she strained it into the large stainless steel bowl at the top of the separator. This bowl had many cone-shaped small parts. As the handle turned these parts in the bowl, the cream, which is lighter than the milk, was thrown to the outside of the bowl and drained off into a container by a spout near the top of the bowl. The heavier milk drained into another container through a drain near the bottom of the bowl. Separating the cream with this device was easy, but oh, washing the separator with its many parts was a job.

Where Blackie's parents lived in Central Texas, the women did the milking, among almost all the other farm tasks. This was new to me. Where I lived, the men did the milking and the ranch work. Blackie's father claimed he couldn't milk a cow because his hands didn't fit the cow's teats. One time Eva had something wrong with her knees, probably fluid in the joint. It was so painful that she felt she could not bear to walk to the corral to milk the cow. Chief, as we called Blackie's father, said he would take her to the corral in the wheelbarrow. He helped her into the wheelbarrow and started pushing her to the corral. About halfway there, he turned the wheelbarrow over and dumped her out. I never heard any details of what happened then. This was just another crisis in their 68 years of marriage, but I am assured he did not milk the cow. After Gran, as we called Eva, was in her eighties we were concerned about her still milking the cow, especially in cold, bad weather. I said to her that I wished she wouldn't milk the cow. She replied, "I like to milk a cow." I did not say any more. I thought if she died milking the cow, at least she was doing something she liked. It had never occurred to me that anyone would like milking a cow. To me it was a chore that had to be done.

Twice in my life I had to milk the cow. Blackie had to be gone one night when we lived at the Burned House. Somehow Beary, six years old, and I milked that cow. In New Mexico when Blackie was called to Santa Fe for his Army physical, he had to be gone overnight, so again it was up to me to milk. Both times I am sure the calves got their fill of milk.

There was a trapper who trapped coyotes on the ranch. Sometimes his son, about nine years of age, lived with him. Mother felt sorry for this little boy. She thought he should have milk to supplement the plain fare his father had, so she would give them milk when they came to our house. Some times in the late spring the cows must have a craving for something green. They are fond of wild onions and gourd vines, which give the milk a horrible taste. You cannot use it. She did not know this milk was not good when she gave it to the trapper. The next visit he told her the milk tasted like the milk bucket was not clean. Mother was insulted. You can be sure he never got any more milk.

Mother made our light bread. She used an everlasting yeast, but not sourdough yeast. Her bread was much lighter and better than sourdough bread. When we were to be away from home for a while, she mixed this yeast with cornmeal and patted it into thin cakes to dry. When she returned home she reconstituted it into the liquid starter yeast. I used to nibble on these yeast patties and really liked the taste.

63

Mother became an excellent cook. Her cakes were the best ever. She followed the recipe exactly so the results were always the same. My sister, Frances, once said of Mother that if a recipe called for two brown eggs and Mother had only white eggs, she couldn't make it. Mother made good biscuits, too, as Dad had taught her. Mother made hot rolls to take to church dinners, bereaved families, or to friends. Everyone looked forward to her delicious rolls.

Around 4 PM was Dad's Coffee Time—coffee accompanied with some of his fruit cobbler or Mother's cake. Each new pastor soon found that was a good time for a visit. Dad made pulled molasses taffy candy. It was heavenly. He pulled the cooked and cooled syrup with his fingertips until it was a golden color and was very porous when he stretched it into a long narrow strip and broke it into pieces. After Dad developed emphysema and Mother would have to call the doctor to come, when Dr. Lipsey came in he would take a piece of that molasses candy from the plate Dad kept handy on his way in to check on Dad. Doc really liked that molasses candy.

**The first lights I remember were gas lights**. The gas was formed in a separate house and piped into the houses. The chemical used was calcium carbide, white chalky lumps that when put in a large circular trough and water added, emitted a flammable gas caught in a round chamber in the center of this trough. This gas was piped from the ceiling's center in each room to the fixture with dainty orifices which, when lighted, gave a bright light through the glass globes.

After these gas lights we had electric lights from a gasoline powered generator which charged a myriad of batteries in glass jars. I have one of these glass jars. My dad became an expert mechanic from working to keep this generator operating. There were several generators through the years, each one smaller and more efficient.

At one time we had a wind charger, a turbine to charge the batteries when the wind blew and turned the rotor. It was not as efficient or dependable as the generators, though there was the advantage of free power and no cost of gasoline or mechanical maintenance.

We had kerosene lamps to use when the generator would not run despite all Dad's efforts. Then the Aladdin lamp which had a delicate "mantle" over the flame gave an excellent light. There were gasoline lanterns which had a pump to build pressure in the gasoline tank and burned brightly with a buzzing noise. They are still available for camping.

Dad installed a master switch which would turn off all lights in the house to keep from draining power from the batteries. Reading was my favorite pastime. After so long of reading in bed, Dad would call, "Lottie, turn off your light." I would reply, "Just let me finish this chapter." This chapter led to another until after the second or third warning. Dad would pull the master switch, and that was the end of reading that night.

Electricity from REA did not reach this ranch until 1967. Then we could have electric appliances. The generator supplied only lights.

**In my childhood, and many years before**, children were introduced to horseback riding at an early age. When Dad came in from riding the range and was met by his wife and baby, he would put Baby in the saddle in front of him and sometimes, when Baby could sit alone, after he had dismounted. Thus the child got an early introduction to the feel and scent of saddle leather. By the time a child was one year old he or she could ride holding to the saddle horn while Dad led the horse to the corral. At four years old a child could ride a horse alone riding close by his dad, and age five he was considered able to go on the fall and spring roundups, where he would stay out in camp with the other cowboys for three weeks, or until the open range was worked, with his bedroll and extra clothes in a flour sack (his war bag) tied on behind his saddle.

The rancher knew which horses would tolerate this tiny rider. Not all the horses would. A horse gentle enough for a young rider was highly prized. Though full-grown in size, they were usually called "kid ponies." Horses are smart, and when he has smelled of this small rider this horse seems to know this small cowboy is special.

For his fourth birthday my brother, Paul, was given the custom made saddle that his uncle Rube Evens had made for him by the Miller Saddlery in El Paso. Now he had a saddle that fit him. He was equipped to go on the spring and fall roundups when he was five years old, as had his father before him.

My father told me that at five years old he was on the fall roundup that drove the cattle to Van Horn as the shipping point. He said only one man, the railroad agent, lived at Van Horn at that time. There were four or five houses not lived in—they had been built by surrounding ranch owners to stay in when shipping their cattle, for sometimes it might be several days after they ordered the railroad cars before enough cars were brought there. The ranchers had to ride herd on the cattle until then—herd them on good grazing ground and take them to water by day and ride guard on them at night during that time. There were large pens with a loading chute next to the railroad where the cattle would be held and loaded into the cattle cars. Sometimes the steam locomotive would scare the cattle into a stampede, making more dangerous work for the cowboys.

The cattle from EV Ranch had to cross the railroad tracks to get to the shipping pens at Valentine. Dad told me of one bunch which refused to lift their hooves over the rails, so Dad roped one calf and pulled it onto the crossing. As the calf bawled, its mother cow's instincts brought her to the crying calf, and the other cattle could be driven to follow after her across the rails.

**My favorite time to walk is in the summer evenings** just before the sun goes down. As a teenager, after the supper dishes were done I would climb the Indian trail of the North Mountain. This trail was so named because soon after my Grandfather Evans settled in Panther Canyon in 1888 he and his oldest sons, Will and Joe, were starting down this trail after looking about the cattle in the mountain pasture. They met four Indian braves coming up the trail. Grandfather must have had some anxious moments—he was unarmed (he never carried a gun) with two very young sons, versus four husky Indians. They conversed enough to reveal that the Indians were peaceful. They were traveling to this area in quest of certain herbs that did not grow in Mexico where they now lived.

This trail angled up the side of the mountain and across a plateau ending about a mile away at a rim rock. This rim rock was a special place for me. There I could sit hundreds of feet above the foot of the mountain. From there I could see the Eagle Mountains fifty or sixty miles to the southwest; the towering Guadalupe Mountains were visible more than seventy miles to the northwest; the Diablo Mountains fifty miles west. Many times dark would overtake me before I reached home. One night I sensed something as I walked on the last stretch home. Looking down, I identified the black and white stripes of a rattlesnake's tail. He was crawling parallel with me. You can be sure I walked a little faster that remaining one-fourth mile home.

**Even as late as the 1940's, women wore hats.** For one reason, cars were not air conditioned then and it was vital to roll windows down in summer to keep from sweltering from the heat. The hats were supposed to keep our hairdos in place. We wore hats to church and on shopping trips to town. The men wore hats almost all their waking hours. They worked out in all weather: hot sunshine, cold winds, and rain, so the hat afforded protection from the elements. Their hats covered their brows, which did not tan as did the rest of their faces.  One old Indian sign for a white man was two fingers drawn across the brow.  When Blackie and I first married, he had been out in camp so much that when he undressed for bed, his hat was the last item of clothing he removed and was the first he put on the next morning.  His hat, next to his boots, represented the greatest expense of his wardrobe.

Naturally, men removed their hats when they entered a house.  When they greeted a woman, that hat was swept off with a flourish of respect for a woman and as the mark of a gentleman.  It is a most complimentary gesture.

A woman who had a grocery store in Van Horn told me that she had wondered why my mother's hat was always dusty until she went to my parents' ranch.  Then she understood.  Fifteen miles of the 35 miles to Van Horn was a country unpaved dirt road.  It had been bladed off to make the road, but was not maintained.  It was rough and very dusty most of the year.

Once, a man called from Ft. Worth to arrange for a lion hunt with my husband.  He asked if it would be all right if he wore a silly hat. I told him, "We don't care what kind of hat you wear, but be sure to wear one."  He was the president of the Wild Turkey Association of Texas and wore a dashing felt hat with a turkey feather stuck in the band.  He was a very nice young man, and he did get a lion.

The cowboy's Stetson hats had the crown creased many different ways, but each cowboy's hat had his own distinctive crease.  No two were exactly alike.  After church one time a man put my husband's hat on and started away.  Blackie knew the hat left on the rack was not his.  He was really disgusted that the man did not know his own hat.  This was a city man, and he was not aware he had the wrong hat.  You can be sure that Blackie overtook him and got his hat back. Another time during a church service on Sunday morning, someone came into the vestibule and took four hats off of the hat rack. There was great consternation when those men found their hats missing. Those hats had cost about $500 each. Luckily, Blackie had left his hat locked in our car.

As a young child I didn't wear a hat, but Mother insisted that my sister and I wear sunbonnets to protect our faces and necks. I did have the type of complexion that, though olive, blistered from exposure to the sun. We hated these bonnets. They were hot and interfered with our scope of vision. Therefore, as soon as we were out of Mother's sight, we would push them off and let them dangle down our backs by the bonnet strings. I am sure that many times I came home from playing in the sun with a red, blistered face and neck, so that Mother knew I had not worn the bonnet. The pain from the sunburn was my punishment.

**A good, dependable automobile** is a necessity for ranchers because of the distances they have to travel. In 1948 Blackie bought two cars, a Ford and a Chevrolet, to see which one he liked best. The Ford gave good gas mileage, so we started to Breckenridge to visit his family. He wanted to see how far that Ford would go on a tank of gas. We were motoring along when west of Colorado City the car sputtered and died. That was how far it would go on a tank of gas. Blackie started walking. He came to what had been a filling station, but was out of business. The man living there still had some gasoline in the storage tank. Blackie bought a can full and put it in the tank. I think it must have been about half water. You could never afford to let the gasoline get low in the tank after that. On a weekend trip to the River to be with Blackie, I was driving pretty fast with that Ford. The hood came unfastened and blew back against the windshield. Somehow I got it stopped, even if I could not see the highway. We kept the Chevrolet, which proved to be an excellent car.

In my childhood days, you always checked to see how much clearance a car had. This was important—for the underbody to be high enough from the ground to travel the roads we had to travel. These roads were made by following the first wheel tracks across the country. Over the years these ruts might become worn quite deep, leaving the center space between the ruts high by comparison, and with occasional rocks on it that might damage the under parts of the car. You didn't want to risk high-centering your car. A rancher in New Mexico was prospering, so he bought a Cadillac and drove it over his ranch. When asked how he liked this car, he replied, "It won't even straddle a cow chip."

**Some of the great advantages of ranch life** are the absolute absence of noise—the powerful quietude of nature—and the almost unlimited visibility in open mountain country. As the sun peeps over the mountain at the east end of the canyon, the twittering of the birds announces their arousal for the search for their daily food. A light breeze wafts up the canyon to stir the creaking of the windmill with the "thunk" of the bottom check in the well as it brings life-sustaining water to the surface for the use of man and animal—sounds of pulsating life beginning the daily routine, but not really noise as such.

When you leave the canyon with the protective, sheltering stability of the surrounding mountains, you have visibility interrupted only by distant mountains from twenty to ninety miles away. You can always know where you are in relation to a mountain. My daughter, Chance, grew up in the mountains, then in adulthood lived in El Paso, then in Albuquerque, New Mexico, each city with its dominant mountain. Last year she moved to Amarillo, Texas, and she is having trouble finding where she needs to be in that flat city. There is no mountain by which you can find your way.

While visiting with a woman who ranched in the forested mountains of New Mexico where you can see only from one tree to the next, I asked her how she found her way. She told me, "You watch the watersheds—which way does the water run?" I think you would have to be very careful to notice and remember, but you would know which side of a mountain you are on by which way the water runs.

**About 1915 one of my father's older brothers** took his inheritance and bought land in northwestern New Mexico adjacent to Indian reservations. He told the Indians he would neighbor with them, but if they didn't keep up the taxes on their land, when it came up for sheriff's sale he would buy it. Indians were notoriously poor money managers (I think nearly every other business in Gallup is a pawn shop) so one after the other as their places came up for sale, he bought them. He and his wife, Lou C, acquired a large ranch this way.

When I was about seven years old they had a seven-passenger Buick. At Bloys Campmeeting Aunt Lou C would gather all her nieces and nephews to go with her in that Buick to Ft. Davis to buy ice cream. This was a real treat that we looked forward to. We climbed into this Buick and were off to Ft. Davis, 16 miles away. She drove that big car with a flourish. It was an exciting trip.

Two years later on a trip to another uncle's ranch, the V+Ts in New Mexico far west of Winston, my sister and I learned to roller skate. Our cousins a little older than we were had these magic roller skates. Learning to skate was easy when you straddled a broom—if you started to fall you could just sit down on the broom handle and get your balance. This house at V+Ts had a wooden porch around three sides with the planks laid at right angles to the walls. I know it made a terrible noise as we skated across these boards, but at least our mothers knew where we were and what we were doing. I liked to skate and became really adept at it. For Christmas that year my brother, sister, and I received roller skates. What fun we had skating on the only concrete available—the center section of the big barn which was about 50 feet long and 10 feet wide, and which was also where we held our dances when we were older.  I spent much time skating there after I had swept the floor free of hay and dirt.

While at V+Ts, all of us went to Cooney Tanks to gather wild grapes.  The men, older children and Aunt Lou C rode horseback; the other women and children rode in a wagon.  Aunt Lou C rode sidesaddle, wearing a calf-length leather skirt.  She was an excellent rider.  When we returned to V+T headquarters after that day's jaunt, the women made the wild grapes into a most delicious jelly.

Much later, in the 1950's, two of my cousins worked for our mutual uncle, Lee Evans, on his New Mexico ranch.  The situation was such in that area that these two young cowboys wore their holstered pistols as they rode the range. Once they surprised some men in the act of stealing their uncle's cattle.  They were not intimidated by this dangerous encounter—both of them were WWII veterans.  Johnny Evans had served in the Pacific zone against the Japanese.  Joe M. Evans Jr. served in Italy where his platoon was under fire from some German soldiers ensconced in a house on a hill above them.  Jodie, as leader, climbed the hill with his unit covering for him.  At the house, Jodie pulled the pin of a grenade and threw it into a window. The Germans threw it back out, so Jodie pulled the pin on another grenade and held it long enough before throwing it that it would explode inside the house, which it did.  The twenty-six Germans surrendered, and the vantage point of that house on the hill was secured.  Four or five Mexican cattle rustlers did not scare these veterans.  They disarmed the rustlers and while one held them at gunpoint, the other rode to the nearby town for the sheriff.  When this case came to trial, the trial was conducted entirely in Spanish with a Mexican judge and all Mexican jurors.  The rustlers were ruled not guilty and acquitted despite being caught red-handed by two witnesses. Such was justice in New Mexico at that time.

The good ending is that uranium was found on part of Lee's ranch and he and Lou C became wealthy. They did many good deeds with their money, establishing and endowing a retirement ranch for old pastors, sending young people to college, and leaving a trust for a new larger Tabernacle at Bloys Campmeeting, which was built to seat 1500 to 2000 people, and which we enjoy each year.

**Weather is a large factor in the life of ranching**. A rancher is completely dependent on the weather for his well-being. My Uncle Graves Evans told me of an experience he had when he and his brothers, Paul and Rube, were caught by a Blue Norther. They had ridden horseback some 15 miles from headquarters to work cattle in the flatland pasture. That morning the weather was not very cold, so they all wore light jackets. While they were working the cattle a Blue Norther moved in. You can see these cold winds approaching. They actually look like a dense blue cloud reaching from the ground to the stratosphere. They move very rapidly, and lower temperatures even more quickly.

They quickly left that pasture, but still had to ride 15 miles horseback to reach home. After riding about 12 miles, they came to a shallow water trough that had already frozen over. One lone cow stood at this trough unable to drink. Feeling sorry for her, Graves dismounted, broke the ice so this cow could drink, and rode on to overtake his brothers. The brothers were all sitting on their horses at a closed gate. Graves chided them for not opening the gate and they replied, "We can't get off our horses—our legs are too stiff and numb from the cold." Graves opened the gate and they rode the two miles home, where they were helped off their horses. Graves was convinced they might have all perished at that gate two miles from home if he had not felt pity for that cow and by dismounting then kept his legs and arms moveable.

# Bloys

The first meeting of Bloys Campmeeting was held October 10 through October 13, 1890. There are supposed to have been 47 people in attendance. My grandmother, Kate Evans, one of the founders of this meeting, told me that her family, composed of Kate, her husband, George W. Evans, and sons, Will, Joe, Lee, George W. Jr., and Rube, were the only ones who camped at the first meeting. They lived so far away that they had to camp, while the other people attending came from Marfa, Fort Davis, or surrounding ranches just for the day and returned home at night. - These people lived close enough to Skillman Grove to come in hacks, wagons and on horseback for the day's preaching.

What are my early memories of Bloys Camp Meeting? Bloys has ever been in my memory. My parents, Paul and Wertie Evans, brought me, Lottie Virginia, their first child, to Bloys Camp Meeting in August 1917, when I was one month old. My very first memories are of the specialness of this space. Of the awesome thrill of the first hymn of the opening church service Tuesday evening: "How firm a foundation, ye saints of the Lord, is laid for your faith in His excellent Word." Each year of one's life to hear a group of people sing with such joy, reverence, conviction and dedication, "How Firm a Foundation," you know beyond doubt that God is real, supreme and everlasting, and that Bloys will be perpetuated. That puts a child's roots down solidly in the faith of God.

Memories come to mind of the wonderful aroma of wood fires and coffee brewing, steak frying even for breakfast; of the pristine freshness of the campgrounds each year—the grass knee high and untracked except for the faint outline of where a tent had been

*Typical chuck wagon campfire scene*

pitched and ditched the year before, the wonderful aroma of oak and pinon trees and grass and the pure fresh air untainted by automobile exhaust. The memory of the grateful happiness of greeting friends and relatives, most of whom you had not seen since last Campmeeting a year ago, and the wrenching sadness of parting when on the following Tuesday morning it was time to return, each one to his own home. No one left without a "goodbye," usually tearful, to each other one in our camp, for it was almost certain to be another year before we, "*Sí Dios quiere,*" would be together again. The sunrise service at 8 a.m. each day was a time for sharing favorite Bible passages and affirmations of faith from Bible promises. On that last Tuesday morning it was also a farewell service and time of sharing decisions and dedication before we sang, "God be with you 'til we meet again," and meant it.

Our years were not reckoned from January, but from AC or BC—

After Campmeeting or Before Campmeeting. The anticipation and preparation built up such excitement that I felt I could not wait until that date. By the time we actually drove over the pass at Crow's Nest west of the Campground, I was so keyed up, excited and tense that if you had thumped me, I would have twanged like an electric guitar. It was a contest between us as children to see which one could see the Campground first. Naturally, each one claimed that distinction, and who could disprove it?

The new dresses Mother had made for us were for Bloys and only incidentally for school and other wear. The many cakes to serve as dessert at the cook shed were baked and packed.

Each bed roll was prepared with a mattress and many "covers" or blankets, for it is cold even in August sleeping on the ground or on a cot in a tent at over a mile altitude. The bedding was laid on the canvas tarp and rolled and fastened with two leather straps. Tents, bedrolls and suitcases were loaded in the bed wagon early on the Monday morning of departure, for it took longer for Elisandro Valdez and his helper with the mule-drawn wagons—one for beds and luggage and one for the chuck wagon—to reach the Y6 Ranch than it did for us in our speedy 1920's automobiles. Although Elisandro left the EV Ranch before we did, we always passed him—except for one time. It was our custom to spend that Monday night at Uncle John Means' Y6 Ranch, for it broke the long trip of some 85 miles and, I strongly suspect, gave the families extra time for visiting and just being together.

That evening after the chuck wagon supper that Elisandro and "Ole Cladio" had prepared, there was music and dancing and singing to the violin, piano and guitars. Everyone who played guitar or violin brought them to Bloys. My father, Paul Evans, played both but was more adept on guitar and brought it to Bloys. Huling Means played violin, Cole and Bug (M.O.) Means both played guitars.

These instruments were not used in special music for church as they are now—we had only piano—but for group singing after church. The men would spread a large heavy tarp on the hillside about where James Mims' cabin now is. There, we were far enough away not to bother the cooks and the older folks, who probably listened with pleasure from the warmth of their beds while we grew colder and colder sitting flat on the tarp as the chill of the night assailed us from the ground below and from the air above and around us.

We would not have left the group before the last note of "Goodnight Ladies" was sung, no matter how cold we were. We did not use chairs even for the musicians, who just "hunkered" on their heels, cowboy fashion. We sang old songs, the latest popular songs, hymns, funny songs, and songs in Spanish, all without books or sheet music.

### The Darkie's Sunday school
(one song we sang with its many verses)

Young folks, old folks, come one and all
Join the Darkie's Sunday school and make yourself to home,
Park yo' slug o' chewing gum and razors at the door
And you'll hear more Bible stories than you ever heard before.
Adam was the first man and
Eve she was his spouse
They joined together and started keeping house
They lived together happily and peaceful in the main
'Til they had a little son and started raising Cain.

As a matter of fact, it **was dark**. We could not have seen words or music. This was before we had any overhead lights on the grounds and flashlights were a must to walk from evening church to your tent. We had electricity in the first cabins when they were built about 1926. Before then there was electricity only in the Tabernacle, provided by a gasoline-powered generator. When the generator broke its steady rhythm or the lights flickered, some man, usually Terrell Smith, would grab his hat and run, hopefully to restore our source of power. Very seldom did the lights go out during the evening church service, which was the only time lights were used in the Tabernacle, for it was small enough to be well lighted by daylight.

We did not have the freedom at Bloys that children have now. We were dressed in our best clothes, as were the adults. Everyone dressed as though attending Sunday church services, for this *was* our church. I still feel that way. I wish the word "camp" was not in the name of Bloys. Too many are acting as though it is only a camp.

Climbing the mountain was no big deal for us. At home the rocky hillsides were our playground. Going through the "Cave" was special, for we had to have a chaperone to go with us—some tall boy a little older than we were. We promptly ran off and left him before we got to the cave. In later years I asked Mother if she went through the cave when she was young. "Oh, yes," she answered, "and if I couldn't get anyone to go with me, I would go by myself." "Then why," I asked, "did we have to have a chaperone?" "I don't know," she replied. But I knew. That was the age of, "What will people think of me if I let my girls run wild?"

The boys brought their ropes and they knew how to use them. Lacking anything else, the girls were their prey. When we crossed an open space there was a boy lurking in wait with his loop built. Rarely could we outrun him to the safety zone of a big tree where we could stand against the trunk so that he could not get his loop over us. One year Coley Means roped my sister, Frances, who did not stop in time and received a bad rope burn around her neck. She was very conscious of this in her pretty dresses. Usually the boys roped us around the waist, but if they jerked their slack too quickly and the girl didn't stop in time, it was a neck catch. Frances' was the only really bad rope burn I recall. Rope burns are very painful!

Bro. Hogg had come to Bloys as the Methodist preacher for a number of years. He was a great favorite with the children, as he had traveled with Houdini and knew all kinds of tricks, such as beans coming out of his eyes and ears, being able to get untied from ropes, and so on. The children rushed to get the front seats when he preached. He acted out the Bible stories as he told them—such as making rowing motions when he told about the disciples in a boat on the Sea of Galilee. It was easy to visualize the scenes of his Bible stories.

As we reached teenage and almost every boy in Means and Evans Camp was a first or second cousin, we found there were lots of non-cousins in the other camps. Somehow young people have a feeling for this. The big thing was to have a "date" to take you to church. These boys in their best clothes would come to our cabins and escort us to evening church services and after-church activities.

About this time Mrs. Jessie Jones Mueller asked us to meet to select a site for a young people's evening church service. From Means and Evans Camp came Coley Means, Charles Carpenter, Frances Evans, Kittie Carpenter, Paul Evans Jr., and Lottie Evans. From other camps were Ben Medley, Otis Grubb, "Booger" Smith—all I can think of now. This group chose the site of the first shed we called the "Nabertacle." This must have been about 1933. I am sure there are records of this with correct date and list of young people participating.

After the earthquake experience I had so recently been through, I was very receptive to the preaching at Bloys. Bro. William Hogg was preaching the night I made my decision for Christ. We were singing, "Oh, Happy Day When Jesus Washed My Sins Away." I left my date without explanation to make my decision public at the front of the Tabernacle.

One incident of going to Campmeeting that I remember as if it were yesterday happened when I was four years old.  It was raining that Monday morning when it was time to start to Bloys Campmeeting.  But we had "curtains" for the cars—small ising glass (mica) windows to enclose the open-sided cars, so we set out.  These curtains gave an eerie feeling to me.  They crackled and popped and intensified the sound of the rain as it pelted against them.  They gave me a claustrophobic feeling because I could not see out.  When on the Means Y6 Ranch we came to Bunton Draw, a deep, usually dry, creek we had to cross.  It was running some water.  My dad, always the first car in the caravan, thought he could cross it in his powerful Overland, a product of Oldsmobile.  But this powerful Overland had its motor drowned out by the water splashed on it and we stalled in the creek with the water level rising.  It was still raining and the ground was so wet and slick that his brother's cars could not get enough traction to pull our Overland out of the creek.  As the water began to seep into the car, the men carried us, my mother, sister Frances, baby brother Paul and me and the cakes to safety.  Uncles, aunts and cousins made room for us in their cars. Sadly, we returned to the EV Ranch to spend the night and start anew the next morning.  I have since wondered how we had beds that night, because we did not have extra mattresses but had sent ours in the bed wagon.  That was the time we did not pass Elisandro's bed wagon in our speedy automobiles.

The next morning with the sun shining we started again.  Imagine our dismay to discover that a wall of water must have hit the Overland, for it was turned upside down and covered with gravel so that only the wheels were showing.  Such a disaster!  But it did not prevent us from going to Bloys Campmeeting.  The men dug the car out with shovels, with which all early travelers' cars were equipped.

Mules pulled the car to Valentine, our post office and trading center. The wheels worked, but the motor was full of sand, water and gravel, and was ruined. We didn't stay at the Y6 that night but went on to Bloys. Camp meeting started that day.

My father bought a Model T Ford, the first of a long line of Fords for us. I always felt the Model T was quite a come-down from the Overland. (Are we status-conscious at age 4?)

I do remember one time at Y6 Mrs. George W. Truett teaching me some of the first lengthy Bible verses that I learned. "Study to show thyself approved unto God, a workman who needeth not to be ashamed, rightly dividing the word of Truth" (II Timothy 2:15.) And I Thessalonians 5:22 tells us exactly what to do, "Abstain from all appearance of evil." Dr. and Mrs. Truett were frequent guests and good friends of the Means and Evans families. Dr. Truett was one of the preachers at Bloys for a number of years. At Y6 Ranch Grandmother Kate Means Evans said to Dr. Truett, "You see what these young people are doing with music and dancing." Dr. Truett replied, "I see nothing wrong with it."

**At Bloys there is only one collection of money taken in the Tabernacle.** This collection is equally divided by the four participating denominations for their Orphan Homes. This account tells how it was started:

"It stands to reason that it takes large sums of money to foot the bills for a campmeeting conducted on such a large scale. But each man carries a checkbook and he makes use of it. At one of the afternoon prayer meetings for men, George Evans, owner of the EV Ranch, made the suggestion that those present—twenty-eight in number—make a little donation for the Buckner's Orphan Home, to help relieve an epidemic of typhoid fever prevalent among the orphans. The checkbooks were called into play and four hundred dollars were raised in less time than it takes to tell it. That is the way these people do things."

—*Copied from "The Romance of the Davis Mountains and the Big Bend Country," p. 343, by Carlysle Graham Raht.*

## Emergency 1925

"An emergency arose in the Means and Evans Camp today and was averted only by the resourcefulness of the women in camp. It was discovered that the sweet tooth of the large crowds of people in attendance had depleted the supply of cakes brought from their homes to serve for dessert at the chuck shed. They realized there were not enough cakes remaining to serve after dinner and supper each day through the rest of the meeting. Something had to be done!

Several carloads of women and children drove to the Gillettes' Barrel Springs Ranch and the women spent the afternoon baking while the children climbed the hills, the trees in the orchard, the windmill, and explored any other interesting places. Attendance at the afternoon services was less than usual, but disgrace was avoided because of the Gillettes' well-stocked pantry and the willingness of the women to spend a hot afternoon baking on a wood stove; there was now an ample supply of cakes. The emergency was resolved and everyone saved from great embarrassment."

—Written as a news item for the centennial celebration of Bloys Campmeeting 1990 by Lottie Woods.

# Family

*(left to right) Blackie Woods, JP Woods, Lottie Woods, David Fritts, Chance Hart, Morris Woods, Betty Woods, Tim Woods, Beary Woods, Judy Roach, Mary Sue Woods*

## BEARY ALLEN (BLACKIE) WOODS

**John Arnsby Woods and Eva Gertrude Bratton** were married January 10, 1900. He would be twenty-one January 31, 1900. She was sixteen November 10, 1899. The children of John A. (born 1-31-1879; died April 1974) and Eva Bratton Woods (born 11-10-1884; died March 1968):

| | |
|---|---|
| Nannie Elizabeth | b. March 7, 1902 |
| William Tim | b. July 26, 1904 |

| | |
|---|---|
| John Mills | b. November 20, 1905 |
| (infant death) | ? |
| Beary Allen | b. October 10, 1908 |
| (infant death) | ? |
| Amanda Martha | b. January 29, 1910 |
| Mary Artie | b. February 7, 1913 |
| Willie Belle | b. April 4, 1915 |
| Eva Faye | b. September 14, 1919 |
| John Thomas | b. January 20, 1921 |

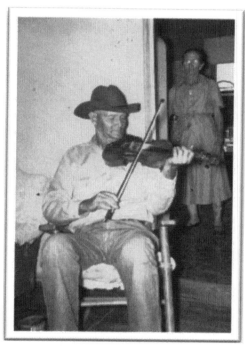

*John and Eva Woods*

**Beary Allen Woods was born October 10, 1908,** at the little community of La Casa in Stephens County, Texas. He was named for the doctor who delivered him, Dr. Beary. His father was a man of strong likes and dislikes, especially dislikes. He disliked Dr. Beary, so he would never call his son Beary. He was prone to give veryone a nickname, so he sought a nickname for his son. He tried several, one of which was "Nig." I am thankful that didn't stick. Evidently this new son had lots of black hair—his early pictures show this to be so. His father settled on the nickname, "Black." Two of his brothers called him Black, but his mother, sisters and one brother always called him Beary. He was evidently quite young when the family moved from La Casa to Murray, a community near Graham, Texas. He told me when they were ready to move, he couldn't find his little gun and had to leave without it. This was a great loss. It probably was his only possession.

The school house was about five miles away from their home, so Beary could not start to school until he was able to walk that distance. When his little sister, Faye, started to school he would carry her on his back a good part of the way when she would get tired.

When they started long division in math, he could figure it so fast in his head that he would just write the answer on the blackboard, omitting all the steps of long division. Instead of recognizing and encouraging his superior mathematical ability, the teacher accused him of cheating. That did not make him like school any better. He said when they started algebra, they lost him. Evidently the teacher did not know how to teach algebra.

The Woods brothers were innovative and seemed to have a penchant for cars and adventure. The family had two .22 caliber rifles. In one the shell was prone to hang after the gun was shot and had to be dug and pried out. When Blackie was about nine years old and his brother Mills some two and a half years older, they took these two rifles and went hunting. Sure enough, after they shot their rifles, the empty shell hung in that gun and they could not pry it out. They decided to shoot it out with the working gun. Mills held the ends of the gun barrels together and Black fired the gun. Somehow no one was injured.

When Blackie's older brother, Tim, was a young boy he had amassed a collection of boards, wheels, metal rods, and wire to build a go-cart. This go-cart would have four wheels and a place for the boy to sit. It was steered with the feet on the front axle. When finished, he was downright proud of his creation. Like a sled, it had to be pushed to a high rise from which he could coast downhill. His mother, Eva, was churning to make butter for the family. Since it was cool in the shade of a tree in front of the house she had carried the earthenware churn with its wooden dasher to the tree to take advantage of this refreshing shade. Before air conditioning you did what you could to make life bearable.

Tim prepared to show his mother how well this amazing go-cart would come downhill. He pushed it to the top of the hill, mounted it, and started downhill, gaining speed. The foot-powered steering lacked a lot in accuracy and maneuverability. He intended to come close enough for his mother to admire his go-cart. His calculation for steering was amiss. At full speed the go-cart crashed into the churn. His mother jumped to safety as the cream poured out of the broken churn. Tim knew he was in trouble. He abandoned the go-cart and took off running to escape the situation and the inevitable consequences. Eva called after him, "I will whip you when you come back if your beard is white as snow and dragging on the ground." Tim's inventive career was thwarted. The family had no butter on their hot biscuits until another churn was procured.

I asked Blackie's brother, Tim, why his mother named two sons John—John Mills and John Thomas. I learned that Gran, as we called her, did not name Thomas, the eleventh child she bore. (Two sons had died in early childhood.) A good friend, Mrs. Tom Hamilton, named him for her husband, John Thomas Hamilton, a very good friend of John Woods. Obviously John Mills was named for his father.  He did not know who the Mills was for.  This Mrs. Hamilton was a dynamic character.  Her main interest in life was the race horses she bred and trained.  These filled her thoughts and conversation.  At the first Woods reunion we attended in the early 1960's Elsie Woods and I were sitting near where Mrs. Hamilton was visiting with a friend when she said, "I just have arthritis so bad in my hind leg."  Elsie looked at me and I looked at her, and we knew that was really what we had heard.  We had to go outside until we got our giggles under control.  We knew she was not being facetious; she just lived and thought and talked horses.

Blackie and Mills decided to strip down a 1928 Chevy.  They got it stripped down to the frame, the front seats and the running boards. Then they could not get the motor started even with much working on it.  Finally they went to do something else.  Their little sister, Faye, who was nine or ten years old, told her younger brother, Thomas, "You give me a push down this hill and I will start this car. Then hang on and I'll give you a ride."  Thomas pushed and the motor started, but Faye didn't know how to stop it.  She steered it by one tree, knocking the passenger seat off.  Her brother Beary was running to overtake her and save his car.  Their mother was looking out the kitchen window calling, "You're going to kill that child," not realizing "that child" had started the whole show.  Beary did overtake her before she wrecked the car.  Another time with this car Beary and Mills found it needed brakes.  They made some brake shoes out of leather.  They seemed to work, but with use they caught fire.  So much for that!

Still another time they were working on this stripped-down car to go to a dance.  They did not have it ready when the rest of the family left to go to the dance.  It was already dark when they were ready. The lights on this car were not very bright, and there were no warning signs when they drove into the gap where the bridge was out.  The sudden jolt threw Beary out, where he landed on his feet on the road bed on the far side of this gap. As I recall, he said it blew some of the tires out, broke some springs, and maybe some other damage. I don't think they made it to that dance. Blackie told me that car exactly fit through that space.

Years later, Eva (Gran) had a model A Ford that she drove to the feed store and A&P grocery store. She also used it to deliver butter and eggs to some customers. After Gran got older Fay, the younger daughter, scolded her about that. "Gran, you should not deliver to those folks. Let them come and get it." Gran replied, "Oh, honey, I just take it to the old folks." Many of those "old folks" were younger than she was.

One time Gran decided to drive to see her son, Tim, who lived at Hobbs, New Mexico, more than 400 miles from her home in Breckenridge, Texas. Faye asked if Tim was at home when she arrived that afternoon. She replied, "Oh, honey, I got there by noon." This was before wide highways and Interstate freeways. Tim gave her a young dogie calf which she tied down and took home with her in the back of that 4-door Model A.

John Woods, "Chief" to his family, had a pickup in which he took his July hound dogs and hunted wolves at night. It was not practical to follow the dogs at night on foot, so a fire was built for warmth in winter, or in summer to help ward off the mosquitoes and to make coffee. The hunters knew the voices of their dogs. The progression of the hunt was gauged by the barking of the dogs, as to where they were and what they were doing. Sometimes when the dogs "treed" or cornered a wolf the men would walk to that place, but at times the dogs would kill the wolf before they arrived. John became deaf when he was quite young. He had various styles of hearing aids through the years, but he used them only when he went hunting.

After I married into the Woods family, Blackie's older brother, Tim, told me that their great grandmother Woods was an Indian woman. She cooked meat over an outdoor fire. When he and the other boys tried to snitch some of it, she would throw hot ashes on them with her shovel. She was probably Cherokee or Choctaw Indian. I have a picture of Blackie's family that shows strong Indian likeness, especially Tim and Nannie, his older brother and sister. Tim could have passed as full-blood Indian in looks and mannerisms.

**When he left school, Black started working as a cowboy.** He bought his first pair of long pants with money he earned. He must have had only knickers, the garb of young boys of that time. He worked cowboying in the Graham area now covered by Possum Kingdom Lake. Later he worked on ranches in the Albany area. There a horse he was riding started pitching along a barbed wire fence and fell into the fence, throwing Blackie into the barbed wire. He sustained a deep gash eight inches long on his left shoulder which left a scar three-fourths of an inch wide. It should have been sutured, but was not. More than one doctor was startled on seeing that scar and wanted to know what made it.

Blackie always saved his wage and didn't blow it in like some did. He soon had accumulated his saddle and gear, a bedroll and a car. His older brother, Tim, was working in far West Texas in the Davis Mountains. There were jobs for his brothers if they could get there. Blackie and Mills set out in Blackie's car for West Texas. They arrived in Toyah with $1.27 and the promise of jobs. I think they day-worked on ranches around Toyah. When he and Mills worked together they shared Blackie's bed roll. Mills snored very loudly. Blackie said he would wake Mills and then try to go to sleep before Mills did and the snoring started.

Blackie worked for a while at Kent helping to build Highway 80. He drove mules pulling a Fresno scraper to haul dirt for the road bed. That is very hard work. After only a few days of this work he got a ranch job at the Nunn Ranch owned by Cliff Caldwell. Cliff had turned this ranch over to his son, Guy, who was really not a rancher. He lived then in Abilene and only occasionally came to the ranch. Sometimes between his visits the groceries would get used up. The cowboys would have to kill a deer to have something to eat. Deer were plentiful. Tim told me that once they had killed a deer and had a skillet full of good venison frying, looking forward to a real meal. He saw the game warden drive up. He turned the skillet full of grease and meat upside down into the fire in the wood stove. The fire really roared, but there was no incriminating evidence. The cowboys were not furnished much but flour and beans. Blackie was not fond of beans. For several years he had beans for breakfast, beans for lunch, and beans for supper. He had his fill of beans. He did learn to make very good biscuits. He did not make biscuits after we married. He had batched for a number of years and was ready to turn all the cooking over to me.

When Blackie worked on a ranch near Albany, Texas, in 1926 a high school boy about Blackie's age was in the crew of cowboys. He claimed to be the best athlete in the county and was quick to regale the other cowboys with his athletic feats. The cowboys soon tired of his boasting. Real cowboys don't brag about themselves. Their philosophy is that if you are good at a thing it will be noticed. It seemed this boy was especially proud of his ability to win races. The 100 yard dash was his forte. The cowboys matched a race between him and Blackie. A site was chosen and the time was set. There might have been a few bets laid. The distance for a 100 yard dash was stepped off through the pasture grass. The runners took their positions. Blackie pulled his boots off. The starting gun sounded and they were off, Blackie running in his sock feet. At the 100 yard mark Blackie was ahead by a good distance, clearly the winner.

# Beary Allen—Our Life Together

Beary Allen Woods and Lottie Evans were married August 19 at 7:30 AM Wednesday, the first day of Bloys Campmeeting. My sister, Frances, was my attendant and his brother, Tim Woods, was best man. Mrs. Huling Means (Hester) played, "I Love You Truly" and Mrs. Sam Means (Dora) sang. The service was performed by Dr. R. L. Irving.

My dad, Paul Evans, insisted that we take his new Ford V8 for our honeymoon trip. For that trip Blackie took me to meet his parents, whom I had never seen. They lived on a farm near Breckenridge, Texas. They welcomed me warmly, she with a hug. His mother had evidently been written of Blackie's plans, for she had the nicest room in their house ready for us. It is the only time I ever knew of Blackie's father giving up his room to anyone. Blackie was a son who pleased his mother. He caused her no worry or grief. He was so much like her.

We returned to Bloys for the rest of the meeting. Our family and good friends at Bloys chipped in and gave us a set of Community Plate flatware. Other friends in the Valentine area gave a bridal shower where we received sheets, basic cookware and some Depression glassware. Blackie's family gave pink Depression glass bowls and cake plates.

Newly married, we packed our worldly possessions in the Chevy Roadster Blackie had bought. He strapped the new saddle he had just had made to the hood of that Roadster, which had a hood about the size of a horse's back. There was a hinged cover on each side that opened for access to the motor and closed with some kind of spring-held catch. We set out for the Breckenridge area to look for work and a place to live. We spent one night visiting friends in Olden, Angie and Everett Everett. Angie had introduced me to Blackie when she taught at Cowden's Ranch and he worked there. To protect that new saddle from the weather and someone's possible covetousness, Blackie brought it into their living room for the night. Everett thought that was hilarious, but that saddle represented several months' wages and his means of livelihood to Blackie.

We rented an apartment in Ranger that was between where the Woods reunion now meets and the brushy hill southwest of it. We were hardly unpacked when Blackie had this job offer at Crane, Texas, on the Jax Cowden Ranch, but the house for us to live in was not finished. So Blackie went to Crane and I stayed in Ranger. Soon Blackie's Aunt Manda came over and insisted that I come and stay with them. Her husband, Pink Stafford, had a car dealership in Ranger. They had a daughter about my age. Aunt Manda cooked the best pork and sweet potatoes I ever ate. Aunt Manda was so good to me.

Blackie was very adept with a rope, dating back to when he, as a small boy, roped his mother's chickens and turkeys. He got in big trouble when he one turkey he roped got loose with the rope on his leg and hung up out in the bushes. Blackie always carried a nylon cord or light rope in his pocket—anything he could build a loop in. There are a lot of things you can do with a light rope. He roped any and everything, including me. As I was cooking or washing dishes, he would rope me and pull me to him for a hug or a kiss. When the house at Crane was finished, he came to Ranger for me. We moved into the new house, but I had not put up curtains in the kitchen-dining area yet. The black man who worked for Jax Cowden thought Blackie was the best cowboy in the world, especially as a roper. He saw Blackie make some spectacular catches and remarked on how well Blackie roped. Blackie told him, "It takes practice, man, practice."  To which the black man replied, "Yassuh, I seed you ropin' yo' wife."

The Lord God said, "It is not good for man to be alone. I will make him a helpmeet."  Genesis 2:18.  I married a man who was intelligent, competent, forceful and capable of handling any situation that arose in ranch life pertaining to cattle, horses, windmills—even wild animals, including coyotes, bobcats or mountain lions.  Hunting mountain lions with his well-trained dogs later became his obsessive hobby.  He was the master of the art.

**During our time at Crane our first child was born December 7, a son, Beary Allen Jr**.  I found this man I had married was kind, gentle, and as awed by this new life we had created as I was.

One of the early steps in my training of what he expected of me as a helpmeet was when we moved from Crane, Texas.  With our two-month-old son, Beary, I was to drive our pickup with all our possessions over a dim road through the sand and mesquites to a certain gate where I had never been, while my mate rode the horse he had acquired to turn through that gate into a friend's pasture.  We did not have a horse trailer yet, so he would return for his horse later.  Lacking a trailer, he probably rode his horse from Crane to Monahans after he started work at Monahans.

This move was all after dark; for if Blackie was employed by someone, he put in a full day's work for them before he gave any time to his own needs or pleasures, even on his last day of employment.  From Crane we went to a Toyah ranch where I stayed with Blackie's sister, Mary.  Her husband, Herb Pate, worked with Blackie day working on ranches around Monahans.

When day working slowed down, Blackie went to work for Walter McElroy at his beautiful but rough mountain ranch at Balmorhea.

Mary McElroy was so good to me. She was a good woman. There we got our first furniture—a beautiful antique oak dresser with beveled oval mirror, which I still have, a tall narrow wooden cabinet which served variously through the years as dish or linen cabinet, and Beary still has it. There was a bed, table and two chairs long gone. Blackie purchased these in Pecos and did a good job. The oak dresser drawer bottoms show to have been sawn with a type of saw that has not been used in 150 or more years.

Blackie did a lot of hunting bobcats with Walter's dogs. Walter had goats, and bobcats are very fond of eating goats. In this hunting Blackie learned the location of the mountain trails that he still knew how to find fifty or more years later. This ability amazed Jim Moore, for in that length of time Blackie had not used these trails, and they were grown up with brush from not being used and maintained. That summer Bill Cowden asked Blackie to come back and work for him. Blackie had worked for him before we married. I don't recall that Blackie ever asked for a job; he was always offered one. He usually took part of his wages in cattle, which was a good arrangement for ranchers. They had more cattle than money at that time.

Again I drove the pickup with our worldly goods, in daylight this time, while Blackie and Wallace Leatherman drove the cattle Blackie had acquired from McElroy Ranch around Gomez Peak to Cowden's Ranch. The next morning when we waked at Cowden's, Walter's old hound dog was lying on our doorstep. Somehow he knew Blackie was leaving McElroy's and he chose to follow Blackie. He chose to stay, and he and Blackie hunted bobcats on the catclaw and oak brush-covered west side of Gomez Peak at night after Blackie had put in a full day's work. Blackie had the uncanny ability to find his way in the dark. Sometimes it may have taken him a while to get back to the location where he had left his horse. But horses always give themselves away by snuffing or saddle creaks.

At Cowden's we had a bedroom nine by twenty-two feet in a separate house and shared kitchen and bath in the big house. I cooked for us and Uncle Bill during the week while Aunt Grace lived in Pecos so their two girls, Nell and Josephine, and son, Billy, could be in school. I helped her on weekends when she came to the ranch. I learned a lot about cooking and life from her. She was a wonderful person.

Once when we had taken dinner to the men working cattle in a pasture north of the railroad and we were home unloading the lunch gear, I missed Beary and went around the house looking for him. He was about two and a half years old. When I found him he was face-to-face with a very big coiled rattlesnake; not three feet separated them. I grabbed Beary and ran. I don't know why that snake didn't strike. I guess because Beary stopped and stood still. Beary still remembers that incident. Aunt Grace shot the snake, avowing it was the first one ever found there, as she did each other one we found. You can understand why she felt this mountain ranch was so snake-free when you consider that she had lived in the sand country at Crane from the time she married Bill Cowden in 1917 to the time they bought this mountain ranch in 1931. At Crane every morning Bill Cowden would make the rounds of the house and yard to kill all the snakes that had crawled up in the night. Out in the pastures there were big pits where the snakes denned. My dad said you could smell them from a great distance, a putrid, nasty odor. Bill Cowden killed rattlesnakes with the loop of his rope. He would hit the snake right behind the head and break its neck with the loop of his rope.

As children, my siblings and I never found a rattlesnake in all our prowling in the rocks on our mountains. When I was older and able to climb higher in the bluffs, I did see some whitish yellow deposits under the rocky overhangs. I did not know what that was until I visited a reptile garden and saw what rattlesnake offal looked like.

96

One time at Cowden's Blackie came in from riding horseback and asked if I wanted to go with him. He had come for the pickup and trailer. I always enjoyed going with him. What he was going for was a nine-point buck deer he had roped and tied to a Spanish dagger. I helped him and we loaded that big deer into the trailer. He did not cooperate. It is amazing what you can do with a rope or two. We took him home and Blackie unloaded him by himself into a horse stall. Bill Cowden had heard that a neutered buck deer would grow an extra-large set of antlers. Sadly, this buck did not survive. Blackie found him later where he had died.

Aunt Grace taught me to make a type of yeast bread that was very delicious. We made all of our bread. Later I modified the recipe a little, and the hot rolls became my culinary masterpiece. Everyone clamored for my hot rolls. An aunt gave me a bread maker—a bucket with a dough hook suspended from a crosspiece. A handle turned the dough hook and saved me a lot of hand- kneading the dough.

**Our second child, a dainty little girl, was born December 16, 1938.** I named her Chance Ann, after my beloved aunt. Since I knew this baby would arrive right before Christmas, I had made an effort to buy and wrap gifts and have everything ready. That may have been the only time I was ready with everything before Christmas.

Despite freezing winter weather, it was still necessary to wash diapers. They would not dry outside, so I hung them on lines I rigged in the bathroom. We used a kerosene heater in the bathroom. I lighted it and was busy with my little children out in our bedroom. When I went in to check on whether the diapers were dry, imagine my horror to see them—great hanging black, soot-covered, unrecognizable things. That heater had malfunctioned, covering everything in that room with greasy black soot—the walls, the

97

ceiling, and the fixtures. It even penetrated into the linen closet. I have never seen such a mess. I don't know how I ever got it cleaned up, but there was nothing else to do about it but to clean it up, and somehow I did. It took a lot of soap and elbow grease and desperation. I never trusted that heater again.

Blackie rode a horse named Revenue. He was a good horse, but on some occasions he would buck. Blackie was riding him once when it was necessary to rope a cow. After he roped the cow, Revenue started bucking in a circle, winding Blackie's rope around the horse and Blackie's legs. He had wound up almost all of the rope with his bucking and Blackie was reaching into his pocket for his knife to cut the rope. Amazingly, Revenue started bucking around in the opposite direction and unwound the rope. Not all bucking horse wrecks turn out that well.

Bill and Grace Evans Cowden's Gomez Peak Ranch consisted of the entire western slope of Gomez Peak to and including a large pasture north of Highway 80 and the Texas and Pacific Railroad. There were gates to be opened and closed on each side of the highway and the railroad—four gates to be transversed between headquarters and Levison Lake pasture, the northern part of the ranch, a distance of 8 or 10 miles. Bill sent Blackie to bring the mares and stallion from Levison Lake pasture to headquarters. This stallion was not saddle-broke—perhaps had been ridden a saddle or two as a colt. Since he would not be used as a ranch horse, his training was not continued— he was still a bronc. Everyone with a knowledge of horses knows you cannot drive a stallion and his harem of mares. He will keep them circling and you can't go anywhere with them.

Blackie saddled a good ranch horse and rode to Levison Lake pasture where the stallion and twenty mares were grazing. He managed somehow to drive the stallion away from the mares and through a gate opened into another pasture. There he roped the stallion and tied him to a fencepost. He then unsaddled his horse and put his saddle on the stallion. There were no observers, so no one ever knew what this feat entailed. It had to be a contest of strength, skill, and determination.

After mounting the stallion, he drove his horse with the mares through each of the gates at the railroad and the highway. To do this, Blackie had to dismount, open the gate, drive the mares through after re-mounting the stallion, dismount and close the gate, then re-mount the uncooperative stallion at each of the four gates. This itself was an amazing feat. Bill Cowden was watching as Blackie approached headquarters. When he saw Blackie riding the stallion and driving the mares and his horse, Bill just turned and went into the house. Blackie had accomplished the impossible again.

Blackie worked for W. H. "Bill" Cowden and his wife, Grace Evans Cowden, on their Gomez Peak ranch before I knew him. Their cattle were being gathered on the rough Gomez Peak pasture with their neighbors, the Stocks family, and cowboys helping. When the cattle were herded together, fourteen-year-old Banky Stocks was missing. They began a search for him. He was found where his horse had fallen or thrown him, unconscious but breathing. Blackie was the youngest and strongest man in the group, so he volunteered to carry Banky on his horse to a place where an automobile could be brought, five or six miles away. Somehow Blackie held that limp form in his arm and carried Banky to the automobile which took Banky to the hospital where he lay in a coma for three or four months. His family had no assurance he would ever wake up, but he did rally. Banky became an avid student of history and the Bible and was a popular speaker for civic clubs and churches. Each time he spoke to a group he told them how Blackie had saved his life by carrying him on his horse off that rough and dangerous mountain.

Before I met Blackie he was working for the man who had bought the Nunn Ranch from the Evans'. They now called it the Caldwell Ranch after the owner. Blackie liked to rope and was very adept at it. To rope an animal was a challenge to him. While at Caldwell he tried to rope an elk, but the elk jumped a fence before Blackie's horse could overtake him. He roped a buffalo, but learned that when you draw a loop around a buffalo's neck, its windpipe does not reopen when the noose is loosened—you have a dead buffalo on your hands.

It was customary to keep one horse in the corral at night to rustle the other horses the next morning. They did not feed the horses grain, so it was necessary to rotate them in this way to have a strong, fresh horse to ride. The horse pasture at this ranch had been a large prairie dog town at one time. The prairie dogs had been exterminated several years before, leaving their network of holes to deteriorate and become deadly traps for horsemen. Each morning as Blackie rustled the horses, a big buck deer came pretty close and trotted around in front of him. After a number of times of this buck daring him, Blackie decided he would rope him the next morning. Blackie kept the horse he considered the fastest on the ranch as the night horse. He would have a try at roping that buck.

Sure enough, as he neared the usual place, the buck was there challenging him. Blackie built a loop and took after the buck at full speed. Just as he overtook the buck and started to throw his loop, his horse stepped in one of those decaying prairie dog holes and took a terrible fall. When the horse got up, the loop was fastened around Blackie's wrist and Blackie was knocked unconscious. The frightened horse took off running, dragging Blackie, still unconscious, by the rope on his wrist. This horse had been used to rope calves, so when the rope tightened, he stopped and turned his head parallel with the rope as he had been trained to do. Blackie had no idea how long they must have stayed in this position. It was a blessing the other horses did not come running by, for Blackie's horse would have joined them. The loop was still around Blackie's wrist. Later when Blackie told me about this he said, "I guess the Lord decided I was hurt a little worse than He had thought, so he sent a little cold mountain rain to wake me up."

When he stood up, his chaps were down around his knees where they had been pushed while he was being dragged. Cowboy-like, his first thought was to get his horse's bridle reins. He started toward the horse, but was still so addled he didn't think to take the rope off of his wrist. Perhaps he was not really aware of it being on yet. He caught the bridle reins and then thought about the rope on his wrist and removed it. The horse stood still as Blackie approached him, in spite of the spectacle Blackie must have been—covered with dirt and blood, his chaps down around his knees, his clothes in rags. He rode the horse to the corral, tended to him, made it the considerable distance to the house, and passed out on his bed.

There was a telephone line from the house where he "batched" to the owner's house. The telephone rang, but when he answered it what he said didn't make sense, and that alerted the owner's wife that something was wrong. It was about 2 miles between the houses and she was some 8 months pregnant, but she walked the distance to see what had happened. In those days each person in the family did not have his own car. Her husband was gone in theirs. She got Blackie cleaned up and put back to bed. When the ranch owner came home he was not happy. This man would not take Blackie to a doctor, so it was a good thing that he was not injured internally nor had any broken bones. Being unconscious while he was being dragged had kept him a limp as a sack of feed. I saw Blackie the next day in Kent, but at the time I didn't know who he was. His face was as red and raw as a beefsteak; I am sure his body was too. I don't know why his face was not scarred; thankfully it was not. He was a very handsome man. His mother-in-law said he was the handsomest man she ever saw, and my dad was a good-looking man.

We had spring water at Cowden's.  It was so good.  It came from springs above the house.  At this time this ranch was watered by springs.  There were pipelines that gravity-flowed the water to the whole ranch.  After the drought of the 1950s, some of these springs dried up.

When we married, Blackie did all of his bookkeeping in his head, and he never forgot or got mixed up.  He had a remarkable mind and the most unfailing memory of anyone I ever knew.  If I ever made a remark I shouldn't have, it was brought up to haunt me later.  I learned to be careful what I said.

Blackie never learned to make "small talk."  What he said was direct and to the point.  When he expressed a conclusion, there was nothing more to be said.  His selective and precise use of words was one thing that attracted me to him.  He had one bad habit, that of using sarcasm.  After I told him I was afraid of his sarcasm, he never used it again.  He had a wonderful but subtle sense of humor.  He expressed his appreciation of humor with a lift of his eyebrows.

My baby sister, Mary Sue, was the joy of our lives.  She was such a happy, loving child.  After Frances and I had married and Paul was staying with Grandmother Evans attending Austin High School, Mother and Dad had Mary Sue at home.  She brought them much happiness.  When she was about seven years old she started having sick spells that were diagnosed as biliousness.  These became more frequent until she died one night in her sleep.  We were devastated by this tragedy.  The death of a child is so very heartbreaking.  I feel sure her problem was a quick-acting form of leukemia, before that was recognized and given a name.  To help cope with her grief, Mother worked with her flowers and yard.  It was a memorial to Mary Sue, and working to the point of physical exhaustion was a type of therapy.

**During a snowstorm our third child, a son, was born January 18, 1940**, in Pecos, Texas. He was named Timothy Graves Woods. There had been a Tim Woods in every generation back to the Tim who came to America from Ireland in the 1700s. Blackie was there the night he was born, but the snow got too deep for him to come back for a week.

1940 was a time of change. Bill Cowden leased his ranch to Cole Means. I moved with my little children to my parents' at EV Ranch. Blackie worked for Cole a very short time. Then he worked for Frank Jones driving a bulldozer making stock tanks and diversion dams—commonly called "dirt work." He made enough money at that to buy the net wire to sheep-fence my dad's ranch. I think he built that fence by himself. Then he bought sheep from a Mr. Mills who had been pasturing the sheep at Cowden's, and put them on this newly fenced ranch. They did so well that the other owners of EV land sheep-fenced their pastures.

In 1941 Rube Evans and Guy Cowden stocked Rube's country with sheep and hired Blackie to care for them. Blackie still had his sheep on Paul's ranch. The house on Rube's land had burned, and the two-car garage had been converted into make-shift living quarters. The garage doors had been nailed shut and a door for access cut into one of them. The building was not ceiled and the rafters sat on the walls with nothing to close the space between them. There was a sheep pen built around three sides of the building. The water from the well was not fit for human consumption. The sheep would not drink it. There was a small wood-burning cook stove. It was into this that I moved to be with my husband.

Rains were unusually good that year. By the last of September, clear water was running the seven miles from Panther Canyon to this Burned House where we lived, and beyond. Blackie had to make a dike of dirt to keep the water out of our house. All this rain made exceptionally good grass, so we were planning to put up prairie hay. Dad was cleaning and getting the chuck box ready, putting the contents out on a table. Tim, at 18 months of age, was looking into everything. When I took him into Mother's house, he couldn't stand up. He kept staggering and falling. His coordination was not good. Something was very wrong. Blackie was out in the pasture, so my brother-in-law, Charles, took us to Van Horn to the doctor. That doctor sent us on to El Paso. When we got to El Paso, they had called that they had discovered that Tim had eaten we-never-knew-how-many sulfanilamide tablets that Blackie had for a dog and had put in that chuck box for safekeeping.

On the way to El Paso, Tim had literally died in my arms. He gasped, went limp, and his eyes rolled back in his head. I firmly believe that because of my frantic, fervent appeal to God that God gave his life back. We could tell the doctor the source of the trouble, though Tim was over the worst symptoms. Now the doctor could advise us what to do. Tim was not to eat eggs or any foods with sulfur for a good while.

Dad was working getting the hay baler and the mowing machine ready. I remember he always had to sharpen the blades on the sickle. We started making hay. Dad was driving the mules pulling the mowing machine. Something happened that he had to stop to see about. He got careless and stepped in front of the sickle. The mules gave a start and his foot was caught by the sickle and badly cut. So he was rushed to El Paso. His foot was saved, but it took a long time for it to heal.

Now we were really short-handed. I was spreading the mown grass as it was thrown up into the pickup. Blackie had a very high rack on his pickup bed. The pickup was almost loaded and I was spreading a bunch of hay when I stepped back one step too far. I landed flat on my back from that fall of eight feet. It took me a while to get my breath back and get up and back and get up and back to work. My back was extremely sore for some time.

It did not take long for the coyotes to learn how good sheep were to eat and how easy and fun they were to kill. Blackie was working overtime trying to trap coyotes. His father had dogs that he ran and caught wolves with. These wolves were similar to coyotes, maybe a little larger. Blackie got some dogs from his father. These dogs were bred to run game, not just trail. Blackie ran down and caught a good number of coyotes with these dogs, but not enough. Death loss of sheep to coyotes was still great.

There was an aviator who had rigged his plane with a shotgun mounted on a tripod so he could shoot coyotes and Mexican eagles. The American bald eagle was illegal to kill, but they liked lambs too. There were not many bald eagles in this area. Eagles were very prone to kill lambs. An eagle could pick up a baby lamb with his talons and fly off with the lamb. McCasland killed lots of eagles from his plane. Mac sold the wing and tail feathers to some Indians in Oklahoma for their ceremonial costumes, but only those of the golden eagles.

The ranchers would meet at a ranch on a designated day for a coyote drive. They would ride horses and spread out across the pasture to rouse the coyotes. Sometimes one of them got a chance to kill a coyote, but mostly they roused the coyote so this pilot, McCasland, could kill him. My part in these drives was to provide a meal for them. I always like to cook for men because they enjoyed and appreciated it.

One daily task in this Burned House was to wipe down everything to clean off the dust that blew in. My brother, Paul, was attending Texas A & M College. One holiday he and Bill Bell from Valentine caught a ride home. Bill brought a friend from the city. I knew they would reach my house at noon, so I prepared lunch as well as doing the usual daily cleaning out the dirt. I remember I made my signature hot rolls. This little wood stove cooked pretty well. There would be eight or ten people for lunch. There was the care for my three little children interspersed with cooking lunch for that many extra people. Since there were no stores to go shopping or movies to attend, this city friend of Bill's asked him, "What does she do with her spare time?" Bill, whose mother had five children, wisely replied, "A woman with three children doesn't have any spare time." How true!

Beary had always liked a rope or a string to play with. As a baby he played with the strings on his pull toys instead of the toy itself. By the time he was four years he was adept with either hand—just whichever hand he picked the rope up with. By the time he was teenaged Blackie encouraged him to rope right-handed, for a left-handed roper is at odds with the world. Horses are not used to left-handed roping. I think that is the only thing Beary does with his right hand. He said he ate with his right hand while in the armed services because it was not worth bucking all the elbows to eat left-handed.

I am basically left-handed, but I am sure it never occurred to my mother that she might have a left-handed child, so I was taught to use my right hand. Things I do instinctively, as opening doors or reaching for something, I always use the left hand. My father had two very left-handed brothers.

Chance, despite her delicate, dainty appearance, was a leader. She would play cowboys with her brothers, but then they had to play at housekeeping with her. When very young, Beary would take her dolls from her. He wanted a doll, too, so I made him a boy doll. He named this doll Thomas. He loved Thomas and left Chance's dolls alone. Tim enjoyed a book about a little black boy, Little Brown

106

Koko, so I made a little boy doll of brown satin with big round eyes and mouth. He was a real favorite.

The children were playing out at the woodpile. Beary had a hatchet, and Chance was in the way of where he planned to chop. He told her that if she didn't move, he would hit her. She didn't move and he did hit her, and cut a gash in the top of her head. I came to the scene of two wailing children—Chance because she was hurt, and Beary scared and contrite. (I think he was too young to realize that hitting her would cut her.) I had to comfort both of them.

At the Burned House I had gotten the children a pup tent for a play house. A rain and wind had collapsed this tent. They went out to raise it up, but immediately came running back calling "rattlesnake!" I went to investigate. Gingerly, I pried open the tent flap. There was a big bull snake that had taken refuge in that tent. When he was disturbed he made that blowing noise they make that sounds very much like a rattlesnake. At least my little children were alert to danger at that young age.

The lower portion of the wooden windmill tower had been enclosed to make a room to be used for a barn. Blackie had bought a load of oats in burlap bags to feed his horses. Our children had found that these stacked, slick bags made a great place to slide from the topmost bags down to the bottom. Tim was not yet three years old, but he was in on the sliding too. Somehow he got started head first and hit the edge of the metal oat barrel head-on. When Blackie came in carrying him, limp and bleeding, I didn't know if he was alive. It had knocked him out and cut a nasty gash on his forehead.

Tim was fascinated with the corrals. Before he was fifteen months old, he would run off to the corral when he could get out of the yard. He tore holes in his diapers crawling under the gate to the corral. He was not afraid of horses or livestock. I really had to watch him.

At this time, Blackie bought a kerosene-burning Servel refrigerator. It was a humongous thing, at least 40 inches wide, thirty-two deep, and six feet high, with coils on top. But if every evening you filled the little tank with kerosene, trimmed the wick just right, and lit the burner, this refrigerator would make ice by morning—two little trays 2 ¼ by 2 ¼ by 10 inches. If I worked it just right, I could empty the ice cubes early in the morning and fill the trays with ice cream custard, and they would freeze by noon. What a delight! I have fed ten or twelve people with iced tea and ice cream from those little trays. It is easy for me to accept the account of the loaves and fishes.

It seems I always had a number of people to cook for, starting with the five in my family. It was not unusual for 3 to 5 or more people to arrive unannounced right at mealtime. With no telephone, there was no way to let me know. Distance was a factor, too. From nearly anywhere it took until noon to make the trip. I always managed to feed however many and have enough. I was brought up that way. My mother had coped with the same situation. One unexpected guest told her, "I don't want to impose on you." Mother replied, "Oh, I'm used to it," not thinking how it sounded. But it was true. Sometimes hospitality became an imposition on a woman.

When we lived at the Burned House Beary had a little one-eyed horse named Canela to ride. One afternoon when he started riding this horse to go get the milk cow, this pony didn't want to leave the corral. Blackie had to make him leave the corral. Beary was six and one-half years old. He was riding a man's size saddle with polo-type stirrups. After they got a good distance from the house, the horse shied at a stick on the ground. When he jumped, it threw Beary out of the saddle on the pony's blind side, but his foot hung in the stirrup. This spooked the horse, and he began to run with Beary hanging from the stirrup, his head hitting the ground and bushes. He was trying to climb up. Blackie ran for his gun to shoot the horse. Just as he aimed, Beary's foot came out of the stirrup. Beary's face was bruised and scratched. Chance thought her dad was mean to make Beary get back on the horse. That is harsh, but it is the best way to overcome fear from a wreck like that. And Beary did go on to liking riding horses.

When our son, Tim, was four years old, he was helping round up sheep at EV Ranch when a blue norther (cold north wind) blew in, causing the temperature to rapidly drop to below freezing. His granddad, Paul Evans, brought him to the house, where his hands were held in a pan of ice cold water to start them warming and prevent frostbite. Tim still remembers how that warming process hurt. I, too, can remember being so cold that I first had to immerse my hands in very cold water to start the warming process. It is painful, but not as painful as hold them out to the fireplace heat first. We must not have had gloves to wear.

I was driving from the Burned House to my parents' home at EV to have a birthday party for Beary on December 7, 1942, when on the pickup radio I heard the news of Pearl Harbor. Our country was at war. I have always had a horror of war, perhaps because I was a wartime baby. I know that Mother feared Dad would have to go to war. I think these strong emotions are transmitted to an infant even while in the womb.

# New Mexico Fiasco

In 1943 Blackie had the opportunity to lease a ranch in New Mexico. He looked at it and found it was good grass country of open hills at about 7000 feet altitude. Our sheep were still on Dad's pasture, but there were getting to be too many sheep for the country. I packed and crated our belongings. Blackie had engaged a friend who had a bobtail truck to move us.

Blackie drove the 600-plus sheep to the shipping pens at Kent, loaded them in the railroad cars, and rushed to load our things into this truck. We loaded the household things, including that huge refrigerator, in the front of the truck, fixed a partition, and loaded the horses and the milk cow. He had the pickup loaded and the dogs in the trailer. It was night when we arrived at our destination. Friend Joe helped unload the animals first, then household goods, all by light of the vehicles. I got beds made and we slept some.

Blackie left long before daylight to receive the sheep off the train at Magdalena, fifty miles away. The State had a fenced driveway so ranchers could drive their livestock to shipping points. There were corrals and a windmill about a day's drive apart. There was just a barbed wire fence, not net wire. Blackie hired a young boy to help him, but he knew nothing about sheep. When those sheep were turned out of the shipping pens, they were hungry. They scattered in every direction, even with Blackie trying to keep them bunched. That barbed wire fence didn't mean a thing to them. Blackie rode and looked and asked, but he never recovered any of those 300 sheep he was short. People in that area were not like those in Texas. Their policy must have been "Finders, Keepers." Three hundred sheep didn't evaporate. They were somewhere, but nobody ever admitted

110

it. That was the first disaster, the loss of half our sheep.

At daylight that first morning I waked in this isolated log house needing to find things to fix breakfast for my little children. There were three rooms—a kitchen with a small wood burning cook stove and two good-sized rooms, one with a wood burning heater. The water was down the hill at the windmill. Somehow I got the children fed and began unpacking. We really didn't have much to unpack.

It did not rain, it did not snow. The wind blew—not just with velocity, but with ferocity. It even blew Blackie's glasses off once, and he wore the kind that the temple pieces hooked completely around his ears. He was walking, leading his horse and driving a bunch of sheep. Lightning knocked him and twenty-five sheep down. It was dry lightning—it brought no rain. It may have been a good thing Blackie was not on his horse. He would have then been the highest object around.

That fall I started Beary in school. Chance wanted to do what Beary was doing. I gave her a little something to do, but it was not enough. She learned as Beary did.

The coyotes and bobcats were killing sheep and eagles were carrying off lambs. The dust storms were terrible. When it looked like every bad thing that could happen had happened, Blackie got his draft notice to go to Santa Fe for his Army physical. He had to be gone overnight because it was so far away. It was up to me to milk the cow. I had only once milked a cow before. Milking was always done by men. But the cow had to be milked and the children needed milk, so I milked the cow. I think the calf got a good fill that night.

Thankfully, Blackie was not accepted into the Army.

One day I realized the puppies had been barking for a long time and went to see what they were barking at. A rattlesnake was coiled under the pickup. Blackie was gone, so it was up to me to kill that snake. I couldn't let him go to be where my little children played. I assessed the situation and realized he was coiled under the motor portion of the pickup. I could safely get in the pickup and back it off of him, which I did. Blackie had a very large, heavy hoe with a long handle. I got that hoe, took aim, and hit hard. Then I got tickled because it looked so funny. I had sliced that snake across all the coils. There were just little half circles of snake. He was yellow. The snakes there were yellow because the rocks on the hills were yellow. After that, Blackie showed me how to shoot the .410 shotgun, and I used that to kill many snakes.

My brother, Paul, had enlisted in the Air Force. He took his basic flight training at Fort D. A. Russell at Marfa, Texas. He was to receive his wings at a base at Phoenix, Arizona. Paul loved little children and had been especially close to Tim because we lived at EVs. Our parents and sister and brother-in-law planned to go to Phoenix for the occasion and they wanted to take Tim. They did take him and said that at three years old he made a good traveler.

A redeeming feature of this New Mexico fiasco was the very good neighbors who lived about three miles away. They had two boys, one older than Beary and one just the age of Tim. He and Tim could have passed for identical twins—hair, eyes, skin color were just the same. They even had burn scars on their left arms in the same place. At a little distance the only way his mother and I could tell them apart was by their clothing. They were really good buddies.

There was a fenced space under the lead pipe where the good corral dirt had blown in. I planted chard and beets there. They did amazingly well; even in that short growing season we had chard in abundance and shared it with our neighbors. There had been an icicle from the lead pipe the 27th of June, and we had frost and another icicle from the lead pipe the 27th of September.

The Presbyterian Church had missionaries in that western part of New Mexico. It was not long after we arrived that the missionary for that area, Roger Sherman, came to visit. He was a cowboy and a wonderful man. As a cowboy he could relate to ranchers in that area. If they were branding or doing any ranch work, he would pitch in and make a hand. On one visit, while I fixed lunch, he repaired Tim's little wagon and made one little boy happy. He held church services one Sunday a month at a school house at Dusty, a community about 30 miles from us. We had church and everyone had brought a basket lunch for a community meal. It was a time of good fellowship.

There was a camp meeting patterned after Bloys that met at Montosa, west of Magdalena. We had started to attend it when we met our good friends, Teague and Kirk Hutchinson, on the road. They were coming to help us, Teague to help Blackie and Kirk to help me with whatever we needed to do to enable us to attend Montosa—really true friends. Teague said he had a bed so the children and I could stay that night. Blackie had to go feed and care for the animals. I stayed, but I am sure that was Teague's bed and that he stayed up at the campfire that night.

Our association with old and new friends in New Mexico was good, but financially for us this move was utter disaster. We sold 27 lambs. We had left Texas with money and more than 600 good young sheep all paid for and clear. We had to borrow money to go back to Texas. Blackie drove the sheep, nearly 300, and I drove the pickup. At night we camped at these driveway corrals where we could pen the sheep. I cooked our meals over a campfire in a cast iron Dutch skillet. We unrolled our bedrolls on the pine needles and slept under the stars.

Blackie needed to go to Magdalena in the pickup. He took Chance and Tim, and Beary and I drove the sheep.  It came a cold mountain rain, the only rain we saw the whole year.  We were near a ranch house.  Beary was hurting with the cold, so we penned the sheep, and those kind folks took us in and gave us something dry to put on. I ironed our clothes dry with sad irons heated on a wood stove.

In New Mexico that winter, if the wind wasn't blowing, Blackie would go to milk the cow and do chores in his shirt sleeves—no coat—though the thermometer registered zero.  That January we went to Breckenridge to visit his parents and we nearly froze.  It seemed so much colder there.  I think the difference in altitude affected it.

Blackie's brother, Thomas, was stationed at Carlsbad, New Mexico, in the Air Force.  We went by Carlsbad to pick up Thomas and his wife, Charlcie.  The dogs were in the back of the pickup, our luggage on a rack above them, and we four adults and three little children were in the cab of the pickup.  It was a good thing we were all slender.  With gas rationing, you did what you could.  Somehow we rode that way to Breckenridge.  Thomas and Charlcie did not return with us.

While we were there Blackie's sister, Nannie, gave our children some ducks.  To return, we loaded the dogs in the back of the pickup, the luggage and ducks went on the shelf above the dogs, and we started home late in the afternoon.  It was night and a light rain was falling when we reached Abilene.  Blackie missed the turn that bypassed downtown Abilene.  We arrived in downtown Abilene just as people were coming out of the movie theaters.  The dogs got in a fight, Blackie was hollering at the dogs, the ducks started quacking, the children started crying, and I wanted to disappear.  We created quite a spectacle.

Those ducks became quite a nuisance. They learned to get under a horse's morral and make a quacking fuss so the horse would throw his head up and shake oats out of the morral. Ducks are really nasty to have around corrals. They gradually disappeared. Maybe the coyotes caught them.

After the sheep were loaded onto the train headed for Van Horn, Texas, we rushed to load our things in the pickup and trailer. We took that huge refrigerator, but we never used it again. Blackie sold it to someone. Driving the sheep from Van Horn to EV Ranch, we spent one night at Michigan Flat Ranch where a friend worked. He had only one arm; his left arm had been shot off at the shoulder in a shotgun accident when he was quite young. He had made his living working as a cowboy. He could rope and saddle a horse and do any other ranch work. That night he fixed supper for us. I saw him peel potatoes with one hand. He did a good job of it.

We moved in with my parents again and put the sheep in Dad's pasture. I continued to teach Beary and Chance. It was wartime, and sugar and canned fruit were rationed. You could only buy what you had ration stamps for. I always bought the maximum, but still had to have it only for special occasions. I came into the kitchen to find that Tim, at age 4 ½ years, had prepared lunch. He knew how to use the manual can opener and had opened most of my rationed canned goods. I immediately started him to school where I could keep an eye on him.

**In World War II Paul Jr. was a co-pilot of a B-29** bomber plane in the Pacific zone. He was based on several islands, including Guam, from which they bombed Iwo Jima so the Marines could go in to capture it, as well as bombing Japan before the atomic bombs were dropped. His crew flew forty missions without getting a scratch on their plane. Paulie flew these missions with his Bible open on his lap.

115

Mother and Dad had been to California to see Paul, who was stationed at Fort Ord, near Bakersfield. At the café where they ate, a very attractive young girl was their waitress. Dad liked her black eyes and dark hair and pleasing manner. He told Paul, "You ought to build a smoke for that girl." Paul took his advice, and they corresponded while he was overseas. When he came home on leave Myrtle came from Dallas to see him. One afternoon she went with him to feed the bulls. They were still gone at dark. Mother feared they had car trouble. Dad just smiled. When they returned, they announced their plans to marry while he was on leave.

We got busy getting ready for a wedding. Word was sent to relatives and friends. Frances, a cousin Claylia, and I made the wedding cake. Ration stamps were allotted on the number of people in a family, not on ages, so I had accumulated a good supply of sugars, plain and powdered. As we made and iced this big cake I was able to supply the sugars we needed. We decorated it with blue Air Force wings. It turned out really well. Mother sent Paul's dress uniform and a white dress Myrtle had brought to have them pressed by the Marfa Cleaners.

Then it began to rain. Rain was unheard of in the last week of March. It rained and the creeks began to run. The flat country through which the road came was overflowed. On the wedding day, March 31, 1945, people started to come but were stopped at a running creek. A spunky ranch woman driving a big Buick said, "I can cross it," and she did. Some of the drivers made it through, but some cars were stuck in the mud, including the pastor who was to officiate at the ceremony. Blackie brought him and others on to EV Ranch. He was kept busy pulling cars out of the mud and ferrying people from their mired cars. He didn't make it to the wedding. Neither did the nice clothes that had been sent to Marfa.

Aunt Grace had brought her car loaded with bridal wreath and iris blooms to bank the altar. We had a lovely wedding for this couple despite the unexpected happenings. Ranch people are always happy any time it rains.

After the war Paulie worked in maintenance for Standard Oil's refinery in El Paso. He was so efficient that he was sent to the Bahamas to inspect the welds of the Trans-Atlantic pipeline before it was lowered into the ocean. Myrtle was able to go with him. Then Paulie had the opportunity to go to India to oversee the construction of a fertilizer plant that Standard Oil was building there on India's east coast. He and Myrtle lived in India for three years. When this plant was finished, Paulie had to write a manual in British English for its maintenance.

# The Circles

**Blackie leased a ranch north of Plateau** and 17 miles east of Van Horn. He sold the sheep to my dad and bought cattle to put on this ranch. Now we could have a home of our own. This house had two bedrooms and bath, kitchen, and a large dining-living room. It had a room upstairs that the children stayed and played in. Blackie's brother, Tim, had recently married and brought his wife to meet us. As she told me later, Tim thought her nieces and nephews were little hellions. His brother Blackie's children were good, well-behaved children. As we were visiting in the living room that evening and the children were upstairs, we heard the most terrific noise of something falling, crashing and bouncing down the stairs. Blackie and I rushed to see how many children were killed or hurt. The children just looked sheepish. It was Chance's big wooden doll house that had fallen, or been pushed, down the stairs. Elsie said Tim never talked any more about his brother's well-behaved children.

Beary was eight years old when we moved to the Circle Ranch. This ranch was not sheep fenced, and we bought cattle for this ranch. Beary helped Blackie tend and work the cattle while riding a big black jackass with a man's saddle. This jack could be ridden like a horse to work cattle, but he would always kick at Beary trying to mount him until Blackie would hit the jack with a big board. Only then would he let Beary get in the saddle. There were two burros at this ranch, and a discarded two-wheeled cart. The children hitched one of the burros to this two-wheeled cart, and they had transportation. They just had to persuade the burro to keep going to pull the cart. They were very young to be able to know how to hitch up the burro, but children on ranches learn many skills at a young age. After all, Beary was eight, Chance six, and Tim five. They were very innovative in their recreation. They were never without something to do, for they were filled with creative ideas.

This house had a butane cook stove. The old bachelor who had lived there bragged to me about how fast that stove would make coffee. When I started cleaning, I discovered the entire space under the burners was packed solid with coffee grounds where his coffee had boiled over. It was great to have butane gas. We bought a gas-burning Servel refrigerator. Those were the greatest boon to ranchers, to have refrigeration when there was no electricity. They were so dependable. We used that one for more than forty years.

I continued to teach my children.

We arose early one morning to go to my parents' ranch for breakfast and to work sheep. About 15 miles from their ranch our car stopped and Blackie couldn't get it to start. He walked back about 4 miles to his brother Mills' filling station. He was gone until long after daylight. I think they had to go to Van Horn for a part. My children were too restless to stay in the car. They were prowling out in the bushes. They decided to show me how hungry they were by eating greasewood. I don't think they ate much. Blackie bought a classy little Studebaker car to replace the one that stopped on us.

**Our fourth child, a darling little 6 ½ pound girl, was born May 17, 1947.** Blackie named her Myrtle Judith, or Judy, as she became.

We enrolled the children in the Van Horn School in September, and started driving to Van Horn twice a day. Sometimes Blackie could take them, but it usually fell to me to get the baby ready and pick them up in the afternoon. Educating children is always a problem for ranchers.

When we moved to the Circle Ranch, it was feasible to drive to Sunday school and church on Sunday mornings. Though Blackie had not been reared in a church-attending family, he was brought up by Biblical standards of honesty, truth, and integrity. He had made his decision for Christ the year before we married. I had never attended Sunday school at a church, but Mother had Sunday school for her three children on the ranch. Blackie and I believed it was the right thing to do that our children attend Sunday school and church with us. But as long as we approached the question of "should we go to church in the morning or not," we usually didn't go. Then we decided that if it was Sunday, we would go to church. There was no question of "whether or not." We went.

In 1944 a young couple, Johnny and Margaret Fitzgerald, leased part of the EV Ranch to pasture sheep. They had two children, Johnny II and Elizabeth, who were the same ages as our children. We enjoyed doing things together. Blackie and Johnny both had dogs and liked to hunt bobcats. Margaret suggested we go fishing on her father's ranch close to Balmorhea, where there was a spring-fed lake in the mountains. This lake supplied water for the small town of Toyah, Texas, through a twenty-mile pipeline. The lake was stocked with fish and there was a rowboat there. Margaret said she could borrow an outboard motor from her uncle to power the boat. We set a date and drove the seventy-five miles to the lake.

To avoid scaring the fish, Margaret, Johnny, and Blackie rowed to the deepest area of the lake. They were not having any luck catching fish, so they decided to attach the motor and move to a different place. With the motor on the boat, Johnny pulled the rope to start the motor. When he jerked the rope, the motor came off the boat and sank in twenty feet of water. Quickly Blackie handed his glasses and wallet to Margaret and dived after the motor, which he found and brought to the surface, hoping it was not ruined. Blackie poured the water out of his boots and was glad that it was a warm sunshiny day to dry his clothes. After this mishap, our enthusiasm for fishing was as dampened as the motor was. What was Margaret going to tell her uncle?

**A friend let me borrow her treadle Singer sewing machine** so that I could make dresses for my daughters. I decided to see if I could make a shirt for my husband. I bought fabric and a shirt pattern, cut and sewed it together by the pattern directions. It was really funny-looking. The sleeves were so full that they looked like clown's sleeves; the collar was too wide and not shaped right; the body was too big. Bless him—he actually wore it a time or two, but it soon disappeared.

I measured one of his well-fitting shirts and took his measurements and cut a pattern for him. The resulting shirt looked and fit the way I had in mind. I made his custom-fitted shirts the rest of his life. With the success of Blackie's shirts, I tried making shirts for our sons. They were successful, too. As I gained expertise, I designed the yokes and sleeve plackets fancier and more elaborate. Western and rodeo shirts were the rage then. Other boys and girls wanted me to make shirts for them, too. I made shirts for Jim and Sandy Neal, Blackie's employer's sons. A black woman was ironing these shirts and remarked she had never seen any so fancy. The boys' mother, Beth, told her that I had made them. Her comment was, "They look just like factory-made." I took that as a compliment—that they did not look "homemade." At that time factory-made garments were precision sewn. Years later, at a Van Horn class reunion, a fellow classmate told how he and the other boys envied Tim and Beary while in school because they had those fancy shirts and the other boys did not.

I sewed dresses and suits for women. One customer would have clothes sent on approval from Neiman Marcus in Dallas, and if I could alter them to fit her, she would buy them. I could always make the alterations. I learned many ways to make clothing more professional-looking by seeing how these expensive dresses were made. I sewed girls' festive gowns for the school proms, costumes for the dancing class recitals, and pants, jackets and shirts for girls who rodeoed. For each shirt, I measured the person and drafted a custom pattern.

# The River

The U. S. Government through the Department of Agriculture set up a program to patrol the entire US—Mexico border to prevent the spread of Hoof and Mouth Disease to the U. S. from Mexico. There was an outbreak of the disease in Mexico. The entire border was divided into 50 or 60-mile sectors with four or five riders, each patrolling a 10 or 15 mile stretch. A friend of Blackie's told him of the job opportunity and wanted Blackie to work there, so Blackie made application and was hired as a Range Rider. He was also a Customs Officer. He sold the cattle we had on the Circle Ranch. The children and I moved into town into a little open air house. Blackie stayed in a tent on the river. Each rider had to furnish his horses and gear and a place to stay.

That was a very cold winter. The Rio Grande River froze solid, so a horse could be ridden across it. The cold wind blew from the northeast for two or three days; then it would blow from the west several days, bringing back the dust that the northeast wind had blown in. In this little house there would be drifts of sand across the floors. I resorted to taping the front door, which was on the west. That helped some.

Our children were exposed to all the ills of public school. Beary and Judy had the mumps. Blackie had never had the mumps, so when he came to town, he didn't come into the house.

The woman who owned the drug store in Van Horn asked me to manage her store. I didn't see how I could do that and care for my four children. Also, I knew that I would go to be where my husband was as soon as it was possible, to keep our family together.

Blackie bought a trailer house 22 feet long and 7 feet wide for us to move into when school was out for the summer. With four children, it was very cozy. We lived at Sierra Alta, southwest of Sierra Blanca and south of Fort Quitman. This trailer had a door less than six feet high. Sometimes my six foot husband would forget to duck his head when he entered. I really think that was one reason he sold that trailer.

About two months after Blackie started work as a Range Rider, he was promoted to Foreman of Range Riders of the sector from Bosque Bonita and the Box to the Sierra Alta sector. The Riders were to kill and burn every hoofed animal that crossed the Rio Grande River to the United States.

There was an old Mexican man who lived just across the river in Mexico who had a houseful of children and one old milk cow. That cow found there was good grass across the river. Those kind-hearted Range Riders would chunk rocks at her and do whatever it took to drive her back to Mexico. The next day she would be back where the good grass grew. Those Riders knew that sometimes her milk was all those children had to eat. They risked their jobs to keep from having to kill that cow. There really was not much danger—the closest Hoof and Mouth infection was 200 miles from this area.

Judy was one year old when we moved to the River. I had washed some of her clothes, and lacking a clothes line, I strung them on the broom handle and was wedging the broom in the cap of the butane bottle. I kept hearing what I thought was locusts, or cicadas. When I looked down, a rattlesnake was singing under the butane bottle. I was really alarmed that I had mistaken a rattlesnake for a locust.

I knew the snakes were bad along the River, so I asked our pharmacist what to do if someone was bitten. We were 70 miles from the nearest doctor. He highly recommended an antivenin kit, complete with syringe, powdered venom, and horse serum to mix the venom in for injection. He said, "You may or may not be sensitive to the horse serum, but for sure you will be sensitive to the rattlesnake venom." I bought that kit for $4.50 and kept a replacement in my refrigerator as each one was used for a dog. I never had to use one for a person, but they worked magic on dogs. Within minutes after injection you could see the dog getting better. That made me a believer in those antivenin kits. Every time I had to use one I would quickly get a replacement. For over 50 years I kept a kit in my refrigerator. Then they found some kind of antihistamine would work, and Blackie kept that antihistamine and a syringe in the pocket of his chaps. It did not have to be refrigerated. This was an improvement because the last antivenin kit I priced was $75. I paid $45 for the last one I bought. In fifty years they had increased over sixteen fold in price.

After selling that trailer house we moved into a one room flat-roofed rock house at Mule Canyon farther down the river, but more centrally located in Blackie's sector. There were many lecheguilla plants on the hillsides. My children gathered the stalks for stick horses, as my siblings and I had done. Duncan Freeman was at Mule Canyon years later and said those piles of lecheguilla stalks were still there.

The government furnished materials for a camp house, and the men built it. It was 12 by 15 feet, with a wooden floor and three-feet-high walls. Above that it was screened with copper screens which had plastic-covered flaps that could be raised or lowered. It had a sheet iron roof. We also had a 14 by 16 foot wooden platform over which was stretched an army tent.

When we lived on the banks of the Rio Grande my cooking facilities were very limited. I had a two-burner gas hot plate and no oven. Butane was our fuel because there was no electricity. It is surprising

*Our house on the Rio Grande. Beary, Tim, Blackie, Chance, and Judy*

what you can do with a 10-inch aluminum skillet. I even made cookies occasionally. I had to turn them like pancakes to brown the second side. They were very good. French toast was an easy, nourishing breakfast that my children liked. It was quick to prepare in my skillet, and the children could put lots of syrup on it. We had four children, so that was six people to cook for. What made life bearable in the hot summers were the butane refrigerators we had. One four cubic foot Servel was in my kitchen area. Later we had a full-sized Servel that had to be kept outside our dwelling because it wouldn't go through the door. It made ice and chilled foods even when its outside was so hot it would burn you when touched.

When we lived close to Guerra's Farm on the Rio Grande, Blackie built a brush arbor adjacent to our government house. This gave us more room and a welcome shade to sit under. Our sons, Beary and Tim, had their cots and slept there. It was a good place to be in case an infrequent breeze came by. I don't remember it ever raining while we lived there. The farms were irrigated with water from the river. One night before Beary and Tim went to bed we heard a rattlesnake under the brush arbor. We must not have had a flashlight; anyway, no one wanted to go out into the darkness to locate this snake. There was no question of our boys sleeping under the brush arbor that night. They were glad to let the rattlesnake have their usual bedroom. Somehow I fixed pallets for them in our house. The next morning Blackie found where the snake had coiled up in his bed and at daylight had left his trail as he slithered his way to the bosque. Blackie could even trail a rattlesnake by the little pieces of grass or twigs moved out of place as the snake slithered over the ground. A patch of sand or soft dirt made it easy to follow the trail. This way Blackie made sure the snake was not still at our house. He had left to make his way to the bosque to join the rest of his family.

In 1950 Santa brought three bicycles and a tricycle to the Woods home above the bosque at Guerra's Farm on the Rio Grande. It didn't take long for our children to master riding a bicycle. Judy, age 3, rode the tricycle at top speed around in our house. The road made a slope of about 50 yards to the level of our home. Blackie offered a quarter (back when 25 cents was real money) to the first one to ride his bicycle to the top of the slope. Competition was keen as each one attempted to ride to the top, only to tire and have to give up. But Chance kept trying until she rode her bicycle to the top of the slope and claimed the quarter, much to her brothers' chagrin. Little thorns picked up by the bicycle tires caused many flat tires, hampering the pleasure of riding their bikes. They found that a gravel-bottomed creek bed was a good place to ride that did not have so many thorns. Chance was riding her bike along one of these creeks when she saw a snake trying to climb up the creek bank. She reached out and caught him near the tail. He whipped back down and bit her hand. There was quite a lot of excitement until it was determined that it was not a poisonous snake and her hand was only scratched. Why she wanted to touch him, no one could understand.

**Blackie needed a new saddle**. There was a good saddle maker called Bobo in Van Horn, but he had one deterrent to his business. When he was given a down payment to buy leather for a saddle, instead of buying leather he would visit a local bar until the money was gone. To avoid this, Blackie took Bobo to El Paso where he picked out what he needed to make a saddle. Blackie paid for the supplies. Back in Van Horn Blackie loaded all Bobo's saddle-making equipment and supplies, and Bobo, into the pickup and brought him to where we lived at Mule Canyon. Bobo was not real happy about being 70 miles from any bar, but that was the only way to keep him sober and working on the saddle. He had a little house to stay in and work in and we furnished his meals. He told Blackie, "Your wife makes the best damn toast I ever ate." He really liked that French toast.

**The government's area supervisor was coming for an inspection tour**. He brought his own cot and bedding. He was to take his meals with us. He was a city man. When time to prepare his bed, he got out his army regulation folding canvas cot. He said to Blackie, "This is where we separate the men from the boys." Those stretchers at each end of the cot were very hard to get in place. Blackie very easily put those stretchers in place. The supervisor had nothing else to say. I had known this man was to come, so I was glad to have some fresh eggs. Because of our infrequent trips to town 70 miles away, I did not always have eggs for breakfast. That morning, trying to be polite and treat this man with the deference due a supervisor, I asked him, "How do you like your eggs cooked?" He replied, "It don't make no difference. I can't stand the taste of them no how."

**When we moved from Mule Canyon** to Guerra's farm, we moved the government house we were using. Blackie and Beary worked and worked at jacking this house up so that it could be loaded on my dad's 4-wheel trailer we had borrowed. This trailer was not like the flat-bed trailers of the present. This trailer had big wheels and must have been 40 inches high. How they ever got that 12 x 15 foot house high enough to load onto that trailer, I don't know. When Blackie started to do something there was never any giving up. He just figured a way to get it done. Fastening the house onto the trailer was another challenge. The trailer was only five feet wide. Maneuvering that wide load over the winding mountain road took some doing. Beary rode with the Range Rider who pulled the trailer with his pickup.

There was a school for the Mexican farm workers' children within walking distance of where we lived at Guerra's farm on the Rio Grande. It was taught by an old woman who was lame and used a very large limb of salt cedar as a cane or crutch. I enrolled Beary, Chance and Tim in that school. Everyone else in the school was Mexican and they made life miserable for my children. It took very little of such treatment for my children to decide they did not have to tolerate it. Their solution was to remove themselves from the situation. They would take the lunches I prepared each morning and leave our home. They would then spend the day out in the hills until they thought school should be over. When this subterfuge was discovered, I secretly had to admire their initiative in handling a situation that was demeaning, discriminatory, and abusive, and which they did not have to tolerate.

Blackie was paid twice a month. We lived on one paycheck and put the other in a savings account until we had enough to buy a government bond. That way, when we had an opportunity to lease a pasture, we had the money to buy the livestock for it, too.

I was expecting our fifth child, and everything seemed to be normal. I had been going to the same doctor I saw before Judy was born two years before. We never knew why, but at six and one-half months into the pregnancy, I went into labor. I sent my son, Beary, who was 12 years old, to saddle a horse and go find his dad, who was patrolling his sector of the river. We rushed the 125 miles to El Paso. The doctor put me in the hospital and began everything they knew to postpone labor. It didn't work. This doctor used a controversial method of spinal anesthesia in childbirth. He had used this method in delivering my daughter two years before. It was wonderful. I was completely conscious and relaxed. I felt no pain, and the baby was not traumatized. The same method of pain control was used this time. No other medication was given to me. I was completely conscious and aware. There was the shock of knowing the baby might not live.

Just before she was born, I had the sensation of being out of my body— that my conscious self was somewhere above my body but still in the delivery room. I felt sad about leaving my husband and children, but it still seemed to be all right. When she was born, she cried and I snapped back into my body. She was perfectly formed, a beautiful little 3-pound doll. She looked just like Judy had as a baby, but was only half as big. The pediatrician was in attendance at her birth, saw her at least twice a day for the seven days she lived, and was with her from the time she developed respiratory problems until she died. The bill for those services was $4.

While I was in the hospital, Blackie bought a house in Van Horn. Our abode on the River would not have been a good place for a tiny baby had she lived. Since we had electricity in Van Horn, I bought an automatic washer. Such joy! It took all the work out of laundry. In talking to the dealer about this washer, I asked about any new improvements GE had made. He replied, "They made a good washer to start with." I found this to be true.

Laundry was a problem on the Rio Grande. We had to haul all the water we used. We had a heavy 55 gallon barrel to haul our water in. It had a faucet, so we had running water when we ran out to the barrel to get it. Blackie had made a wooden rack to lay the barrel in and put it right outside the door. That was very handy. This barrel must have weighed nearly a hundred pounds empty. Filled with water, that was at least 500 pounds. We used several barrels a week. I don't know how Blackie managed to unload it from the pickup to the rack. He did this many, many times. We did have good, soft water, which was a rarity along the River.

For laundry, I either had to wash the clothes on a rub board or take them to Van Horn. For that I had to get four children and the clothes loaded in the car. This with a little girl who got so car sick over that crooked road that we had to watch her closely to get stopped just before she turned green. It was 70 miles to the Laundromat which had electric washers and tubs for rinse water. No dryer. Back at the River it would be too late to hang the clothes out to dry. That had to be done the next day.

Some of the River Riders' wives had their laundry done by the Mexican women. Blackie insisted that I do that. I was all for it. I got the laundry ready and Blackie took it to this Mexican woman. It came back washed, beautifully starched and ironed, but it smelled like something putrefied. I tried rewashing those clothes several times, but I never got that odor out. We couldn't wear them; we had to throw them away. I know what happened. With the dearth of water, that woman had saved the water from washing someone's clothes before, and the soap had soured. She had ironed that stench into the fibers of that clothing, and there was no way to get it out. So much for having my laundry done!

As Foreman of the Range Riders, Blackie had some vacation time coming. He decided to have a hernia repaired during this time, while he had government insurance. He had this surgery done in El Paso and I brought him to Van Horn where we had a house where the children and I lived during the week so that they could attend school. We went to the River for weekends. After one day of staying in town, Blackie got a severe case of cabin fever. He assured me that he would be perfectly all right on the River—that he would not drive the pickup or ride a horse. I knew he would be careful, so I drove him to Mule Canyon and left him. That evening one of the River Riders came to my house with a message. Naturally, he thought Blackie would be in town. The message was that a family of very unsavory people had leased the Mule Canyon, and Blackie had four days to get moved.

I got my sister to keep my children and drove back to Mule Canyon, arriving about midnight and waking Blackie, who knew nothing of this ultimatum. The afternoon before, he had gone walking for exercise. Because the rattlesnakes were so numerous there, he stuck his pistol in his belt. While he was walking, the old woman and two of her sons who had leased Mule Canyon drove up. They thought Blackie was in Van Horn. They were really surprised to see him. They had several guns in their pickup and seemed very nervous as they briefly talked to Blackie. I feel sure they thought Blackie had received their ultimatum and that was why he had a pistol. They were cowards, so they left without saying anything about their order for Blackie to move. Early the next morning we drove to their house, where Blackie told them he would move, but he could not move in four days. They were very nervous. They had some cattle in the corral that they didn't want us to see.

## Hunting

The first mountain lion Blackie trailed with his dogs and killed was in New Mexico about 1942. The bobcats were very fond of eating our sheep. Lambs were just play for a bobcat to kill. Blackie trailed and caught many bobcats. This day it seemed the bobcat his dogs were trailing was traveling an unusually long distance. The trail led to an isolated little hill and the dogs started baying. Imagine Blackie's surprise to see a large mountain lion on a rock instead of a bobcat! He liked the way the dogs had worked the trail. There was something different about it. A lion hunter was born. He killed this lion, that I am sure knew the taste of Running W sheep.

When we lived at Mule Canyon, Blackie and his best hunting buddy, Duncan Freeman, who was a River Rider in Blackie's sector, did a lot of hunting across the Rio Grande. There were more lions in that area. There were some bushes, but no trees on the mountains. What they had to watch for and avoid were the Mexican Rurales.

On one hunt, the dogs had trailed a lion and crowded him until he crawled up in a bush. The dogs were bunched so closely, fighting and baying the lion, that it was impossible to shoot the lion without hitting a dog. The lion was biting and clawing the dogs, so to protect the dogs Blackie grasped the lion's tail and pulled him away from the cluster of dogs enough to shoot him.

The climax of these stories after the dogs have the lion stopped in a tree, a cave, a bush or a bluff does not take long to tell. The hunt itself is the long story. It started before daylight, and many times it might be late afternoon before the trail was worked out and the lion overtaken. Not every lion they trailed was caught; there were a lot of dry runs. The lions have every advantage in the mountains where they make their homes. Some days the dogs might not even find a workable trail.

Beary tells of a time he was hunting with his dad. After a chase the dogs were baying the lion in a cave where he had taken refuge. The dogs were crowding the lion so closely that the lion turned from facing them to go deeper into the cave. As the lion turned, Blackie grabbed him by the tail with his left hand and shot with his right. One more lion that would not escape.

Blackie really did not enjoy killing lions. His pleasure was in seeing and hearing the dogs work the trail. He would have much preferred to allow the lion to escape and go free to be trailed again. But it is necessary for the dogs to complete their work; else they lose their enthusiasm for the chase. Also, the ranchers on whose land Blackie hunted wanted the lions killed. The mainstay of a lion's diet is a deer a week on the average. When the lion population increases, the deer can be rapidly depleted. Hunters who pay well to kill a deer make a good part of many ranchers' incomes. They do not welcome the lions' competition. If Blackie did not kill the lion his dogs cornered, he would soon have not been welcome to hunt on that ranch. In his billfold he had a long list of combination numbers of locked gates to ranches where he was trusted to hunt.

One Saturday evening in 1955 our closest neighbor called to tell Blackie he had found a freshly killed calf. Could Blackie come and catch this lion? This was a call Blackie always responded to. He did not hunt on Sunday except in the case of such an emergency. The best chance of catching a lion is from a fresh kill the lion has made. He will eat his fill and lay up nearby. In one more day the lion may have covered the kill and moved on to another place. Early the next morning Blackie drove to the place the neighbor had told him the kill was, with mule and dogs. About 10 am he returned home and said, "Let's go to church." We quickly showered and dressed. He drove past the church where our children were and went on to the church our neighbor attended. We were a little late. Every seat in that small church was filled except for the front pew. I felt conspicuous in my new maternity dress as we walked the full length of the aisle. The rest of the congregation may have wondered why we were there, but not neighbor Bill; he knew why. His attention may not have been completely on the pastor's sermon, but on what was sure to be in

Blackie's pickup. After church I think everyone there came to look at that big male calf-killing lion. The Woods' were the talk of the town that day.

In 1978 while hunting high in the Eagle Mountains, Blackie was leading his mule around the steep side of a mountain. Blackie crossed a narrow ledge—the mule didn't make it across. This ledge caved off under the mule's weight, causing an avalanche of rocks, dirt, and mule to go crashing down the mountain. When the avalanche subsided far below, the mule was very dead. Blackie was miles from his pickup where he had unloaded his mule and dogs to start hunting. He was much closer to a friend's weekend house in the top of the mountain. He removed his saddle and bridle from the dead mule. He would return for them later. He started walking to this house where no one lived. A Jeep which remained at the ranch just might have the key left in it. He was in luck—the key was in the Jeep, but not much gasoline. Blackie drove to another friend's unoccupied ranch and borrowed gasoline enough to drive around the Eagles to his pickup.

When Blackie had not returned home by 9 pm, I began to get uneasy. 10 pm, 11 pm—I was wondering if this time he would not come back. Was he injured or dead in some inaccessible canyon in those mountains? No one knew where his hunting would take him; not even he knew that. After midnight he came home and ate his first food since his breakfast at 3 am the day before, and possibly had his first drink of water.

Early that morning he called the owner of the Jeep to tell Kit that he had taken the Jeep, and why. Blackie took his gooseneck trailer to where the Jeep was, loaded it in the trailer and returned it. Then came the task of recovering his saddle and dogs. The dogs would return to the place he had unloaded them if they were not too sore-footed. Sometimes the pads of their feet would be worn raw and bleeding from running in that rocky mountain country.  They would rest where they were until they could travel.  Dogs can find the little hidden seeps of water where the deer drink.  Once one of his best dogs failed to show up until the fourth day after he had been lost, with Blackie looking and waiting for him each day.  Blackie had bought a lunch meat-type sandwich as he came through town.  He never took a lunch with him.  He offered this sandwich to the dog, who refused to eat it, even after four days of not being fed.  We did not eat lunch meat.  Even that hungry dog would not eat it.

Blackie continued to hunt alone after he was 80 years old.  One of his buddies was concerned and told Blackie he should not ride in those mountains alone.  Blackie's reply:  "I like the company."

On one such occasion his dogs were trailing a lion across a narrow slick-rock canyon from where he was.  He looked the lay of the land over and decided a ledge near the top of a steep rock escarpment where he was standing would be wide enough for him and his mule to cross over.  This ledge was at least 75 feet above the lower edge of this escarpment.  He was almost across when he was about to run out of ledge.  It was becoming too narrow for the mule to walk on.  He was debating what to do when his mule got nervous and her left hind foot slipped off the ledge.   As she fell, her head hit Blackie, knocking him off the ledge.  The mule slid backwards on her hocks without turning over.  Blackie rolled over and over and slid and tumbled down the escarpment; at one point his left leg must have gotten under the mule.  From the hip down he was badly bruised, even between the two bones of his leg.  Though he had lost his hat about halfway down, he did not lose his glasses.  His heavy canvas hunting coat, Levis, chaps and gloves had protected his body from cuts and scratches, but not bruises.  His .22 pistol stayed in its holster.  With a long stick he retrieved his hat from the bush where it had lodged.  His mule did not run off.  She was grazing where she had landed. He mounted her and found another way to get to the other side of that slick-rock canyon where his dogs were.

Cowboys have to be some of the hardiest beings ever created. An example of that is my friend Jim. Jim hunted with Blackie even before he got his own hunting dogs. Blackie had introduced Jim to lion hunting, and Jim was sold on the sport. After one hunt Blackie was waiting for one of his dogs to come to him, so Jim decided to go home. He mounted his mule and rode through the mountains. As he rode down a steep rock trail, his mule got boogered at something and started pitching down that trail. Jim's saddle turned, throwing Jim under the mule, with Jim's feet still in the stirrups. Mules are very touchy about the area of their underbelly. Before Jim could get his feet out of the stirrups and while he was still hanging head-down, the mule started kicking to dislodge this object underneath him. A mule's kick is rapid and powerful—not for nothing the comparison "kick like a mule." The mule's kicks were striking Jim's face repeatedly, knocking out teeth, cutting his face, and breaking delicate face bones and jaws while beating his whole body against the rocks underneath him.

When Jim got loose from this precarious position, he had to get the bridle reins and subdue the scared mule to remove the saddle and gear and re-saddle. The mule probably didn't cooperate. With his saddle back in place, Jim mounted the bronc mule to resume the ride back to his pickup. On the way he had to go through a gate, which entailed dismounting, opening the gate, leading the reluctant mule through the gate, closing the gate, and re-mounting. His eyes were swelling almost closed by now, his face still bleeding. When he reached his pickup, he loaded the mule in the trailer and drove to his uncle's ranch for help.

Later when Blackie rode down this steep trail and saw the blood on the dislodged rocks, he knew his buddy had been hurt in some kind of mule wreck.  By that time Jim had been taken to the hospital in Odessa, where he spent months with multiple operations to repair the shattered facial bones, and then with his jaws wired together for them to heal.  I can't imagine how he had endured the pain of his broken jaw and facial bones while he subdued his frightened mule, lifted his heavy saddle in place, and mounted the spooked animal. Talk about "true grit!"

After we bought the little ranch in 1977 and Blackie did not have to work the long hard hours he had before that, he could devote time to hunting mountain lions in earnest instead of only in answer to an urgent call from a rancher who had found a kill.  He had hunted enough to have well-trained dogs in his pack of four or five hounds. The part of the hunt he enjoyed most was watching the dogs find and work out the trail by scent left by the mountain lion.  In this way he learned much about the lions' habits, whether the lion was seeking his next meal, travelling from one mountain range to another, seeking a mate, or just prowling.  Mountain lions are loners—they do not live together as pairs or families.  The female keeps her cubs with her only until they are able to kill small game on their own.

At one time in Blackie's hunting, his dogs would find the trail of a big lion in the Eagle Mountains where ranchers reported losing calves to lions.  Then about a month later a rancher would find calves killed by a lion on his ranch in the Candaleria Mountains over one hundred miles south.  By the similarity of the trails Blackie decided there was only one big lion, who seemed to have a charmed life.  The dogs would find this lion's trail but never fresh enough to overtake him.  Many long days were spent with the dogs working the trail to no avail.

On one trail, the lion went to the Rio Grande and not only got a drink, but killed and ate a beaver.  Few people know there are beavers in Texas.  Blackie and his Range Riders found beavers' dams and lodges on the Rio Grande from one hundred to two hundred miles south of El Paso, but I have never heard or read of beavers along the Big Bend Section of the Rio Grande. Blackie continued to hunt and find the trail of this big elusive lion, who thwarted the dogs' efforts to overtake him.

There is a beautiful canyon on the Miller Ranch with permanent water, a favorite haunt of mountain lions. As Blackie topped out on the north side of this Holland Canyon, his dogs picked up a good lion trail. Blackie soon realized that at last he had a workable trail of this lion. The dogs caught up with the killer lion at Vieja Pass, where Blackie put an end to the calf-killing depredations. He sent word to the ranchers along this one hundred-mile stretch that they would lose no more calves to this big lion.

# Neal Ranch

**October 1, 1951, Blackie resigned his position with the USDA** as Foreman of the Range Riders to be foreman on a ranch for J. A. "Buddy" Neal. Buddy, a recent World Champion Steer Roper, had bought a big ranch ten miles from Van Horn and south of the Southern Pacific Railroad. This ranch included the entire range of the Van Horn Mountains. The house Blackie was to live in had been built by the Cameron Lumber Company as a hunting lodge high in a canyon near the top of these mountains.

It was not a very long climb from the house to the head of the canyon in a gap overlooking Lobo Valley and beyond. From there I could see Boracho Peak, thirty-five miles to the east. Boracho Peak is the highest point on EV Ranch. At the foot of this gap down the almost perpendicular mountainside are Indian petrographs etched into the big rocks. A short distance to the north of the petrographs is a shallow well that had furnished water for the stagecoach stop in the 1800's. The grave of Maggie Graham, who was killed by Indians, is near this well.

This shallow well needs only one sucker rod to pump water from the twenty-foot depth. Blackie or his sons could pull it by hand when the pump needed new leathers. Directly over the mountain to the west there was a well 900 feet to water. It had to be pumped with an oil well pump jack.

The road from Van Horn through the pasture and mountains to the Lodge was our teenage children's practice range for learning to drive a car. We went to the Lodge for weekends from our school home in Van Horn. On one steep mountain the rain had washed the dirt away, leaving the loose flat rocks to drive over. That was tricky driving, with the road so steep you could not see past the hood of the car. These teens were very vigilant in keeping track of whose turn it was to drive. They all became expert drivers, and I did survive.

While living at the Lodge, Blackie looked over the lay of the land and decided water from the reservoir in the canyon the Lodge was in would gravity-flow over a gap in the mountain on the west side of the canyon. The pasture west of that gap was not being utilized because there was no water for the livestock.

The Soil Conservation men came and surveyed the proposed pipeline. Their verdict was that the water would not run over the gap. Blackie insisted it would. Buddy trusted his judgment. Work began on the pipeline ditch. This was extremely hard, rocky digging. When the ditch was completed, they started laying pipe. The pipeline reached the center of the gap about quitting time one afternoon. Blackie screwed one more joint of pipe into an ell fitting and stood the twenty foot joint of pipe vertically at the end of the pipeline. The day's work was done.

The next morning when they came to work, water was pouring out of the top of that twenty foot joint of pipe, over the gap, plus twenty feet.

Soon after Blackie started work at the Neal Ranch, he was alone riding the fence in the Jeep. As he followed the fence line, the mountain it followed became so steep that the Jeep was in danger of sliding down the mountain or turning over. To prevent this Blackie tied the Jeep to a Spanish dagger with a saddle rope. He would choose a Spanish dagger above and a little distance beyond the Jeep, drive the Jeep ahead the length of the rope, scotch the Jeep to keep it from turning over downhill, and pick another dagger to tie it to. There was no way he could have turned around to go back uphill.

141

By winching that Jeep with his saddle rope to the various Spanish daggers, he got it safely past that very steep part of the mountain.

At one time Blackie rode a little red mule that was not very gentle (great understatement).  The reason for riding mules was that the mountains are too steep and rocky to punish a horse by riding him in those places.  Also he is more apt to get nervous and hurt himself or you.  The mules are tougher and more sure-footed in those bad places and won't cripple themselves like a horse will.

Sheep will get themselves into places in the mountains that they will not come out of even to go to water.  Blackie was riding the red mule trying to drive this bunch of sheep off the extremely steep mountainside to water at the foot of the mountain.  The red mule started pitching downhill.  This threw Blackie in front of his saddle. Blackie's weight on the mule's neck while she was pitching downhill caused her to turn a somersault and deposit Blackie into a dense clump of prickly pear cactus.  He was like a human pincushion with all three kinds of prickly pear thorns and stickers in his arms, back, shoulders, and head.  It was a nerve-wracking task to remove them.  The little red stickers are so prone to breaking off when you try to pull them with tweezers, which is the only way you can pull them out.  The other thorns have scales which make them resistant to being pulled out.  I hoped it didn't hurt Blackie when I pulled them out as bad as it hurt me; I was so overcome with compassion for him, though he never complained.  For both of us it was just something that had to be done.

**Deer are the primary food for mountain lions**, though they also eat porcupines, skunks, and other small animals.  They are strictly carnivores.  An adult mountain lion may average eating a deer every week or ten days.  A female with kittens may require more than that to feed her kittens as they grow larger.  Her usual litter is three, rarely four, kittens born with their eyes sealed for the first nine or ten days of life, as all felines are.

Once, Blackie brought a newborn lion kitten home inside his shirt, where the baby was warm and contented. The dogs had killed the mother. Blackie's hunting buddy took another kitten. I fed this tiny baby warm cow's milk with an eye dropper until he was able to nurse a bottle and nipple. We learned that the buddy's kitten died of dysentery. Mine also developed dysentery, but I gave him an injection of an antibiotic that Blackie had for a dog, and he lived and grew. As his large teeth grew in and he had chewed up all the nipples I had, Blackie would kill a rabbit for him. He did not need a mother to show him what to do with it. A little later Blackie would bring in a wounded rabbit for him. Again, he did not need to be taught what to do. Instinct was ingrained in him to kill.

As our youngest son, just over one year old, toddled around the yard we noticed that this lion, about five months old, would crouch and lie in wait for JP. To avoid the probability of the lion pouncing on JP and hurting or killing him, Blackie built a pen of metal landing strip panels, with a top to contain the lion. Every morning as Blackie walked to the front door from our bedroom, the lion would whistle to him. It was a clear, high-pitched whistle like I have never heard elsewhere. Keeping the lion supplied with at least one jackrabbit a day in addition to Blackie's heavy schedule of ranch work proved to be a burden. A friend really wanted a lion, so Blackie gave him our lion.

**In 1953 our baby girl, Judy, started in school.** The house seemed very quiet during the day when all four children were in school. In a sense I was still grieving for the baby girl I had lost. I thought another child would help fill the void. My desire was fulfilled when after an unusually hot summer, our third son was born August 29, 1955. Blackie wanted to name him for his father, so we named him John Paul for both his grandfathers. That winter Judy developed a terrible cough that would not clear up. All the children in her class had this terrible cough. Our three-month-old son, John Paul, developed this cough. The new doctor in town prescribed medicine and the use of a vaporizer. The vaporizer clearly made him worse. We rushed him to the pediatrician in El Paso. I told this doctor that Blackie thought John Paul had whooping cough. But Judy had the same type cough, and she had all her early childhood shots. The doctor was writing a prescription for medicine for bronchitis when John Paul began to cough. The doctor tore up the prescription he was writing and said, "I believe your husband is right." That was the first time that young doctor had heard that "whooping" cough. John Paul was given two injections of gamma globulin that alleviated the cough somewhat. Each injection cost $15, a very steep price at that time. I think the children from Mexico that were Judy's classmates brought this form of the disease that even the American children who had been vaccinated were susceptible to.

**After the birth of my fifth child** something happened to me that I couldn't understand. I no longer had the drive to accomplish even minor household tasks. The creative urges I had always had were no longer there. It was a terrible time in my life. My poor husband never knew when he came home from work whether I would be out on the couch, or reupholstering it.

As I was preparing a meal to take to the cowboys working out in the pasture, I experienced an agonizing pain in the back of my head. It was so extremely painful that I crumpled to the floor. Sometime later I managed to rouse enough to answer a knock at the door. It was a woman I was sewing a dress for. She recognized something was wrong with me and called my daughter, Chance, who was in church. I don't have any memory of the rest of that day. Evidently Chance finished preparing the meal and took it to the cowboys. Chance called my sister Frances, who came, and when she heard my hesitant and slurred speech thought I had suffered a stroke. I was

144

thirty-nine years old. A stroke at 39? Frances called the doctor, who confirmed the diagnosis of stroke. There seemed to be no permanent damage other than I was unusually weak and it was a great effort to talk. My left foot tended to drag, and still does. The periods of deep discouragement continued. I would sit and stare at the dogwood design on the couch. Years later I read about depression, and I realized I had battled depression before it was diagnosed and given a name.

The turning point in my life came when a doctor had a hair analysis done. He asked me if I ever felt moody and discouraged. That was the story of these last number of years. He told me I had a lack of lithium, which caused these mood changes. This contributed to my bipolar disposition. The addition of lithium has evened out my life so I no longer have those black depressive times. I am so thankful for that doctor's knowledge. This time of depression was accompanied by a glandular change. I lost the pigment from my dark olive skin, my blue-black hair turned grey, and my chocolate brown eyes faded to hazel. When I looked in the mirror I didn't know the old woman who looked back at me. Who was I? I no longer knew.

**By 1957 we had REA.** Now we could use appliances and have a water-cooled air conditioner. Chance was working as secretary at the John Deere agency, which sold air conditioners. But where to put it? This house had casement windows—not compatible with installing air conditioners. There was a false chimney between the living room and kitchen. It was filled to below ceiling height—open above that. I decided that bricks could be removed from the chimney to make openings into the kitchen and living room. Chance and I bought a large down-draft air conditioner. Now how to get that huge hulk to the top of the house and onto the chimney?

Blackie to the rescue. His was a history of stepping in to save the situation when the projects I started reached a point beyond my physical capabilities. He always knew what to do and how to get it done. Somehow with the use of ropes and main strength he put that massive air conditioner on top of the red brick chimney, hooked up the water lines and, "Oh, joy!" we had a cool house that summer.

At the beginning of the next summer, I bought new pads for this air conditioner. They were not a good kind. The excelsior worked through the mesh covering. Pieces of it clogged the water pump and pipes. When the atmosphere in the house became less than cool I knew I would have to climb up on that steep sheet iron roof, remove a side panel, and clean out the bits of excelsior that caused the stoppage.

I didn't have a ladder, but the back porch had wrought iron supports. I could clamber up one of these and get on the porch roof and then up that steep and dangerous roof to where the air conditioner sat. I think I spent about as much time on the roof unstopping the water pump and pipes as I did in the house enjoying the cool. It did not take long for this to become too exasperating. New and better pads were the solution.

A big air conditioner on top of a brick chimney did look rather odd, but it worked to cool the house. When a cousin and his family came to see us, he laughed so hard at the sight of that big air conditioner sitting on a red brick chimney, I thought he was going to roll on the ground,

**The Drug Enforcement Agency** tried many ways to combat the bringing of drugs, mainly marijuana and heroin, into the United States through Mexico. They started a plane spotting program manned by volunteers. Since we now had a telephone, and the ranch where we lived on the north slope of a mountain had almost unlimited visibility and was so quiet you could hear a plane a long distance away, I volunteered to join the Ground Observer Corps. I was given a code name and instructed to call this number free of charge when I saw an airplane, giving its location and direction of flight. They were looking for low-flying aircraft not on the regular flight schedules. This program was evidently not successful or feasible, for it was not continued for very long. It was an interesting experience.

**One day in 1958 I was busily sewing when I realized that I did not hear John Paul**, three years old, playing in the yard. I called and began to look for him. He was not in the house or the yard. I went to the barn. He was not at the barn or corral, though there were many little boot tracks where he had been in the past few days. I searched the dry creek behind the house. Again, many little boot tracks, but no little boy. Had he decided to go to the highway some 300 yards from the house to meet his sister on the school bus? He was not allowed to go to the highway alone, but all my children were very venturesome even at an early age. I walked to the highway. There were boot tracks along the road, but no little boy. Had he reached the highway and been picked up by some stranger passing by? I began to panic. I called our pastor who came right away with another man from the church. We were debating what to do when Blackie drove up with John Paul in the pickup. Blackie had returned to the barn for something, and John Paul always enjoyed going to the pasture with his dad. Blackie thought I knew he had taken John Paul with him. We had better communication from then on. I have better empathy for parents whose child is lost or kidnapped—the terrible anguish and heartbreaking loss they must feel.

I had an automatic washer when we lived at the Neal Ranch, but not a dryer. I was hanging sheets on the clothesline when JP, about 2 ½ years old, came to me saying, "I bwoke it, I bwoke it." "What did you break?" I asked, but his vocabulary was not enough to tell me. I envisioned one of my prized purple glass objects shattered. He led me to my sewing machine. There he had unscrewed the entire tension assembly of my Singer sewing machine—this machine that I used to sew for the public to help on college costs for the older children. Thankfully, he had not scattered it. It was intact, lying on the sewing machine just as he had unscrewed it. All I had to do to fix it was to screw it back into place. That was probably the beginning of his interest in finding out how things worked. Through his early years any clock, radio or appliance that failed to work, he dismantled. Blackie, in his orderly thinking, would say, "JP will never get all those things put back together." JP had no intention of putting them back together. He just wanted to find out how they were made and what made them work.

When JP was three years old he had the ability to stand motionless for long periods of time when he was concentrating on something, unusual for a child of that age. He could also move quickly and quietly. One day after I thought he had been playing in the yard he came for me to open the door for him. He had both hands packed full of little yellow butterflies that had been hovering over the flowers. How he had caught that many, I have no idea. He must have had dozens of them packed in his little hands.

We had three kinds of hummingbirds at EV Ranch—Ruby-throated, Black Banded, with a black band around the neck, and Rufus. The Rufus are a rusty red color with a rounder body than other hummingbirds. The Rufus are very aggressive, fighting the other birds away from the feeder or even just the space on the clothesline where they all liked to perch. JP caught a hummingbird in his hand and brought it to show me before he released it unhurt. I don't know how he did, but he was that patient and quick.

When John Paul was a young boy our neighbor gave him a just-weaned kitten, for she wanted him to have one of her long-haired cats. JP named him "Kitty Wyche" for this woman. JP and Kitty

Wyche bonded as best friends. They had many adventures together. Kitty Wyche would follow JP like a dog as they climbed the mountains at EV Ranch. At the Neal ranch while Kitty Wyche was quite young, I noticed him jumping around in some tall grass, but since I did not know much about cats except lion kittens and I was busy, I thought he was just playing. The next day when his head was swollen I knew he had encountered a rattlesnake and I was sorry I had not investigated. He did not seem to be very sick and soon recovered, but he never got over his fascination with rattlesnakes. He was bitten again several times.

When we moved from Neal Ranch to EV's Kitty Wyche was put in a tow sack (burlap bag) and loaded onto the pickup. We had not travelled quite a mile when in the rear view mirror we saw this tow sack bouncing across the highway. Kitty Wyche was retrieved and placed in a more secure place in the pickup. JP and Kitty Wyche had many escapades as they roamed the mountains at EVs. Sometimes Kitty Wyche would be absent from three or four days to three or four months. We never knew where he went, but one day he would be back home. Evidently he had friends somewhere else, though our closest neighbors were eight miles away. After JP went away to college at Tarleton University, Kitty Wyche seemed to have a running feud with me, though I never abused him. He liked to lie in the sun on the steps of our back porch. When I went out the back door it seemed he deliberately tried to run between my legs and trip me. It happened too many times to be coincidence. Luckily he never made me fall down those concrete steps, though I felt he tried. Another of his favorite places was in the rocks above the house that had been my playhouse when I was a child. The rock squirrels lived in those rocks too. Perhaps he feasted on one of them occasionally. JP shot a rock squirrel once and, like any little boy, wanted to skin his trophy. When we laid it down to begin, we saw it was alive with fleas. I had never seen an animal with so many fleas. It was hurriedly burned in our trash barrel.

149

Through the years Kitty Wyche was caught many times in steel traps Blackie had set for bobcats. Blackie always set these traps no closer than two or three miles from our house, but at times as Blackie checked a trap, there would be Kitty Wyche in it. He never seemed to learn and couldn't resist the lure used as bait. Blackie did set traps so that there was no visible indication of anything being hidden there. After Kitty Wyche was old Blackie took him to the Salome Place where there was cattle feed store in the barn. Because of the prevalence of mice and rats, Kitty Wyche was needed there. But before long, he must have used up all nine of his precarious lives. He had lived past seventeen years despite his hazardous life.

By the time he was eight or nine years old JP declared, "I am going to be a research chemist." It was a long and rocky road, but he is now a research chemist. When he was nine years old we gave him a basic chemistry kit complete with microscope and various chemicals. He experimented with making gun powder and hydrogen disulphide working in his bedroom. This was too unpleasant, so we moved his equipment and supplies to a small brick building apart from any other building. This suited his purpose very well and he spent many hours working in his science lab. Needless to say, chemistry was his favorite subject in school. He was fortunate to have a good teacher who took special interest in his ability.

At EV's there was a variety of collared lizard similar to a larger type found in Arizona. They had a head like a horned toad with the rearward spikes on the heads, but black and white stripes around the throat, hence the name "collared lizard." They are fierce-looking but harmless. My father and his seven brothers called them "scaly bucks," which was the only name I knew until I researched reptiles. JP, at about 10 years old, was exploring the big rocks on the mountain in front of EV House and found a scaly buck in a crevice of the rock. As he captured her by pulling her out of the crevice, he saw she had seven tiny babies, replicas of the mother but redder and

150

only about ¾ inch long. Since the collared lizards give birth to live young we didn't know if she had just delivered them or if pulling her out of the crevice in the rock had hastened the process. She had been tightly wedged in the crevice.

That year at Bloys Campmeeting JP and his buddies were one-upping each other by jumping from one big boulder on Mount Bloys to another. As the leaps became longer and more daring, JP attempted the longest leap yet, but he didn't quite make it, and hit the back of his head on a rock as he fell. Blood was flowing from a cut as the other boys hurried to the nurse's station, and some came to tell me of the accident. At Bloys we maintain a first aid station with a nurse always on duty. There are a number of doctors who attend the meeting who can be called if necessary. When I reached the nurse's station JP was dazed, but the bleeding was almost stopped. The cut needed suturing but none of the doctors there on call had the equipment to suture a wound. The nurse advised us to take JP somewhere to see a doctor and cautioned me not to let him go to sleep, as there might be concussion with a head wound, and said to watch the pupils of his eyes. He didn't seem to be so affected.

My brother-in-law, Charles Carpenter, drove me to Van Horn as I held JP. Dr. Lipsey quickly sutured the wound with seven stitches. Because of the location of the wound the bandage had to be placed in a band completely around JP's head. When we returned to Bloys at suppertime JP was the hero with his bandaged head and his seven stitches, which number increased with the boys' retelling of the accident.

About 1970 the Van Horn school district started a course of driver education. A local car dealer furnished a vehicle for the students to learn to drive. It was a very popular course with the teenage students. JP already knew how to drive. On ranches, boys nine or ten years old are driving the ranch pickups or jeeps. They learn to be

151

very good drivers because of the type of roads over the mountain pastures, first driving with their dad with them; and by the time they are twelve years old they can take the pickup anywhere on the ranch by themselves. The school driving instructor had a certain schedule for the students' practice driving sessions. JP was always the student driving before a girl in his class who was just learning to drive. When he finished driving, he would fix the controls for her so that when she turned on the ignition the radio would start at the loudest volume, the windshield wipers start at their fastest speed, and anything activated by the motor would begin to work, and the emergency brake would be set. That poor girl became afraid to start the motor for her practice time. But she was a good sport about this razzing.

Once I saw a town boy trying to back his car into a parking space. He had made several attempts but couldn't get it parked. I thought of my two older boys who could spot a 40-foot semi-truck and trailer at a loading chute or dock on the first try. I guess a lot of it is having the opportunity to learn how, which our sons had.

After graduating from high school in Van Horn, JP went to Tarleton University in Stephenville, Texas; but where he really wanted to be was in Dallas where there were job opportunities in his scientific field. In Dallas he worked for a company that manufactured products for animals. There he formulated a shampoo to keep white-haired dogs and cats white. Though my hair was not white at that time that was the best shampoo I ever used. Since he had formulated it while on company time, he could not patent it. I am sure it has brought that company a lot of income.

While working for Texas Instruments he perfected a method of purifying sulfuric acid, which they used by the tank car loads. When this company received a shipment of sulfuric acid that did not meet their specifications of purity, they had been just dumping it into the

152

Trinity River. His method of purifying it to be usable saved Texas Instruments much money and protected the fish in the Trinity River.

JP was continuing his education while working these jobs. In 1983 he graduated summa cum laude from the University of Texas at Dallas. In the early 1980s he made a discovery about ions and was asked to give a report—"read a paper," as they say in scientific circles—at Symposiums for Ion Chromatology at Denver, San Francisco, and New Orleans. He is so modest about his scientific discoveries that I have had a hard time getting this much information. He is like a young woman who worked at a lab in Houston and when asked what she did, replied, "Even if I told you, you would not know."

In 1997 he went to work for Hyundai in Eugene, Oregon. They sent him and a planeload of new employees to Korea for training at a collage in Seoul during January and February. During this time the temperature never reached above the freezing point. The only time it reached above freezing was the day they left Korea to come back to the United States. The only thing they had been taught to say in the Korean language before they left the United States was how to say, "I don't eat dog." JP has no desire to return to Korea.

Since JP could not come home for Christmas that year, his sister Judy and I flew to Eugene to be with him. While JP was at work, Judy and I drove over the mountains to Florence on the Pacific coast. The hills between Portland and Eugene had been stripped of the pine trees to supply the pulp mills, but the mountain west of Eugene was lush with ferns and thick vegetation. It rains so much that water gushes out of the hillsides and accumulates into a river making its way from the mountains to the Pacific Ocean, where the raging, roaring surf beat against the rocky coast. The powerful surge of the tide was awesome and frightening to this West Texas landlubber. I was amazed at the power of the surf there as compared to the gentle Pacific at Los Angeles.  When at Los Angeles I didn't want to be that close and not at least stand in the Pacific, so I removed my shoes and waded out into the ocean.  What a mistake!  That ever-moving, restless ocean had washed sand inside my nylon hose.  It was a terrible feeling.  I don't like oceans.  Give me a mountain that will be there—you can depend on that.  The ocean is never still—always moving.

# Raising the Children

In 1952, Buddy Neal bought a house in Van Horn and moved his family there. This made the house at headquarters available for us to live in. We sold our house in Van Horn. We could now have our family together and our children in school, too. The school bus ran on Highway 90 just about 300 yards from the house.

Van Horn schools did not then have a cafeteria. They gave a long lunch hour so the ones who lived in town could go home for lunch. Those children who lived in the surrounding country had to bring their lunches to school. When Judy started school I was concerned because she had such a poor appetite. I would try to make their lunches something they liked and would eat—not always just sandwiches. Day after day Judy's lunch box would have her almost-uneaten lunch when she brought it home. I must have scolded her very harshly, but soon she brought her lunch box home empty, and I was so pleased with her. One afternoon I was outside the house when the school bus stopped at the cattle guard to let my children off. Judy didn't at once start up the road toward home. She was bent over and looked to be digging a hole in the soft sand. She was digging—digging a hole into which she emptied the uneaten contents of her lunch and covered them up. Her sister and brothers were not tattle-tales. They would never have reported her little ruse that had fooled me for a while.

Chance continued piano lessons. My dad bought a beautiful oak piano for her so she could practice at home. She took dance lessons—tap dancing, some ballet—good experience in coordination. She was salutatorian of her eighth grade class, and later also of her high school graduating class. In high school Chance

155

played center in basketball, as she was tall. She played the xylophone in the school band.

Chance took part in the Girls' Auxiliary in our church. This was a program of Bible study, memorizing Bible verses and studying about missionaries. She progressed to the status of Queen in the auxiliary. She was the first girl in the history of First Baptist Church Van Horn to attain this honor. Her family all went to Paisano Encampment at Alpine for this recognition service. We were so proud of her.

Chance wanted to go to Baylor University at Waco. The Davis Mountain Federation of Women's Clubs gave her a scholarship through the Twentieth Century Club of Van Horn. This scholarship was for $180. I am not sure we would have had the courage to enroll her without that scholarship. It was very important to Blackie to give his children the educational advantages he had not had. We had a wonderful place furnished to live, but not much cash income. We tithed our salary and there was always enough. God keeps His word.

**The first Livestock Show in Van Horn** was held in January 1949. Boys 9 to 18 years old could participate. Tim qualified because he would be nine a few days before the event. Beary and Tim fed, groomed, and exercised their lambs for several months in order to be ready. One of Tim's lambs was judged First Place of its class. The prize was $4. Immediately upon the conclusion of the Livestock Show, Tim went to the dry goods store where he bought a pair of *real* Levi's for $4.

After the livestock show in Van Horn, the county agent would take the boys and their lambs to the larger El Paso livestock show. I would sew overtime to make them fancy shirts for this. The rest of the family would drive to El Paso for the day they would show their lambs. They would then come home with us. From the bedding straw and sawdust in their clothes and suitcases, I am sure they slept with their lambs in the livestock barn.

These livestock shows were held in January, which is always our coldest, worst weather. One year our boys had not gone to El Paso with their lambs. We were all driving to El Paso for the lamb showing day. It had snowed and the road was icy. We had just passed a big semi-truck that had skidded off the road and was upside down in the irrigation ditch of water next to the highway. As we approached a two-lane bridge our car skidded, made three complete revolutions within that bridge, and came to rest with the rear of the car against the bank of that irrigation ditch. We all shook for a while. Blackie drove very cautiously the rest of the way to El Paso.

As soon as Beary and Tim arrived home from school they changed into work clothes for whatever tasks were to be done on the ranch. They worked like men, even as teenagers. There was a roping arena at headquarters where they sometimes could practice roping calves with Buddy's sons, Jim and Sandy. Buddy Neal, a former World Champion steer roper, was very good to help them take part in the Junior Rodeos of this western area. I was glad my sons did not want to go out for football—a very dangerous and inane activity.

Tim liked the ranch life. He somehow had a hard time adjusting to the school schedule. He made pretty good grades, but he just didn't like school. When he reached high school English, he could not see any reason for what they studied. Chaucer, perhaps? Tim and the high school English teacher, Mrs. Tanner, had a running feud all four years. He nicknamed her "Granny Tanny," a term the other students quickly picked up on.

When Judy reached high school in 1961, Mrs. Tanner was reading the list of freshman students. When she reached "Judy Woods" she said in an alarmed voice, "Not Tim Woods' sister?" Judy and Mrs. Tanner became very good friends. Judy was a model student.

About halfway through high school Tim decided to quit school. When he told his dad he was going to quit school, there was no protest or lecture. Blackie just looked at Tim a long time and said, "It sure is going to be hard to make a living." Tim realized his dad really knew how hard it would be. We heard no more about quitting school. Tim went on to graduate and attend Tarleton University in Stephenville, Texas. He was smart enough to get by in high school without learning to study. In college he wasn't prepared for the studying he needed to do. He had to learn to study.

About a month after he went to college, he called home. He told me he had to come home—that he was not doing any good in school. He needed to come home. My heart ached for him, but I had to tell him he couldn't come home—that he needed to stay there in college and that he could do the work of studying. I would really have liked to have him at home, but he was a big boy now and had to adapt to his present situation. There were tears on each end of the telephone line. He stayed in college.

Cleaning out the chicken house was the most hated chore on the ranch. I often wondered if Blackie used it as a manner of discipline for Beary or Tim. Anyway those boys felt that cleaning out the chicken house was beneath their status as cowboys. When instructed to clean the chicken house, whichever one designated would reluctantly gather the rake, shovel and wheelbarrow to get the job done as soon as possible so he could resume cowboying. Especially if Tim was the designated cleaner, I would hear cackling, squawking and banging from the direction of the henhouse. This day for the hens was completely disrupted. Feathers flew; hens ran to the far side of the pen in terror. Even the rooster was disgruntled by this activity. He flapped around in dismay. His flock of hens could not settle down in their nests. The chicken house was left clean but there were no eggs to gather that day.

On a sheep ranch there are always dogie lambs. The mother ewe might have died or just forgot she had a lamb and left him at the water trough. Ewes are not the protective mothers that cows are. When found, the dogie lamb is brought to headquarters to try to save him. If there is no child to assume the task of giving the dogie bottles of cow's milk, this chore falls to the ranch wife.

Beary had a pet lamb when he was not quite three years old. I would prepare the bottles of milk and Beary would call "Lambie" and feed him the bottle of milk. Lambie would come only when Beary called—he paid no attention to any else's call. One morning we were to leave the ranch before daylight to go help a neighbor, but Lambie had to be fed before we left. I prepared the bottle of milk which Blackie took to feed Lambie. He could not find the lamb in the dark and Lambie did not come when he called. I had to bring Beary into the dark yard. When he called, Lambie came and was fed.

JP had a dogie lamb but one morning when he took the bottle of milk to feed his Lambie, Lambie's head was gone. A pig that had been bought at the 4H Livestock Auction had feasted on Lambie. The next day someone took the pig to El Paso to be processed at the locker plant and put in our freezer for us to feast on. The very last thing needed on a sheep ranch was a pig with a taste for lamb.

**In 1956 Blackie went to Marfa shopping for a car.** What he bought was a good, clean low-mileage '55 Bel Air Chevrolet. This was a classy yellow-with-green-interior courtesy car furnished to Elizabeth Taylor during the filming of the movie "Giant" at Marfa. Blackie was not impressed with its former use. It suited his purpose and was affordable. It was a different story when our children drove it to school and their high school classmates learned the car had been Elizabeth Taylor's personal car. Such prestige to own and drive the car that had been Elizabeth Taylor's!

Access to the pasture at the Neal Ranch was north along Highway 90 a mile and a half to a gate south of the Southern Pacific Railroad just south of the underpass. There was also a road on the north side of this railroad that intersected the highway just north of the underpass. Tim had asked to use this 1955 Chevy for a date in Van Horn, 10 miles north of the ranch headquarters. His dad was about due to return home from work in the pasture and might be at the gate south of the railroad. Tim drove very conservatively until he passed that gate. As he drove through the underpass, he gave that Chevy the gas and was rapidly burning rubber. Above the noise of the motor and the road, he heard an unmistakable whistle. His dad had just come through the gate north of the railroad. Blackie had a whistle that could be heard a mile or more in the mountains. Tim knew he was in trouble. Blackie had Tim follow him home and sit in the living room for a while. After about fifteen minutes Blackie said, "If you can drive at a decent speed you may go on to your date now."

Beary's forte was grass judging and he won many medals in these competitions. He qualified for the blue corduroy FFA club jacket, of which he was very proud. For some reason—jealousy or plain orneriness—a Mexican boy cut that jacket into small pieces. It must have been cut—that new corduroy could not have been torn. Beary was so enraged at the destruction of his coat that he began to fight with this larger boy. Only years later was I told the details of this fight by one of Beary's classmates. Beary had the boy down, beating his head on the sidewalk, when the other boys pulled him off, lest the Mexican be killed.

During the summer vacations Beary worked for a very fine farmer, Mr. Hughes, at Lobo Valley. There he learned the art of farming, which he liked and was very good at doing. As a small boy he had graded roads and done dirt work with his toy trucks and grader. He had a natural aptitude for working with the soil, and still today he is a very fine gardener.

160

When Beary graduated from high school, he chose to attend Tarleton College in Stephenville, Texas. He had learned to study while in high school, so he did well in college even though it was hard for him. Something was not filled out right for his college deferment papers, so he was drafted into the army in 1960. I was really upset that he was taken out of college. His basic training was at Fort Ord, California. He was then stationed at Fort Lewis near Tacoma, Washington. He was the only man in his unit who knew how to drive a 4-speed manual shift transmission truck, so one of his tasks was to drive the trucks as necessary. Ranch boys know how to do many useful things. This was the time of the Berlin air lift. His unit was on alert to go to Germany. He drove many trucks onto the railroad cars to be shipped to Germany. This crisis was settled before they went so he did not see overseas duty.

Living in Van Horn for the school year had made it possible for Chance to have piano lessons from the local music teacher. Since we did not have a piano, it was arranged for her to practice after school in an assembly room of the church. The churches did not have to be locked at that time; neither were they heated except on Sunday, and Wednesday evening. One bitterly cold and windy day the dust was blowing until the visibility was zero. Chance did not come home from school at the usual time. I was concerned for her because of the cold and dust. When she arrived over an hour later I asked, "Where have you been?" Her reply, "Practicing the piano, of course." I thought of that frigid room and marveled at her dedication to learning piano. Her dedication persisted, and she is an accomplished pianist today.

Chance had been in school at Baylor about four weeks when we received a pitiful homesick letter from her. We did not yet have a telephone—letters were our means of communication. She wrote that she had realized she did not belong in college—that she should be home washing dishes. Now, if there was anything she hated to do

161

worse than washing dishes, I don't know what it was. We laughed about that letter. Judy, then 10 years old, decided we would never have occasion to laugh about her like that. I told her if she did not get homesick at college, I would feel that I had failed as a mother. I am sure she experienced homesickness after she went to Tarleton but she did not write home about it.

Chance transferred from Baylor to North Texas State at Denton. This helped us, for North Texas was not as expensive as Baylor University. After a semester there going to classes and working as secretary for various professors, she decided to come home for the summer and get a job that paid better than those professors did. She was employed as secretary for the John Deere agency and farm store in Van Horn and could live at home and drive the ten miles to work.

**The Chamber of Commerce of El Paso**, Texas—the Sun City— sponsored the Sun Carnival each year in December, climaxing with the Sun Parade and the Sun Bowl football game on January 1. In 1957 Chance was selected to be the Sun Princess from Van Horn. Since there were to be receptions, teas, and other functions from December 26 through January 1 for these girls, Chance and I planned her wardrobe. I purchased fabrics and began to sew suits and dresses. Her dress for the coronation was made by a seamstress in El Paso, as all the princesses' gowns were alike. There was a girl from every town in the Trans-Pecos area as princess to represent her hometown in this Sun Carnival. It was an important affair. The girls stayed at the Cortez Hotel with chaperones.

We drove to El Paso for the pageant and coronation at the Coliseum. That year the theme was Southern plantations. The girls in their white satin hoop skirts, wide-brimmed hats, and sprays of magnolias made a beautiful pageant. It nearly always snows at that time of the year; this year was no exception. Aunt Mary Evans let Chance wear her mink coat for the parade, for it was bitterly cold. The girls wore their coronation gowns on the floats. They could not have stood the cold weather without warm coats, even with the extra layers of clothing under the hoop skirts.

That fall my brother Paul and his wife Myrtle Evans, offered for Chance to live with them in El Paso and get a job there. Having been a Sun Princess gave her status in El Paso. Soon she was hired as secretary for Burroughs Corporation, maker of office machines. She rode the city bus to the office in downtown El Paso and back home after work. One of her duties as secretary was to take the deposit to the bank. As she prepared to go, her boss always said, "Don't forget to bring the paper clip back." He got a lot of mileage out of a paper clip.

Soon Chance rented an apartment with another girl. Chance's roommate applied for a job at White Sands, but when the physical exam showed she had tuberculosis she was hospitalized. She called Chance and explained her dilemma. She had a date with a young man, Bobby Hart, to go to a Halloween party to which she could not go now. She asked Chance, "Would you take my place and go with him to this party? He is so shy he would not ask you but I will set it up with him." Chance agreed to this arrangement. When this tall blond young man called for her that evening she liked his looks and manner. They attended the party and had a good time. Chance kept telling Bobby she needed to catch a bus to go to her parents' home near Van Horn for the weekend. He told her, "I will take you home," probably not realizing it was 125 miles away. He did drive her home to the Neal Ranch, then drove back to El Paso in time to go to work at American Airlines without any sleep.

This date led to other good times with each other. By mid-December they were sure they were in love and wanted to be married. The first weekend that they both had off work was December 29—31, so the date for the wedding was set for December

30, 1959, to be in the First Baptist Church in Van Horn.  I made her wedding dress of white wool with satin collar and cuffs and belt, and trimmed with a yoke of tatted lace made by her great, great grandmother.  Instead of flowers she carried a white satin-covered Bible given to me by my Powell grandmother when I was thirteen. The presiding pastor was Roger Sherman, our friend from our New Mexico stay.  Laura Lou Dod was bridesmaid and Bill Wright, a co-worker at American Airlines, was best man.  JP, 3 years old, was ring-bearer.  Beary and Tim were ushers.

The rehearsal was held that afternoon and went well.  Then we dressed and readied for the wedding.  While we were dressing, Blackie teased me by putting on his greasy work hat and saying, "I'll just wear this hat."  I knew he was teasing and ignored him; but after we left the ranch to drive to Van Horn, I saw that he had forgotten to change to his dress Stetson and still wore the greasy work hat.  It didn't matter that much; he didn't wear a hat in the wedding ceremony anyway.  After Blackie had escorted Chance to the altar and had sat down by me, I saw Judy on the platform with the wedding party.  She looked lovely in her blue velvet dress but this was an unrehearsed surprise.  Oh well, none of the guests knew but that her part in the wedding had been planned and rehearsed.  Bobby assured her that seeing her there had given him confidence.  He became her favorite brother-in-law.

It was 1960, and our family had increased with Chance's marriage to Bobby Hart.  They lived in his house in El Paso at 8120 Harrier Dr. Bobby was employed by American Airlines and Chance by Burroughs Corporation.  The newlyweds had their problems.  A woman ran into the car Bobby had just bought before he obtained insurance on it.  At that time insurance was not compulsory as it is now.  What a shattering loss!  The car was wrecked and unusable, but still had to be paid for.  Now Bobby walked the 5 or 6 miles to his work at American Airlines.  Chance continued to ride the bus to

Burroughs' office in downtown El Paso. Bobby, the only child of a single parent, was not used to the sharing and give-and-take that Chance had experienced in a family of parents and four siblings. Chance was not used to someone who had been the only interest in his mother's life. There was a lot of adjusting for these newlyweds, but love is an overcoming force.

Beary and Tim were in college at Tarleton University in Stephenville, Texas, doing a lot of campusology with their college classes and what jobs they could get around the livestock yards.

**In 1959 at Tarleton, Tim met a cute young girl, Jody Holt**, who attracted him. She liked horses and rodeos and things he liked. That summer he worked for her father who had horses to be trained on his country at Chico, Texas. They were too young, but they decided they were in love and wanted to be married. The date was set for June 6, 1960. Blackie, Judy, JP and I traveled the 550 miles from the Neal Ranch to Chico for the wedding which was held in the home of Jodie's grandmother, Pearl Garrett.

This was a time of a double celebration, for Chance announced we would be grandparents in November. Such a momentous thought, to become grandparents—such joyful anticipation!

Tim and Jody enrolled at Tarleton that fall semester with a job at the college dairy which paid tuition costs. That work of milking cows twice a day proved to be so demanding there was not enough time for studying. It was necessary to find a better source of employment. Tim worked at National Welding and Grinding in Dallas where he learned precision welding and how to weld all metals—even gold and silver. At that time they lived in Farmers Branch. His next employment was at Taylor Publishing Company, also in Dallas. His work was maintaining the various machines for making books. He and his co-worker built a book drying machine which synchronized

165

the varied heat settings as the books traveled through its thirty-two foot length on the conveyer belt. One of his co-workers was a black man who was a good worker with a great sense of humor—always joking. Sometimes as they were washing their hands after repairing machines and the black suds flowed off, he would say, "Oh, I'm fading!"

**We knew we were to become grandparents** in the last part of November, so when the telephone rang that November 19th at 2:30 a.m., I was sure I knew what it was about. It was our son-in-law, Bobby Hart, excitedly telling me he was the father of a healthy son. Such good news! Bobby named him Kippy Read Hart—Kippy because he liked the sound of the name and Read was a family name. Kippy was a beautiful and enjoyable baby. He rarely fretted or cried. He seemed to take life as it happened. He was logical and smart for his age.

Chance had found a Mexican woman from Juarez as a live-in maid to keep him while she resumed her work at Burroughs. After that woman returned to Juarez to care for her own family, Chance tried a number of younger women as live-in maids. Not all of them were dependable, so when one would fail to come on Monday morning to her job, Chance would bring Kippy and his clothes for us, Mamire and Papaw, to care for, which was our great pleasure.

Kippy really enjoyed going in the pickup with Blackie, his Papaw, to check the cattle in the pastures, which took several hours. These pastures totaled about 50,000 acres, so there were no close neighbors. In driving over the ranch you would never see another person, so the cowboys felt no need for porta-potties. When Kippy was not quite three years old Bobby, his father, saw him relieve himself in the yard of their home in El Paso. Bobby was horrified and began to admonish Kippy with, "We don't do that outside." Kippy replied, "Papaw does."

166

In 1962 Jody had announced that she and Tim were going to make us grandparents again in July, so Chance packed all of Kippy's baby things and her maternity clothes and mailed them to Jody. About a month later, Chance realized she had been too hasty—she would need baby things by the end of August.

**Our first granddaughter was born July 13, 1962**, in Decatur, Texas, to Tim and Jody Woods and named Tracey Raenell Woods. How wonderful to have a granddaughter! Less than a month later our second granddaughter, Kimberly Grace, was born August 7, 1962, in El Paso, to Bobby and Chance Hart. Two granddaughters 600 miles apart and as opposite in appearance and temperament as is possible—Tracy with her black eyes and hair and melancholy-phlegmatic temperament, and Kim with blue eyes, fair skin, blond hair and choleric-sanguine temperament. It seemed that Kim couldn't wait to get into this life and start things happening. She had arrived three weeks early.

It was our pleasure to keep our little grandchildren from El Paso, Kippy and Kim Hart, when the live-in maid didn't come on Mondays. On one occasion Bobby and Chance planned a vacation trip to Colorado. I kept the children at Bloys Campmeeting during their absence. Kim, at one year old that week, was unhappy about their leaving. I was trying to attract her attention to some boys playing with their ropes just outside the window. I had said, "See the boys," several times when she said very plainly, "See the boys." It was several months before she really started talking, but she had repeated, "See the boys" that one time as plainly as I had.

Kippy would play quietly, but Kim wanted—even demanded—lots of attention. She hated to have to go to bed and to sleep. Many times after I had finally put her to bed in the guest room, I would wake during the night to find her just standing by my bed. One night I woke to see her sitting on the floor in the circle of light made by

167

the pilot light of our gas Servel refrigerator, the only light in the house, for when we turned off the last light it was DARK—there were no other lights of any kind. Kim evidently inherited my penchant for climbing. When very young she learned to climb up on the kitchen cabinets to reach the higher shelves. She was very fond of bananas and could find them no matter where Chance put them; then she would eat all of them. Chance had just bought bananas and told Kim, "I am going to put these where you can't find them." "Where?" immediately asked Kim. There was nowhere that she could not find them. Once Kim told Chance she wanted a banana. Chance said, "We don't have any." Kim replied, "Yes, we do. I smell them." Kim was very active and athletic. She learned to turn cartwheels at a young age. As soon as her arms became long enough to reach across an open door, she learned to climb the door facings by bracing her hand and foot on each side.

It was our great regret that because of the distance, Blackie's work schedule, and having our children in school, we did not get to spend much time with Tracey when she was young.

Judy had graduated as salutatorian of her class at Van Horn High School. She chose to attend Tarleton University in Stephenville. We found a very nice woman who had a room where she could stay off-campus.

I had been having some very painful attacks that were thought to be from my heart. Actually they were found to be gall bladder attacks. To have the gall bladder operation I chose to go to Alpine where there was reputed to be an excellent surgeon. With Judy gone to college someone had to drive JP to the school bus each morning and meet him every afternoon. JP was ten years old and could drive the ranch pickup, so Blackie bought a car that had been abandoned at the Plateau Service Station and Café. It had been left there long enough to be sold for storage charges. Blackie instructed JP to drive the fifteen miles to Highway 80 and leave the car just inside the pasture—not in the highway right-of-way. JP did this and caught the school bus that morning, but when he returned on the school bus that afternoon there was no car where he had left it. The bus driver took JP on to Kent, and then in his own car brought JP home to EV Ranch. The car was reported to the sheriff's office as stolen. As it turned out, it was not stolen at all. An over-zealous DPS patrolman for some unknown reason had it towed to Kent. Blackie was very irritated and disgusted. That patrolman had seen this car at Plateau as he passed or stopped for a cup of coffee at the café. The car was parked inside a fence on private property where the patrolman had no jurisdiction. It was a very unorthodox and uncalled-for action on the patrolman's part and caused much inconvenience to Blackie. This all happened while I was in the hospital and Blackie was busy working cattle, so they tried to spare me many of the unpleasant details.

My Aunt Grace Evans Cowden knew that if I went from the hospital directly to EV Ranch, I would probably over-exert myself, so she came to Alpine and rented a motel room with a kitchen for us to stay for a week after I was discharged from the hospital. We had a great time together. She was like a second mother to Blackie and me.

Our second grandson was born September 9, 1966, in Decatur, Texas, to Tim and Jody Woods and named Timothy Britton Woods. This carried on a family tradition of a Timothy Woods in every generation since Tim Woods came to the United States from Ireland, but there has never been a Tim Woods Jr. Our Tim Britton had black eyes and hair like his father and his sister, Tracey. Britt was a little dare-devil from an early age. He was adventuresome in his play and liked to have an audience—a real sanguine-choleric temperament. His favorite plaything was a Big Wheelie—a foot-pedaled car with a large front wheel. The house at Roanoke where they lived was on the side of a hill above Highway 377. When Britt started his Big Wheelie down that long slope, he could attain a lot of speed by the time he reached the gate onto the highway. We had to watch to be sure the gate was closed lest Britt on his Big Wheelie dash out onto that busy Highway 377 into the path of a passing car. The Big Wheelie had no brakes.

Britt had a sunny disposition but a very short fuse. It did not take much to tee him off, and when he was mad he was mad all over, but his "mad" didn't last long. When it was over he held no grudge and soon was his happy self again. Tracey was the quite protective big sister to Britt. She played on a soccer team when they lived at Farmers Branch. This was a sport she really liked and was very good at playing. It was my introduction to the game of soccer when I took her to practice and to games.

**Judy had met a young man, James Fritts**, at Tarleton that she was interested enough in that we went to Stephenville to meet him. He was very polite with a great personality. James wanted to go hunting with Blackie, so they set up a time for him to come to EV Ranch. When he came he brought a friend who was not used to riding horseback. Though Blackie never carried a lunch, I fixed sandwiches for the two boys and gave each one a banana. James' friend, who was wearing red coveralls, put his banana in a back pocket. After riding a while he reached for the banana. Alas! Neither the banana nor the red coveralls were in very good shape after the horseback ride.

Judy and James married while in college at Tarleton. James was a good electrician and handy at building so he could always get work. He had grown up on his parents' farm at Lake Proctor. While at Bloys Campmeeting we learned we would be grandparents again. On November 19, 1967, this third grandson was born in Hico, Texas, and named David Alan Fritts. I went to Stephenville to help Judy with the new baby. When I looked into the crib, he looked so tiny at

5 lb. 15 oz. that I said, "Oh, I never have held a baby that small!" James looked at me as if to say, "A fine help you are going to be." When Kippy learned of David's birth on November 19, he said, "Oh, my birthday present!" of their shared birth date.

David was a very intelligent only child who stayed with us on the ranch several times and went lion hunting with his "Papaw" after he got older. When he was quite young, Blackie put David in his lap and let him "drive." At one point, he said, "David, don't you think you'd better slow down?" To which David replied, "I like to go fast. It makes me feel good."

David was an excellent student and graduated from high school as salutatorian and then Magna Cum Laude from Tarleton State University. Today he is a successful Christian businessman.

**Chance introduced her brother, Beary,** to an attractive young woman, Mary Sue Clover, who attended the same church that Chance did. After that introduction and short visit Mary Sue went home and told her foster mother, Mamie Woods, "I have met the man I am going to marry." Mamie replied emphatically, "You will do no such thing." Mamie felt her life style was ideal. She stayed home and managed the household while Mary Sue taught school. She had worked as the school nurse at Howard Payne College while Mary Sue finished college. Now Mary Sue had a teaching position in El Paso and they had bought a house there. Beary, at age 30, was lonely and needing someone to love and someone to love him. So their courtship began.

Beary married Mary Sue Clover, a teacher in El Paso, Texas, in 1968. He was an obliging husband to her wishes and fitted his work to her teaching positions wherever they were. After her death he continues to live in Van Horn, Texas, and work in the Brookshire Pecan Orchards. He has a satisfying life with his successful gardening abilities and carpentry skills.

**Beary worked on a stock farm** near Argyle, Texas, at one time. There was a small lake on the property that was stocked with fish. It was very important to the owner that these fish be well fed to grow to maximum size. Greg Blocker, who worked there, too, and Beary loaded the sacks of fish food in a small motor boat to feed the fish. When Greg started the motor the throttle was wide open. This abrupt start and high speed caused the boat to ship water and sink a distance out from shore. Greg swam to shore. When he looked back to where the boat had sunk, Beary was nowhere to be seen. Greg swam back, located Beary, and hauled him to shore. Beary, with his boots, jeans and big belt buckle, had sunk like a rock. His lungs and stomach were full of water. He was not breathing. Presumably he was drowned.

God's marvelous timing again. Greg had been a medic in the armed service. He was trained to know what to do and how to do it. He immediately started mouth-to-mouth resuscitation and revived Beary. When we heard of this incident, we were so grateful for Greg's knowledge and quick action. He had restored Beary to life to his wife, two little sons, and to his family. I have felt ever thankful for Greg.

**Beary and Mary Sue had made a disastrous move** to Oklahoma where they lost their shirts, so Mary Sue applied for teaching jobs in north Texas cities. One place they lived was Sanger, just north of Denton. There Beary worked for a contractor whose specialty was roofing, so Beary learned roofing to add to his knowledge of carpentry and painting. From Sanger, Mary Sue got a teaching position in Dell City, Texas, east of El Paso. Blackie and I took our four-horse trailer and moved them to Dell City. Mary taught second grade there and their son, Royce, was in her class. He was misbehaving in some way, so Mary sent him to the principal's office. The other students were very impressed that she would send her son to the principal's office for correction.

About 1980 Beary got a job on the Foster Ranch north of Kent, Texas, where he was happy to be on a ranch again. Mary Sue took a job teaching in Balmorhea and driving from Kent. This proved to be too much for her driving experience so they moved to Balmorhea in 1982. There Beary managed the irrigated farm for Dr. George Hoffman who practiced medicine in Fort Stockton.

Grandson Morris was now tall and filling out, so was much desired for Balmorhea's football team. High school football is rated as one of the most dangerous games for young boys whose bones are still growing. Early in a home game Morris was tackled and downed with the inane custom of the rest of the players jumping on a man already down. When they got off of Morris he could not get up. He was hurt, so was taken in the ambulance to the hospital in Odessa. His ankle was broken in three places. The doctors operated and put in pins, screws and plates to hold the bone fragments together until the fracture healed. All these years later it still hurts him, especially when the weather is about to change.

**As I was driving to El Paso the morning of May 24, 1986,** I noticed unusual cloud formations over the Diablo Mountains. There were numerous individual clouds shaped like Dairy Queen ice cream cones. I had never seen clouds like these. Something odd was happening in the atmosphere. Little did I realize how odd.

Chance and I shopped until late afternoon. When we returned to her home the television was on. On the screen I saw my grandson, Morris, as he said, "We got under a game table just as the roof blew off." What did this mean? I called but could not get through to Balmorhea where Morris lived. I called Blackie to see what was going on. He only knew Beary had called from Balmorhea and told him they were alright. The telephone service to that area was suddenly cut off. Blackie was more puzzled than I was. Then the news of a tornado that had demolished the small town of Saragosa was on the television. I learned that Balmorhea had not been hit by the tornado, but did not know how Morris had been involved.

I drove home early the next morning and Blackie and I went to Balmorhea where Beary's family lived. Morris' birthday is May 29. Beary, his wife Mary, and Morris had driven to Pecos the afternoon of the 24th to purchase groceries and supplies for a birthday and graduation party for Morris. For some reason Royce was not with them. He was probably in school when they left. As they drove home to Balmorhea, they saw this ominous cloud to the west of the road. As they neared Saragosa, the cloud developed into a tornado headed right across their route. Beary saw that they were going to be caught in the tornado.

There was a beer joint in a solid cinder block building just ahead. Beary parked there and they rushed into the bar. The wind was so strong that they barely got the door open and inside the building. The only place of safety seemed to be the heavy game tables. Just as the three of them squeezed under a table, the tornado ripped the roof off. They were covered with mud and wet with the rain, but they were alive.

Their new Ford Bronco II did not fare as well. The tornado lifted it, sucked all the glass out, along with the groceries and party supplies. Everything in the vehicle was gone—who knows where—never seen again. The Bronco was deposited approximately where it had been parked, upside down and crushed. The only article that survived unbroken was a glass jar of pineapple juice in a fender well.

The village of Saragosa was demolished. Almost every house in the small, mostly Mexican, town was completely ruined, or had vanished. There was a children's program that evening at the Catholic Church with families attending. This church was totally destroyed. Many people were hurt, and some were killed. It was a terrible tragedy. In the bar where Beary had taken refuge, there was a drunk Mexican man. He stood against the back wall of the building through the whole storm. When the dust and mud settled, he went out the door, weaving his way home as if nothing unusual had happened. Friends passing the bar recognized Beary's family and took them to their home where they could bathe, wash the mud out of their hair, and put on clean clothes. The population of Balmorhea was gathered in the high school gymnasium. That was where Morris was interviewed by the television reporter, which I had seen.

People came from many places to aid the victims of the tornado. There was much compassion and assistance for those unfortunate people in Saragosa. There was also much greed and graft that went on. A program was started for car dealers, individuals, and businesses to donate vehicles to those who had lost theirs. The ones who donated vehicles could claim a tax deduction, which was usually deserved. The county sheriff, who was not in the tornado and did not live at Saragosa, got a new-model pickup. Several other undeserving people benefitted by this program. There was much racial discrimination against the Anglos, and favoring the Mexicans. Toward the end of the program Beary got a rusted-out old-model clunker that he was never even able to keep running as a replacement for his new Ford Bronco that was completely demolished.

**In 1961 my father, Paul Evans, was in very poor health** and financial straits. He decided to sell his ranch and move to a house he had bought in Van Horn. His sister, Grace Cowden, would buy the ranch, contingent on Blackie agreeing to lease and manage it.

Blackie had leased Gracie's Wildcat pasture for several years. It joined Paul's country. Buddy Neal had sold all his sheep and his ranch was for sale. Blackie was not still in his employment but we could live there as long as necessary. Blackie and Grace's son, Bill Cowden, worked out a deal on the lease and cattle. Isn't it amazing how God's timing works?

The date for Paul and Wertie to move to Van Horn was set for January 9, 1962. Friends Robert and Edith Everett came to help. Blackie and I came with two pickups and trailers to help. The night of January 8 a norther blew in. It was bitterly cold. Mother had not been able to pack very many things, so it was not an organized move. The extremely cold wind made loading miserable. When the pickups and trailers were loaded, I was the last one to leave. Mother had many plants in the house. She grouped them in the kitchen around a gas heater burning low. As I made a last check through the house I noticed that butane heater burning. This was the house I was to move into in a few days. I just couldn't leave that open heater burning.

The night of January 9, 1962, registered the lowest temperatures ever recorded for that area. It was -16° at the Neal Ranch where we lived. The Mexican man who worked for Paul at EV Ranch reported -20°. One area in Wild Horse Valley recorded -26°. Coley and Barbara Means' lovely ranch home burned that night. The Van Horn Volunteer Firemen responded to help. The cold wind froze the water from their hoses before it reached the fire. It was a tragic night. All the water pipes and even the butane froze at EV Ranch. It was well that I had turned the gas off at that heater. We could not move until things thawed out and the burst water pipes were repaired. The 3-inch pipe from the water cistern on the mountain froze solid and split. Blackie and Bill Cowden worked long days getting the water system repaired.

This house I moved into was the house I had lived in until I married. It was an exceptional privilege to live again in that canyon I loved. The house had been built in 1919. I set in to make some improvements.

There had been a gas explosion in the kitchen in 1958. My three-year-old son and I were visiting with Mother when we smelled gas and started to look for the source, thinking John Paul, out of curiosity, might have turned the valve of a heater on. John Paul sensed something was wrong and was staying close by my side. I had just checked a heater near the water heater when I saw a flash of flame from the water heater about 1½ feet above the floor. There was a terrific sound of the explosion and fire shot out of the supply pipe to the cook stove. Mother ran outside, to turn the gas off, I supposed. I started throwing water on the wall behind the flame but decided I had better help get the gas turned off. That was all that was burning. I turned the gas off at the supply tank, which extinguished the flame before it caught the wall on fire. Mother didn't even know you could turn the gas off at the tank. She was getting the water hose from the garden, which would have had no effect on a gas fire. Again, the Lord's timing was perfect, that I should be in that place at that time. Now I am wiser and know if you smell gas, get out.

I was wearing a dress and nylon hose that day. The explosion melted my hose from the hem of my dress to the tops of my shoes—they were completely gone. It burned John Paul's eyebrows off, and some of his hair. Mother was in another room. We were so fortunate that no one was burned or hurt and the house did not burn. The cause of the explosion was that the supply pipe to the cook stove had gradually pulled out of the connection. Butane is heavy. When it escaped, it sank toward the floor and was ignited by the pilot of the water heater.

On the way home that evening a rear tire of my car blew out before I reached Van Horn. I wasn't sure I could change a tire. I never had. An old hippie-looking van slowed down. Did I really want him to stop? He stopped. He was a nice man with only one arm. He changed the flat tire to the spare while his buddy with two arms watched. I had no money with me. I told this man if he would follow me to Van Horn to a filling station where we had an account, I would have his gasoline tank filled. He came to thank me and said, "Lady, you don't know how you helped. We have jobs in El Paso and we didn't have enough money for gasoline to get there." *Good* always pays.

The ceilings in the EV Ranch house were tongue-and-groove lumber. The explosion had blown the boards apart, and 40 years of accumulated attic dust began to rain down. Mother had cleaned the house, but after we moved in the dust continued to fall through the cracks. I contracted dust pneumonia from that and bronchial pneumonia from working in the extreme cold. It took many visits to the doctor and seven months to clear the pneumonia.

This house was square with four main rooms—kitchen, dining-living room, and two bedrooms, and a pantry and 1½ baths. A screened porch extended across the front. The kitchen had five doors opening into it. The master bedroom had four doors. The other two rooms had each had three doors. This arrangement of doors helped before air conditioning to create air movement in the hot summers.

I replaced the outside door in the east wall of the kitchen with a window so I could have counter space along that wall. Dad had put that door in so Mother could have direct access to her iris and other flowers in the east yard, and not have to go around the front or back of the house, which would have taken a minute or two longer. I made an adequate pantry in the space where the door from the kitchen to an 8' x 10' pantry had been. There was a door from the pantry to the enclosed back porch. The former pantry became John Paul's bedroom. That was two less doors from the kitchen.

The small closet in the master bedroom was inadequate. I used the door opening to the back porch to make another closet. The door between the bedrooms was closed, as was the door from Judy's front bedroom to the front porch. This was a total of five doors made into usable space that contributed to better furniture arrangement. Plywood is the amateur carpenter's best friend. Paint is right there with it. We put fiberboard ceilings to cover the tongue-and-groove. This stopped the falling dust. The big air conditioner from the chimney at Neal Ranch was adapted to fit a window in this house. I was so happy to be living in this familiar canyon again.

Bill Cowden brought his bulldozer and bladed a road up the south mountain following the worn old cow trail. Cow trails may be crooked but they are always the best way to go. As soon as Bill finished blading this road Blackie got in our 1955 Bel Air Chevrolet and drove it up that mountain road where later only 4-wheel pickups could make it. We did not have a 4-wheel pickup at that time but soon bought one. That direct road was a great time and expense saver in caring for the ranch.

After finishing the south mountain road, Bill started a road up the north mountain following the old Indian trail. This was more challenging, as part of it was only a narrow trail along the steep mountainside just wide enough for one horse to walk. He had to cut into the mountainside to make a ledge wide enough for a vehicle to travel. It was an almost perpendicular drop from this ledge to the bottom of the mountain.

Chance and Bobby had befriended a couple from Norway. He was in the Norwegian Air Force on an exchange program with the USAF at Fort Bliss. He and his wife were very desirous to see a ranch so Chance and Bobby brought them to EV Ranch. We took them on a tour up the south mountain and around the head of the canyons. The two children wanted to ride in the back of the pickup, which had high pipe side rails. I insisted that this woman ride in the cab, but she would not be separated from her children. She was a most protective mother, talking to her children in Norwegian, which sounded almost like birds cooing—very melodic. We showed them cattle, mule deer, and rabbits. When we started down the north road she seemed scared, so I told her, "Just don't look down the mountain." Her reply: "Oh, but I must." I know she was relieved to reach the bottom of the canyon.

Before we moved to EV Ranch I had been teaching Judy, who was barely fourteen years old, to drive the car so she could drive to meet the school bus. The bus ran on Highway 80, now Interstate 10, fifteen miles from EVs and twenty more miles to Van Horn—a long trip to school. John Paul had started 1st grade in the fall of 1961. He was sick so much that he missed 30 school days that year. The whooping cough had left him susceptible to throat and bronchial infections. Judy was late and missed the school bus only one time in four years, when she had a flat tire.

Judy's account at 15 years old of her first flat tire: "Wanting to get all my ducks in a row, I had asked what to do if I had a flat tire. I was told John Paul knew what to do. One day I realized I had indeed had a flat tire and asked JP, "What do we do now?" He began to cry in panic and ran off into the bushes. "A fine help he is," I thought. "I was driving a Chevrolet station wagon. I opened the back to access the spare tire. Inside the cover to the spare tire were most of the instructions for using the jack—part of the instructions had peeled off with age. I could see that you needed to insert a gadget into a slot in the bumper when Dad drove up in his pickup. As he drove through the pasture he had seen my stalled car and came to my rescue."

*Blackie Woods*

# Ranching at EV's

Blackie and Bill Cowden had cattle and sheep on the Boggy and Boracho Peak pastures. Blackie and I had cattle and sheep on the Wildcat Pasture. Blackie also managed the ranch John Moore had leased from Mary Ann Carameros. This was a total of 77 sections of land that he took care of by himself until Beary came home from his tour of duty in the armed services. Beary lived with us and helped Blackie with the ranch work.

It was a continual battle with the coyotes. After adjoining ranchers sold their sheep and there was no combined effort in combating the coyotes, the coyotes moved in on us and were winning. We went to strictly cattle operation, which was less work.

About 1972 the rains had been plentiful and the grass was good. Blackie had contracted his calves in August. At delivery time in early November the calves weighed much more than expected. This buyer took the full number, though he suffered a lot of mental anguish and sweat when they were weighed out. They cost him much more than he had anticipated. Later I heard this buyer tell another man, "That EV Ranch is the best in the country. Those calves of Blackie Woods' were just like they had come off the wheat fields." Many years our calves were in such good shape they were shipped directly to the finishing pens in Kansas or Michigan without being kept on conditioning feed pens as was usual. One rancher-cattle buyer from the Marfa area bought our calves for several years. After the first year he would ask via telephone about the calves. Blackie's usual reply: "They are about like they were last year."

And this man would buy them with only that verbal agreement. He did not even come to look at them until he received them later that fall.

Early 1973 was a good rainfall spring and grew a lot of grass until the rains stopped in August before the grass cured out. The grass was rife but it was just dried up, not cured. It was no good. The spring months of 1974 brought thunderheads and lightning, but no rain. Everywhere the lightning struck, a grass fire was started. Even the sparks from passing trains' wheels started fires along the railroad that spread onto the ranch pastures.

In April Blackie and I were returning from a hunting trip in New Mexico with Graves Evans. We stopped in Van Horn to check on my parents, who told us we had a fire on EV Ranch. We hurried home. On the way we could see the fire was on Boggy pasture on top of the mountain from the house in the canyon. Our neighbors, the Turners, were there fighting the fire. They had seen it from their house. Neighbors came to help. Women made sandwiches to send to the fire fighters. This fire spread to a steep, rocky ridge where many *lecheguillas, sotols,* and Spanish daggers grew. These plants contain oils that burn like gasoline and shoot out flames for quite a distance. This spread the fire rapidly. The road that Bill had bulldozed up that steep mountain really paid off. We could drive from the ranch headquarters directly to the scene of the fire. I was the go-getter, taking water and sandwiches to the firefighters and messages to and from Van Horn. We had no telephone.

The Van Horn Volunteer Fire Department brought their big truck. It would have taken too long to go around through the Wildcat Pasture. That was no road for a big fire truck anyway. Blackie tied the fire truck to the back of his pickup with his nylon saddle rope. With the fire truck doing what it could, Blackie pulled that truck that outweighed his pickup many times up that steep rocky road.

You had to have 4-wheel drive to go up or down that road.  There was one stretch so steep that coming down in 4-wheel low with the brakes on, all four wheels slid.  It was an eerie feeling.  I drove up and down that road many times.  On one of my trips to Van Horn I received word that Blackie's 95-year-old father had died.  I was sorry to have to tell him this when he was fighting to save his pasture.  The next day the fire seemed to be contained, so Blackie and I went to Breckenridge for the funeral.  That day it rained 5 inches during the funeral service—a real cloudburst.  There could be no interment then because the grave had filled with water.

After we left the EV's the west wind blew and restarted the fire.  Friends and the Van Horn firemen fought the fire all the time we were gone.  They finally got it stopped after it had burned across that pasture and through the fence onto the adjoining ranch.    As we drove home that night we could see fires burning in several places in the mountains.  Bill Cowden's ranch had a fire in the high mountain country.

There are always hot spots where a sotol or a bush had burned, leaving embers in the ground.  In the hot afternoons these hot spots come to life, so you have to watch even though the fire looks to be out.  I was keeping our two little grandsons whose mother was a teacher in Van Horn.  Morris was nearly three years old; Royce not quite two.  I had to take them with me to watch for the fire.  A hot spot flared up about a quarter of a mile away and I went to help Blackie get it under control, leaving the boys in the pickup.  I could see them, but I did not realize children that young cannot see that far, so they could not see me.  With the fire under control, I returned to the pickup.  The two little boys had been crying.  Their little tear-stained faces were so pathetic.  Morris said, "I fought (thought) you was wost (lost)."  I felt so sorry for them.  A fire affects everyone.

The fire at EV's was out, but the fire at Bill Cowden's had burned down to very near his house. We went to help. The Van Horn firemen and friends kept the fire from the house, though it burned right up to the yard fence. Bill's stockpile of cedar posts, crossties, and highline poles all burned.

For weeks we watched for smoke and responded when we saw any. There was a big fire on the Pinon and Eagle Mountain Ranches. Blackie and I went to help friends there. My friend Linda and I made sandwiches and waited. A fire in the mountains is an awesome sight. Her son, about 4 years old, was very nervous and upset, so I stayed until rather late. I didn't want to leave Linda there alone. About 3 am her son seemed sleepy so I started home. As I approached Van Horn coming in on a road from the Rio Grande River I saw a car with lights on parked on a side street. As I passed by, this car followed me. I didn't like that. I didn't make a very full stop at a stop sign as I turned onto the access road toward home. The car followed. When he turned on his blinking lights to stop me, I knew it was alright. He was one of our county deputies. He was really surprised when he recognized me. I explained why I was traveling that time of night. He had been waiting there because that road from the Rio Grande was used by drug runners. I thanked him for being vigilant.

**Blackie worked his cattle almost alone.** He usually had extra help to round them up to deliver the calves to be sure they were all accounted for. After the calves were cut off and delivered, the cows needed to be back in their pastures. With between two and three hundred cows in one big corral Blackie would open a gate into each of two or three pastures. As soon as a cow saw the open gate giving her access to her usual grazing ground, out she would go. Blackie stood between the gates but rarely had to turn a cow back. These cows knew where they ranged and Blackie also knew where each cow belonged. I would stay at the rear of the herd to urge them toward the gates if necessary. There was never any agitating the

185

cattle.  The whole process went smoothly.

Supplemental feeding of range cattle in the spring months really pays off.  Not only will the cow stay strong and healthy, she will have a sturdy calf and promptly breed to have a calf the next year.  A dry cow is a liability that loses you money.  Cottonseed cake cubes are the usual supplement, easily fed out on the range.  Blackie bought it ten tons—a trailer load—at a time.  He would drive to an area of the pasture that would make a good feed ground, stop, and call and honk the pickup horn.  The cattle soon learn that the pickup is the feed wagon; they don't need much urging to come.  The cattle in that bunch are counted to determine how much cake to feed, allowing so many pounds for each animal.

I drove the pickup over the feed ground as Blackie stood at the back of the pickup, opened the sacks of cake, and poured a portion of the cubes onto individual clumps of grass.  That makes a very good place for the cattle to eat, but a very rough, uneven place to drive over.  I could not reach the accelerator and clutch or brake from Blackie's seat adjustment.  Moving that seat to fit my needs would have released an avalanche of equipment kept behind the seat—ropes, guns, jackets, chaps, tools, and other needed items.  When these shifted out of place, the seat would not re-adjust to Blackie's needs.  So to drive, I hung from my grasp on the steering wheel to keep in reach of the accelerator, clutch, and brake.  With a standard shift pickup it is hard to drive smoothly at that slow speed over those grass clumps.  I never mastered a standard shift and clutch well; I think automatic transmissions are the answer.  With the lurching of the pickup over the grass bumps, I think I only threw Blackie out of the back of the pickup one time.

When that bunch of cattle was fed, we drove to another area and repeated the process until all the cattle were fed.  At times, using the pickup was the best way to move cattle.  They will follow it several miles. They are accustomed to coming to the pickup for feed and they will follow it quite a distance until they are fed.

Blackie was a very close observer of his cattle—of everything, really. He had a special knack for seeing animal tracks, honed to an art by a life of being out where the animals were. One of his buddies said Blackie could see a lion track while driving down a road at 35 miles per hour. I know he could see a coyote track at that speed; I have witnessed that. He showed me lion tracks in the sandy washes that I would never have noticed. You had to really know what you were looking for. A fellow cowboy told of a time when they had gathered the cattle in a pasture and were debating whether they had missed any. Blackie said, "A calf and a black bull left this windmill going north." Curious, this friend asked, "How can you tell a black bull's track from a red bull's?" Blackie replied, "There is just a *little bit* of difference."

**My husband wanted to see a man who lived on the Rio Grande River.** We enjoyed going places together so I went with him. When we arrived where the man lived, there was only a church building. We could hear piano music at intervals so we assumed there was a church service of some kind. We could hear hymns being played, then intervals of quiet. Since we did not want to interrupt we drove down the river to a ranch house. These people spoke only Spanish but with my very limited Spanish using *"toca musica" and "iglesia."* I learned there was not a church service. The man played the piano for his own pleasure. We returned to the church and learned he lived there. He had the church part built so missionaries could hold services for crowds of people.

When Blackie's business with this man was concluded we started home. On this long stretch of lonely road our car started having trouble. The motor would choke down and almost die. Blackie was able to coax it to run a little further each time until we had to make a stop before turning onto the paved Highway 90. The motor died and there was no way to get it started. It was not getting any gasoline to the motor. We were twenty miles from Van Horn. A friend's ranch headquarters was three miles the other direction. There was a telephone there so we started walking in that direction. I had carried my purse because I had phone numbers in it. We had not walked far when a couple in a small car headed toward Van Horn passed us. There was almost no traffic on that highway at that time.

They stopped and started backing up toward us. The woman stuck her head out the window and called, "We don't pick up hitchhikers but when we saw that grey hair and that purse, we thought it was alright." Their car was loaded to capacity but they made room for us to squeeze in. They were from Michigan, and West Texas was very novel to them. They asked about the mountain we were passing. When I told them it belonged to my cousin, they were impressed that one person could own a whole mountain.

**The best thing our government ever did for ranchers was the screwworm eradication program**. The screwworm flies lay their live maggots in any fresh wound. The navel of a newborn calf made a prime target. To combat this problem, the cowboys had to ride all day every day during the warm months to check for "wormies." When they found one, they had to rope and "doctor" that animal, for the maggots continue to eat the live flesh until they kill the animal. If the victim was a calf, the cowboy would also have to fight the cow off, as well as try to help her calf. Cows are very protective mothers. Our scientists with the Agriculture Department found a way to sterilize male flies so they could not breed. With this program, when a cowboy found a "wormie" he collected specimens in the furnished vial and mailed it to the state laboratory. Some of these men would then bring and release sterile male screwworm flies in the area. It was very effective. They also cooperated in a program with Mexico. That was good—those flies don't know where the border is. After the program was pretty effective, Blackie found a case of worms and made a special trip to town to mail in this specimen. The laboratory wrote him back that the specimen was not screwworms. He was furious. He wrote back that he had doctored screwworm cases for forty years and knew what he saw. They promptly came with the sterile flies. Eradicating screwworms saved ranchers much money, time, and lots of hard, steady riding. They could now enjoy summer.

# Running W Ranch

**In 1977 we had to drive from EV Ranch in Jeff Davis County** through Culberson County and Van Horn to Valentine, a distance of 85 miles, to vote in our county precinct. Because of the distance, I asked Blackie if we should ask the Turners, our neighbors, to accompany us. They voted in Valentine, too. He replied, "No, let's just go by ourselves." I should have guessed he had something up his sleeve. He was always surprising me. On the way home after voting, as we neared Van Horn, he turned off the highway onto a county road that led to a little ranch owned by a dentist. This ranch had been for sale for several years. The pasture had been root-plowed and cleared of brush. Looking from the long slope of Highway 80 west of Van Horn, it looked like a field, covered with the grass that had been planted after the root plowing.

The dentist had moved his practice to Pecos. The house was vacant. The gate at the county road was locked. As we walked the ¼ mile up the lane to the house, I felt as if I were coming home. The house was large—a roofed porch extended across the front to the double carport. My father had been the dowser for the water well, so we knew there was a strong source of water. We called the dentist and arranged a time to meet and look at the house. On that evening I again experienced that feeling of coming home. God was answering.

The house consisted of living room, kitchen, and dining room in the center section of the house. Three bedrooms and two baths were on the west side of that. The dining room was open to a large den with a fireplace. The master bedroom and bath opened into the den. The laundry was accessible from the kitchen, with a room beyond it that could be used for an office. It became my sewing room. There were

190

walk-in closets in two bedrooms, average closets in the other two. This seemed like Utopia to me.

Blackie made an offer, which was accepted. We bought the ranch that night on handshakes with the dentist and his wife. The next week we signed the papers in a lawyer's office and paid for it with a CD and a check.

Blackie had been working much harder than he should have to take care of 35 sections, about 23,000 acres of land. The ranch was not large enough to hire a man to help, even if one could have been found. It was too much for Blackie to do alone. I was concerned for his health. Some other factors signaled it was time for a changed. I just said, "Now, Lord, it looks like it is time for a change. I am trusting you to lead us to a place." This was not quite three months before we looked at this little ranch and bought it. It was less than one section of land but adequate for Blackie's mules and dogs, and to run some cattle. Blackie bought it as a headquarters for the lion hunting he had for many years wanted to do more of than his work responsibilities had allowed. Now he could hunt full time—at least as often as his dogs were able.

For me, it was my dream house. After living and making the best I could of whatever house went with the lease or job, after living in a cramped trailer house, a log house, a makeshift garage, a government screened hut, and a tent, this house was more than I had ever dreamed of. God had answered in His abundant way.

Blackie had caught many goat-killing lions for Jim Espy on his Fort Davis ranches. When Jim learned we were going to move, in gratitude he offered to help us. On moving day Jim brought two pickups, a flatbed and a big gooseneck trailer, and two men to help. Besides the usual furniture, we had two refrigerators and two freezers. Also, Blackie had discovered that old chest-type freezers turned on their sides made good dog houses.  They were insulated and easy to clean.  He had several of these to move.

I knew we would need to have a meal at noon.  Moving would take all day.  What could I feed five people when my cook stove had to be disconnected and loaded among the first things?  I decided I could cook a turkey in my Crockpot.  I don't recall what else I had.  The turkey was a good solution.  It cooked while I slept that last night.  Jim accused me of spoiling his men—they were used to just pinto beans.

After the move Jim told someone that before he offered to help anyone else move, he would ask them first how many ice boxes they had.

**Blackie bought a Dodge pickup** from a dealer in Van Horn, paid for it, and started home to EV Ranch.  Before he reached home he decided he did not like this pickup.  It was paid for, so it was now his.  He built a rack, a shelf over the bed of the pickup so his dogs could have some shade and some protection below, and a load of something could be carried on the shelf.

We had gone to El Paso where Blackie had purchased a ton of dog food which was loaded on this shelf.  My smaller parcels were in the front on the floor.  As we left Chance's house in east El Paso, I was trying to make a place among the packages for my feet.  I had not fastened the seat belt because I needed to bend over to the floor.  Not three blocks from Chance's house a Mexican woman stopped in front of us without signaling.  There was an oncoming car in the left lane and another car in the lane on the right.  There was nothing for Blackie to do but hit the brakes.  The impact threw me so that my head hit the upper corner of the windshield, which opened enough to pull some of my hair out and leave it in the cracked place.  The woman's car trunk was slightly damaged.  She pulled her turn signal on after we hit her. She was not hurt but of course, she sued. We had insurance. I don't remember that she did.

When the dealer repaired our pickup, he told us that ton of dog food almost collapsed the cab of the pickup as it was thrown forward. My neck hurt so the next day, I went to my chiropractor in Marfa. I told him that I hit my head on the windshield, but my neck was what hurt. The x-rays showed there was a cracked neck vertebra. I wore a neck brace for a long time. We attended a friend's Annual Bull Sale, a very gala affair, in Marfa the next day. Since I had to wear the neck brace I pinned a decorative piece of jewelry to the front of the brace. This friend thought that was remarkable.

**There was a telephone in the house we had bought**. After being without the convenience of a telephone for fifteen years—we had to drive 35 miles to Van Horn to make a telephone call—I was welcoming this telephone. The telephone man told me, "Mrs. W is not going to like this." I knew this woman, I thought. She was very friendly and nice when I saw her in Van Horn. I assured him that I knew Mrs. W and that it would be all right to activate the phone. Was I ever mistaken! Each time I made a call, someone would break in with, "Who is this? Who are you?" I learned that this telephone line was privately owned and that this woman wanted no one else using it. Period. We were telephone-less again. Back to those stinking phone booths again.

Blackie was doing a lot of hunting lions for Jim Espy in the Fort Davis area 85 miles away. His son, Jim II, would have to drive that distance to tell Blackie when they had found fresh lion sign. Jim II and Blackie decided to build a telephone line the 1 ½ miles from the main line to our house. Blackie arranged for the telephone company to connect us when it was finished.

Our neighbor who was the district highway superintendent and lived between us and the main line would furnish the tall poles. He wanted a telephone too. Blackie supplied the wire and insulators. A young man who hunted with Blackie and Jim worked for a telephone company in Alpine. He agreed to engineer the project. Blackie borrowed a tractor with a posthole digger and dug the holes. Jim brought a Mexican man and Bill, the engineer. The four men built that line in two days. The telephone representative made the connection and, Oh, Joy, we had a telephone! No more having to use those foul phone booths. Blackie was to maintain the line until it was inspected and approved by the telephone company a few years later. A telephone official told me at that time that it was the best aboveground line in the system.

Before the telephone company assumed its maintenance, during a thunderstorm lightning struck and burned the wire in two. To keep the line from getting slack before he could fix it right, Blackie joined the ends of the wire with baling wire and a boomer. One afternoon as I returned from Van Horn, Blackie told me a man had called but that he couldn't understand him very well. The man said he could call back. When he called, I discovered he was in Saudi Arabia. He wanted to arrange a mountain lion hunt with Blackie. This man called again the next day and wrote a letter or two, but he never managed to set up a lion hunt. How Blackie's fame as a lion hunter reached Saudi Arabia, I don't know, but this man had Blackie's name and telephone number. When we talked I could hear him as plainly as if he were in Van Horn, three airline miles away, through that baling wire splice. Never underestimate the dependability and versatility of baling wire and a boomer.

**Our policy was to live within our income** and not make any major purchase until we could pay for it. We always had plenty to wear and to eat, and a good car to drive. I tried to shop for groceries sensibly; we did not eat junk food. We ate our own beef—really veal. We killed calves weighing 400 or 500 pounds. Once I remember not having a calf ready to butcher and Blackie bought one from a neighbor. This calf had only fed on grass and the mother's milk, but it was the only meat I ever saw that was really too fat to be good. I would have to trim and discard great layers of suet.

After we moved to our newly-acquired little ranch, a man in Van Horn made several allusions as to how rich we were. He tried to sell me several rent houses he had, which were the last things I would want. This puzzled me as to why he thought we were rich. As I knew him better I learned he frequented the County Clerk's office where he could access records of land transactions on file there. Noting that the deed to our land showed "no lien" he assumed we must be rich not to have to borrow money to buy land.

Our back yard was enclosed by a cinder block fence four feet high with only two snugly-fitted gates. It was supposed to be snake-proof except for these adders. I had noticed some round holes about 1 ½ inches in diameter that went straight down. They did not look like frog holes; they were holes these adders had dug. The cinder block fence didn't stop them—they just dug under it. I saw one digging its hole once. The snake was about half its length into its hole so I didn't get to see how it started. As it dug, the ground around its body just jiggled slightly, with some very fine dirt for ¼ inch around its body. I don't know what happened to the dirt its body displaced—it was not brought to the surface. The snake's body was held erect, perpendicular to the ground for about seven inches; the remainder of its body looped over toward the ground. The snake was in my garden, so I killed it, but later wished I had watched it almost finish its hole first, before I killed it. So don't let anyone tell you that snakes can't dig holes. Some of them can.

**My knowledge of honey bees was limited** to a memory before I was six years old of my grandfather, George Wesley Evans, tending his bee hives in his yard. He would wear long sleeves as usual and gloves and a veil over his western hat that hung from the brim to his shoulders. He carried a container to put the honeycomb in. The bees did not seem to be upset, for he had first used a bellows to blow smoke into the hive. I remember how good that sweet honey was on hot buttered biscuits. Then I would chew the wax comb like chewing gum.

At our Running W ranch I had noticed occasional bees in my garden gathering pollen, but I didn't know where they came from. One day as I went out the back door the bees were buzzing around. When I looked up to the porch ceiling there was a swarm of bees hanging from it. Hundreds of bees were clustered in a cone-shaped mass about ten inches long, constantly moving but staying the same shape. I didn't feel that they could be allowed to stay where they were in front of our back door. I called the exterminator business in Pecos and told her I had a problem. But when I said "bees" she answered, "Oh, we don't do bees. It is against the law to exterminate bees." What was I to do? In asking people in Van Horn I was told of a young man who had bees. When I called him, he was glad for the chance to get a new swarm of bees. He came in his protective coveralls and brought a five gallon can which he lifted up to cover the bees and scraped them from the ceiling into the can and quickly put the lid on. As he waited he explained that he needed to be sure he got the queen bee. If he did not have her no bees would go to the can. Thankfully he had the queen bee.

A few years later when I went to my garden a bee stung me on my cheek. A few days later when I came from my sewing room into the den I heard a loud buzzing. The windows were swarming with bees. I quickly sprayed them with Raid; but, where had they come from into the house? Upon watching the bees outside, they seemed to all fly to the chimney of our fireplace in the den. Closer inspection showed they were using one hole, about as big around as a pencil, in the screen of a ventilator to go under the house. But how were they coming into the house? Evidently they were making their hive on the rock foundation of the fireplace. There was no way anyone could get to them to capture them this time. How could we get rid of them? And how were they coming into the den? I discovered there was one place big enough for a bee where the rock fireplace was so irregular the carpet didn't fit smoothly against it. I stopped it up. One day in a store I saw the sprays that you set to spray and leave them in the room. I bought two and figured Blackie could decide how to use them against the bees. He tied one spray bomb onto a very long piece of plastic pipe, put it against the bees' hole, and set it off. It worked. From in the den you could hear a very loud buzzing while the spray bomb was working, then no buzzing bees. I stopped up their hole in the screen ventilator.

Bees are very determined and persistent when they find a place they like. We continued to find that they intended to make their hive between the soffit and the roof of our house. Beary used expanding foam that hardens to close up every crack that a bee could go through, until they finally gave up or cold weather began.

**At EV Ranch I had a garden with good soil and an abundant water supply**. Blackie helped me haul trailer loads of dead, dried sotol which I spread on and tilled into my garden space. As I irrigated it, plants grew amazingly. The squash vines had strong erect stalks and large leaves that grew taller than my waist. I entered four little squashes about seven inches long in the vegetable division of our Culberson County Fair, and the man who judged that division said he would have given them Best of Show if they had not been squashes. They were the most nearly-perfect specimens he had ever seen. But the four "big-as-a-grapefruit" rosy red pomegranates I had entered did win Best of Show that year.

At our Running W Ranch I grew excellent tomatoes. They grew so tall that I had to contain the plants in wire cages nearly as tall as I was.  I canned about one hundred pint jars of tomatoes every summer, enough to supply us and share with our children.  I also made tomato preserves with both the ripe and green tomatoes.  With the addition of lemon slices and sugar they made delicious preserves.  I really liked the preserves made with the green tomatoes—those just turning white—the best for their tangy flavor.  I had a rosemary bush that grew quite large.  I especially enjoyed it because of the little blue flowers that bloomed in the wintertime when nothing else did.

There was a pecan tree with a trunk about as big as Blackie's arm and as tall as he was when we bought our home.  With his care and extra water, it grew rapidly.  In a few years it became taller than our house, or even the electric highline poles.  The trunk became almost as big around as his body.  But the most wonderful thing was the pecans it bore so prolifically with their delicious flavor rivaling those from Comanche, Texas.  Blackie had wished for a pine tree, so I bought a Mondale Pine and brought it home from the nursery in the car.  It was about as tall as I was.  Blackie dug a very large hole and planted this little tree in three or four bags of peat moss.  It grew rapidly and was soon too large for the strings of Christmas lights I had decorated it with at first at Christmas.

Our ranch seemed to be a haven for many species of birds, perhaps because of the tall pine and pecan trees.  There were Mockingbirds with their cheerful songs even on moonlight nights, when they would sing all night, and little brown speckled Wrens with their lovely melodic songs during mating season in the spring, and occasional Blue Jays.  The Blue Grosbeaks and Brown Towhees nestled there as well as Brown Thrashers and the lovely Scarlet Tanager with the male a beautiful soft rosy red and his female counterpart of all yellow.  There were the comical Chaparrals or Roadrunners, Blue Quail, and some Gambrel Quail with their lovely color markings and a plume atop their heads.  I fear these quail have not survived the years of drought we are in.

We had Western Orioles with their bright colors, who built their hanging nests—a marvel of engineering, as all birds' nests are. One year a Blue Grosbeak built her nest in a tomato plant. These birds build a small round nest lined smoothly with horse hair. I did not have a camera then, so I was not able to get a picture of it. She did not choose one of the tallest plants—her nest was only about three and a half feet above the ground. One winter we had a flock of White Egrets stay with us, solemnly perched on the fence posts so far from any body of water. I don't know what or when they ate, for they so rarely left their perch on one leg on the fence posts. The only birds I know of which saved for future meals was the Shrike. These birds would catch grasshoppers and other insects when they were plentiful and impale them on thorns of bushes or the barbs of the barb wire fence so the Shrike could eat them later.

**A neighbor introduced me to a skin care product** that was far better than anything I had ever found. It contained no petroleum products such as mineral oil, petrolatum or Vaseline. All the ingredients are compatible with the human skin. She persuaded me to sell this product. It was to be a party plan for selling to people I knew. She made it sound easy. I bought the demonstration kit and a large order of product. There was a manual, and that was really all the training I received.

I was scared stiff at the thought of selling—of asking people to buy. What had I gotten myself into? But I believed in this skin care. I knew it was better than anything else on the market. Also, I had invested money in this and I was determined to make it pay. Selling did not come easy for me. I dreaded approaching women with the idea of selling them this skin care, but that was the only way to get it sold. It helped to know that they used something they bought, and mine was a better product. I persevered and got the skin care sold. I made some money and received a liberal education in people's personalities.

One year at the annual convention in Dallas I was recognized as fourth in sales in the company and won a fur vest. Blackie supported me in this endeavor and was proud of my success. He flew to Dallas for the awards banquet. I was accused of selling to the jackrabbits, for they knew I lived in a sparsely populated area of only a few small towns. There were five small towns in five different counties. Selling in these small towns within a radius of 100 miles entailed a lot of driving and long distance telephone calls. It was discouraging work but I stuck with it. I recruited a unit of enough women to sell under me to be made Marketing Director. It is hard to keep people motivated and working in sales.

This skin care was developed by a dermatologist and research scientist in his laboratory with test on his wife and friends. He was interested in formulating a product that benefitted the human skin instead of coating it with some petroleum product. Petroleum products are not good for the human skin. The skin care he formulated kept the skin clean, soft and moisturized. His wife suggested he call this skin care "Pene-gen" as it penetrated the skin and generated a healthy condition—a good product but an awkward name.

Chance had decided to sell this skin care in El Paso in addition to her job as secretary of a large church. She was a wonderful help and inspiration to me to overcome my inferiority complex and persist in learning to sell. We attended many seminars on selling techniques and motivation. Her husband's employment with American Airlines was a great aid in being able to fly to the annual conferences in Dallas. She could fly on a pass and I got a good discount on a ticket. One year instead of flying I accompanied several women driving to Anaheim, California, to a conference. One year the annual conference was held in Midland, Texas, in January. When I left Van Horn to attend, I encountered ice on the road at Kent, 40 miles east of Van Horn. As I slowly continued, thinking road conditions would get better, they only continued to worsen. By the time I drove to Toyah, 30 miles farther east, the bushes and the road were covered in ice. I decided I would have to turn back. Then I noticed the trucks and a few cars coming through from the east. If they could, I could. It was hairy driving the 150 miles to Midland, but by being very careful, I made it. I was driving a Chrysler New Yorker, which held the road really well. When I walked into the conference room, I received an ovation. Midland was iced in.

One year the conference was held on a cruise ship from Miami to Nassau in the Bahamas. That was a fun trip, flying from El Paso to Miami and enjoying the cruise to Nassau. I was entranced by the deep blue color of the ocean after we got away from shore. The little whitecaps contrasted with the deep blue and the occasional red seaweed.

In sales you meet all types of people. A fairly attractive woman I met when I had a booth at the County Fair in Pecos was interested in my product and scheduled a class. When I arrived that afternoon, some of her guests had obviously come early and had been partaking freely of her liquid refreshments. I conducted the class as quickly as possible. I sold some skin care and got out of there. This woman continued to purchase skin care products from me. One day when I went to her house, it looked to be vacant. Upon inquiry I learned the police had staged a raid on her house and she didn't live there anymore.

I found the Mexican women of all ages were more interested in and responsive to enhancing their looks than the average Anglo housewife. Women who worked at jobs out of the home were good customers; those who worked only in their homes usually were not.

**An Emergency Care Course** was offered to interest and start training for EMTs for our new hospital. I thought that since we lived

35 miles from the hospital I should take advantage of this training experience and learn what to do in an emergency.  Ranch life has its dangers and the distance from the hospital was a factor.  I drove to Van Horn for the required number of training sessions.  We learned first aid procedures, how to bandage various injuries, and to do artificial respiration on a dummy.  I was never called upon to use this particular knowledge, but it gave me assurance that I could cope if the occasion arose.   I learned great respect for emergency care workers.

Blackie was trying to load an Angus bull into a trailer.  The bull was not cooperating.  He had no intention of going into that trailer. Blackie was down in the pen with this bull trying to force him into the trailer.  This bull weighed about 700 pounds, four times as much as Blackie.  The bull turned, and with his head against Blackie's body, pushed him toward the tall pole-and-pipe fence.  To keep his head from hitting the pipe rail, Blackie put out his left hand.  When his hand reached the fence, Blackie heard and felt the bones in his arm break above the wrist.   He clasped his right hand around the break and came to the house for me to drive him to the hospital.  By holding his hand around the break, the bones did not become displaced.  The doctor only needed to put a cast on the arm.  The x-ray technician was new at the job.  He made the x-rays and as he developed them, he stuck his head out the door and said, "It's broke," something we already knew.

# More Family Stories

**My husband was to have some minor surgery** so we prepared to go to the hospital in Andrews, Texas. Blackie, as a patient, would not need many clothes. His small bag was quickly packed. He put it in the back seat of the car. He was always waiting for me to finish packing a suitcase so he could load it. I finished my packing and went to do something else. I was ready at last. We drove to Andrews.

After he checked in at the hospital, we went to get something to eat and then bring my suitcase from the car. This hospital provided a bed for someone with the patient to stay in the same room. Blackie opened the car trunk and we looked in disbelief at the completely empty trunk. There was no suitcase. There was nothing at all in that trunk. What was I to do?

My daughter, Judy, had recently moved to Lubbock and was coming the next day to be with me during Blackie's surgery. I had not yet memorized her new telephone number and did not have it with me. I called Chance, whose phone number I knew, and asked her to contact Judy so that she could bring me some items. The nurse brought a pair of men's large pajamas for me to sleep in that night.

After the surgery was done and Blackie was sleeping, Judy and I went shopping for something for me to wear. At that time there was not much choice of petite size clothing in Andrews. I managed to find pajamas and a couple of changes of clothes. You can be sure that from that time on I carefully checked to see that my suitcase went with me on any trip.

**One cold Saturday night Blackie and I arrived at Tim and Jody's home at Roanoke** to find that no one was home. This was long before cell phones. We thought that they would be home soon so we decided to wait. Waiting soon became very cold even with running the car motor at intervals to give a little heat. After about eleven p.m. we decided to drive to Denton and stay in a motel. When we got to Denton it was wild—it was Homecoming at North Texas, I think. Every motel in Denton was full—no vacancy. Young couples were walking around looking for friends' cars they might recognize. So staying in Denton was out. We decided to drive the 50 miles to Decatur and find a motel there. It was the same situation in Decatur. No vacancy in the only three motels there. Blackie drove out a highway north from Decatur and there was a motel. When he went into the office to register and pay, no one was there. He drove through the parking lot looking for someone to pay. There were vehicles parked at every room except one. Maybe this was an office. I went to the door, which was slightly ajar so I could see light from it, but no one answered my knock or call; so I went in. All the lights were on and the room was warm. I checked the sheets on the beds. They were clean; clean towels in the bath. I went back to the car and told Blackie, "I am going in here and go to bed. I am so tired, and my restless legs are giving me fits from sitting in the car so long. I may die if I don't lie down soon." We went in, locked the door, and had a good night's (what was left of it) sleep. We were aware of vehicles starting and driving by early that morning, but we were enjoying our rest. After a good shower, Blackie went to find someone to pay for the room. There was no one in the office or anywhere in the motel complex; it was completely deserted.

**Tim's son Bob decided when he was about fourteen years** old that he would trap some of the numerous coyotes in the area where they lived near Chico, Texas. When they visited us at Van Horn, Blackie gave Bob four or five coyote traps and some snares and showed him how to set them to catch the coyotes. When Bob returned to Chico he set the traps as Blackie had shown him. A day or two later Bob and little brother, Jett, set out in the Gremlin hatchback car the boys had learned to drive. In one of his traps he had a coyote caught. They had a .22 rifle, so Bob shot the coyote and threw him in the hatchback. The other traps had not caught anything so Bob and Jett started home with their prize, the dead coyote. On the way home they heard something behind them. Looking back they saw this "dead" coyote standing up in the hatchback. Immediately the boys abandoned the Gremlin as if jet-propelled. They were driving uphill so the car didn't go far without a driver until it stopped. Hours later they decided the coyote had probably left the hatchback so they fearfully and cautiously approached the hatchback. The coyote was lying in the back, dead for sure this time.

Several years later Jett and a friend decided that a discarded small camper trailer out in the pasture would make a good hideout for them. They packed up blankets and food—plenty of salsa and chips—and prepared to spend the night in this camper trailer. The camper had several windows broken out, including a small window in the door which left an open space. The weather was mild, so that didn't matter. During this moonlit night they heard something that waked them. To their horror, a coyote had stuck his head through this opening in the door. With the coyote at the only exit, the boys cowered in their bunks in terror. Finally they decided the coyote was gone, so they took their blankets and retreated to the safety of the house, leaving the camper trailer to the coyotes. They had enough of camping out.

**Sometime in the 1950's when we were at the Neal Ranch**, now Lado, a neighbor east of Van Horn who had a ranch in the foothills of the Delaware Mountains had some steers they could not pen. They had tried many times, for several years. Working steers is very different from working cows and calves. These steers were more like wild animals. They spooked at the corral gate and turned en masse back toward the hills and canyons which were their stomping grounds. They just got away. Buddy Neal, a former World Champion Steer Roper, volunteered to pen those steers. On the appointed day Buddy, Burton Meeker and Blackie Woods trailered their horses to help.

This morning the cowboys were just getting the rounded-up steers into a herd. One big old steer, obviously the ring-leader, quit the bunch and started in a high run for the canyons. But he had not met Blackie Woods before. When the steer started to run off, Blackie, riding a real good short coupled horse named Brady, took after him. The old steer was running for all he was worth—his tail sticking straight up in the air. When Blackie overtook the steer, he grabbed said steer's tail, dallied it around his saddle horn and rode on by. When the fairgrounded steer got his breath back, he got up off the ground, shook his head and trotted back to the herd. He gave no more trouble and the steers were penned without further incident.

—*Blackie Woods as told to Lottie Woods*

**I had ever prayed that my children would find mates to complete their lives**. Now that Tim was single again, I especially prayed that he would meet a good woman. This prayer was answered when he met Betty Gilstrap, a nurse working in the pharmacy at Wal-Mart in Decatur, Texas. He called me to invite us to their wedding. We learned that Betty had four children—three daughters and a son. With Tim's three sons and a daughter, that made a combined family of eight children. But only two, her daughter in high school and Tim's ten-year-old son, lived with them. Betty keeps relationships congenial by all eight meeting for holiday meals in their home, and with frequent communications. She is truly the helpmeet for Tim that I had prayed for.

*Our children: Chance, JP, Tim, Beary, Judy*

**After Judy and James' marriage ended**, Judy continued to work for Leatherwood Insurance in Dublin and further her education and knowledge of the insurance business by attending seminars and insurance schools. At one of these, the man conducting the school, upon seeing her thought, "She is the most beautiful woman I have ever seen. I am going to marry her." Thus began his courtship of her. Monte Lee Roach was in the insurance business and was talented and successful in recruiting and training people as insurance agents. He rewarded his high achievers with paid vacation trips to various places—Acapulco and Cancun, Mexico, Banff and Whistler, Canada, and cruises to the Caribbean and Alaska. Judy helped arrange and went on these trips. Monte is a very thoughtful and caring person. He and Judy were married June 30, 1995.

**As with my other children, I had prayed much for John Paul** to find the helpmeet he needed. This was accomplished through this computerized age. While playing games on the computer with a partner, he found they had much in common. But she was in Idaho and he was in Oregon. They arranged to meet and found they had much more in common than just computer games. Her job after she moved to Eugene, Oregon, was testing computer games before they were marketed to be sure they were compatible with all brands of computers. One of her hobbies was growing gardenias. JP Woods and Susan Garner were married in his cabin at Bloys Campmeeting August 4, 1999. Sue has helped JP to become the man of his potential as a research chemist.

**Needle crafts and handwork** have always fascinated me. I learned to embroider when I was quite young, but use for embroidered items was limited to tea towels and luncheon cloths. I learned to crochet when I was teenaged, but use for crocheted things seemed to be afghans or throws. I wanted to knit because the finished product was soft and supple. Sweaters were knitted. My mother and sister could knit and tried to show me how. It seemed to me that there was much shoulder motion in making the stitches the way they did it. I was having a lot of pain from bursitis in my right shoulder, so I didn't think I could bear the strain. I put the idea of knitting on hold.

About 1960-something Mother's sister-in-law from California came to visit. She was left-handed. When I saw her knitting by holding the yarn through the fingers of her left hand like I did to crochet I thought, "I can do that to knit." My desire to knit was rekindled, so I shopped for a book of knitting patterns and was fortunately able to find one with good illustrations, one of a very attractive sweater with a design like a chain in the center front and back and the length of each sleeve. I read the directions, which seemed simple enough— just knit so many stitches and purl so many stitches. The only trouble was I didn't know which was a purl stitch or a knit stitch. No problem; I would get Mother to show me.

I purchased the yarn and the size knitting needles the pattern specified. I was ready to knit if only I knew how. I knew I needed to have some loops on one needle to start, but how to get them there? Just wrapping the yarn around the needle didn't work. Then I remembered when my sister was having a problem doing was called casting on stitches. My brother took one look at the illustration and began to put half-hitches on the needle. That was the solution! I put the number of half-hitches the instructions said to have on one needle. Now what to do?

I drove to Mother's home in Van Horn for help. She was at a complete loss to show me how to make the stitches the way I held the yarn. She did give me the key to knitting when she said, "You hold the yarn in front of the work to purl and at the back of the work to knit. Try knitting a dish cloth first." With these instructions I went home to knit. I didn't want to knit a dish cloth—I wanted to knit a sweater. I had heard it said, "Fools rush in where angels fear to tread." That described me.

The instructions read, "To begin, knit the first stitch, purl the next stitch. Continue in this manner to the end of the row. Turn the work and continue purling each purl stitch and knitting each knit stitch." As I followed these instructions I could see that an area of ribbing was developing—a nice border for the bottom edge of the sweater. I continued to do as the instructions specified with only a few glitches which I was able to correct. To make sure the sleeves became the same length I used two skeins of yarn simultaneously on one set of needles. That turned out so satisfactorily that I continued this method on each of the many sweaters I knitted. I now had knitted a front, back and two sleeves. I sewed them together and gave the finished sweater to my teenaged daughter, Judy. She wore it to school and later when she went to Tarleton University. As I obtained books about knitting and learned more about it, I found that the chain-looking part was a form of cable stitch, which was considered a challenge for experienced knitters. Oh, well…

**Visitors from Mexico**  I was doing laundry when we lived at EV's. My washer and dryer were installed on the plank floor where they made a lot of vibration noise that masked any other sound. I looked up to see five Mexican men in my kitchen headed toward the refrigerator. I was not afraid—I was startled, but mainly furious because they had come into my house with me there. I feel sure they had made that peculiar, distinctly different call they make to announce their presence. It is like no other sound I have ever heard. I had not heard it because of the washer noise. They must have decided no one was there and they were hungry.

The man in the lead motioned they wanted food. I only wanted them out of my house. I was so upset that I couldn't think of what little Spanish I knew. They weren't leaving quickly enough, so I picked up the broom and brandished it in their direction. They got the message and quickly reversed their path back out the front of the house, but looking back over their shoulders at me holding the broom. I followed to the front yard gate. They were only eager to get into the creek where the brush would hide them. Blackie later saw their tracks going on up the canyon.

We often missed food from our refrigerator after we had been away from home. They always took the margarine. I don't know if they ate it or rubbed it on their sore feet. My sister, Frances, and her husband, Charles, decided to build an adobe house on the land he had inherited. A crew of Mexican men was making the adobes on the site. When they sent to town for groceries, they always requested butter—*manteca*. Charles was furnishing their groceries. To save money, he bought margarine. They were very upset about the margarine. It would not take the place of butter to use on their hands to keep the adobe dirt from chapping them. Since butter is an animal fat, it is compatible with human skin.

One night about 9 pm I heard a knock at the back door. I had not heard a car drive up. Anyone arriving in a car would have come to the front door. Blackie had already gone to bed. I turned on the porch light and saw a young Mexican man. Of course, he wanted "*un lunche.*" I fixed him some food and visited with him while he ate. He had a stick about 15 inches long in his hand and noticed me looking at it. "Oh, *el palo.*" He threw it down and explained it was for killing "*biverras.*" I thought that was not much of a weapon for killing rattlesnakes, but that is what the Mexicans use. I gave him a Bible tract in Spanish. He said he could not read, but he had a friend who could. He carefully put it in an inside pocket of his coat as if it was a great treasure. He asked if he could sleep in our barn, and Blackie saw where he had. He was gone when we arose the next morning.

When we were living on our ranch near Van Horn, Blackie came into the house and asked if I had anything to feed some wets. There were three walking on the road, but one looked like a child. It took them a long time to reach our house—they walked unusually slowly. There was a young man, his wife, and their 3-year-old son. I fixed something for them to eat. The young man asked if his wife and baby could take a bath. This was a most unusual request, but I showed them to a front bathroom and offered towels. No, he said, they had "*towelas.*" The woman bathed herself and her son. Then the husband bathed. They came out dressed in clean clothes.

Then he wanted to use our telephone. He assured us that it would not cost us anything. He called relatives who were to come from Odessa and pick them up. They had not come by late bedtime, so I showed them to a guest room. When he saw a quilt I had, he told me his wife had many like it in their home in Ojinaga, Mexico. They had walked from Ojinaga to our house, at least 300 miles. She was wearing the flimsy high-heeled shoes like the Mexican women wear, certainly not shoes for walking. She had a terrible blister on the bottom of one foot. It was a water blister as large as a big pecan.

She didn't want me to drain it. Her husband persuaded her to let me. I sterilized a needle and drained and bandaged it. No wonder they walked so slowly. I don't know how she walked at all. He was a stonemason and had a job if he could get to Odessa. Since their friends had still not come, I insisted they go to bed. They just lay down on the bed in their clothes. I hope they slept, for he told me they had slept on the ground under a bush at times. Their friends did come about 7 a.m. They were a nice couple just trying to better their life.

Blackie was an unusual cowboy, for he did a lot of walking, something most cowboys are averse to. Blackie was not a person to sit idly. When he was not riding a horse or mule or involved in some work that needed to be done, he walked. He would walk around the fence line of our ranch and even out into our neighbor's, the doctor's land which joined ours. He made lots of tracks. Van Horn is a training area for new Border Patrol agents, *"chotas."* One day a new trainee came to my east door and was sure we had a "wetback" in our house. They had been trailing this man all day and trailed him to our door. Blackie was very disgusted that the border patrolmen didn't notice the tracks they were trailing were the same ones that were in the corral and all around the house and yard.

I had fixed a meal for a Mexican when we lived on the Rio Grande. One of the foods I served was stewed prunes. My children really got tickled when this Mexican man spat the prune seeds out onto the floor.

**In 1970 Blackie was hunting in the Davis Mountains with his friend, Jim White**. The dogs struck a lion's trail on Mount Livermore, the 3rd highest peak in Texas. The dogs worked the trail out and cornered the lion in a pour-off, where the rushing rain water through countless ages had eroded a basin in the solid rock of a canyon. Blackie and Jim left their horses and climbed to where the dogs had the lion bayed, but neither had brought a gun. This lion had been killing sheep for some time on this rancher's land and needed killing. Blackie volunteered to hold the lion at bay with the dogs' help while Jim went for a gun. To keep the lion's attention so he would not leave, Blackie chose a sturdy oak limb about six feet long, which he thrust in the lion's mouth. The lion bit some chunks off the limb, making it much shorter; but with Blackie continuing to thrust it into the lion's mouth, he held the lion until Jim returned with a gun. I think at this time Blackie had only a rifle in a saddle scabbard, but he soon secured a .22 pistol and had a holster-like pocket sewn into his chaps so he always had it with him after that. Then he never used any gun except that .22 pistol to kill lions. Bill Cowden gave him a .222 rifle which he kept in his pickup to shoot coyotes.

**Jim White wanted to go bear hunting**, so Blackie arranged for Jim and his wife, Jane Brite, to go to Graves Evans' HOK Ranch in New Mexico. While the men hunted, Jane and I took in the sights of T or C. Jane's hobby was collecting mineral crystals, of which she was very knowledgeable. We visited several rock shops—there are many in this tourist-oriented town. She bought specimens of several mineral crystals and a big geode that had been sawed in half to reveal a star-shaped cavity of crystals. These are beautiful and make good bookends. I discovered and bought four sun-purpled serving sized bowls to add to my collection. That evening as we were showing our purchases to the men, Jane was justifying what she had bought. In my turn I merely said, "I bought these bowls because they are beautiful and I liked them." Jim seemed to appreciate that. Blackie was never critical of anything I bought. He spent money on his hunting and he respected my using money for things I liked.

As Jane drove around T or C we heard a siren that sounded some distance away; but when she looked in her rear view mirror she was being followed by a police car with its light and siren on. This

213

policeman asked her, "Didn't you see that school zone sign? You were exceeding the speed limit." Jane began to apologize and told him she was on the school board in her home town of Marfa, Texas. She would never do anything to harm or endanger a school child, and on and on. He just waved her on as he told her to be careful and enjoy her trip. It was the slickest job I have ever heard.

The three men did have a successful bear chase and Jim killed a nice fat, young bear. We saved the fat and one ham of this bear. Jim wanted the skin. Blackie and I took the meat and fat and I rendered the fat into lard. It is like hog lard, but even greasier, and makes good pie crust and biscuits. The meat was like pork but much sweeter. It made almost a caramel-y crust when pan fried. I liked it. I kept the lard in my freezer.

Later I learned from a saddle maker that bear lard was the best substance there was to oil dry leather, much better even than neat's-foot oil. When my daughter-in-law wanted the saddle of my grandfather's that I rode when I was young I thought of what this saddle maker had told me. This saddle was very old, probably over one hundred years, as my grandfather died in 1926 at age 75. I feel that he had not ridden this saddle for at least 10 years at that time. I am sure the saddle was made before 1900. This saddle had a high cantle, narrow pommel, metal horn and stirrups. It had become very dry from disuse. I gave the bear lard to her to have the saddle restored. The saddle is now displayed in their new living room on a wrought iron saddle rack made by her husband, my son Tim.

*Mountain Lion killed on EV Ranch, 148 pounds*

**A New Mexico Hunt**   The dogs quiver with excitement as they see Blackie loading the five-gallon can containing their feed pans and light tie-chains into the pickup along with a sack of Purina Dog Chow.   Then his saddle and riding gear are taken from the nose cubicle of the horse trailer and placed on the luggage shelf in the pickup camper. They know they will be hunting somewhere distant from the usual area and they are agog with anticipation.   Blackie unlatches the gate to each dog's pen and they rush outside.   As he calls they jump into the camper which Blackie closes as each of the five dogs finds his place on the camper bed.   Our luggage has already been loaded on the camper shelf.   I take my place in the cab of the pickup, eager for the trip's destination but dreading the long hot section we must travel to reach the mountains of New Mexico's Black Range.

215

We stop for Cokes at Hatch, New Mexico. The man at the station notices we have dogs in the camper. He has hunted and he is very interested in seeing the dogs. Blackie opens the camper; the dogs stand, wanting out but holding their places until Blackie gives permission. The man wants to see the lead dog, which has chosen his place next to the pickup cab. Blackie calls softly, "Rowdy," and only Rowdy responds. The man is impressed at dogs that well-trained. He asks about the dogs' breeding. Blackie responds that breed is not that important for his type of hunting. It just takes a dog with a good nose to keep the trail and the stamina to carry it to the quarry. Rowdy is a July hound descended from Blackie's father's line of Julys. The two young dogs are his pups. Obviously, the blue dog is Blue Tick hound; the white dog's lineage is unknown—just picked him up in town where someone had lost him or kicked him out. He has proven to be the workhorse of the pack.

We continue our journey. About ten miles from T or C we realize the pickup's alternator is not functioning. Nothing to do but keep going as long as the battery furnishes power. We got a late start and it is just dark when we reach T or C. The garages are closed. I call my uncle, Graves Evans, who has a house in T or C and is waiting for us to go on to his HOK Ranch with him. He knows a mechanic who will open his shop this evening. We meet him there where he furnishes and installs a new alternator. We follow Graves on to his ranch, feeling we had bought a gold-plated alternator, but that is just the way it is when you are over a barrel.

Upon reaching the HOK Ranch, Blackie stops at the barn to unload, stake, feed and water his dogs. Graves' dogs have been cared for earlier by an employee. My uncle and I go to the big house built on the side of the hill, up the many steps to the porch across the front. As Graves unlocks and opens the door, the most delectable aroma of fires past in the large fireplace wafts out to greet us. The fireplace doesn't smoke—it was just that the oak, juniper, cedar and pine wood that had fueled many fires through the years had perfumed the whole room with a scent like no other—woodsy, warm, comforting, welcoming, and promising rest and contentment.

In the kitchen he unpacks the food his wife, Gene, had prepared—roast beef, vegetables, a delicious pound cake, and her unequalled yeast bread, while I set the table in the kitchen. For the three of us we prefer this over the four by twelve-foot rectangular polished table imported from Italy that is in the front room. Supper over, we do not spend much time sitting by the fire in the living room; a 4 a.m. wakeup time comes swiftly. Though I do not ride on these hunts, I rise when Blackie does and help Graves prepare breakfast and a lunch if he wishes one. Blackie does not ever carry a lunch or water. While Graves and I are busy with breakfast, Blackie goes to the barn to feed the horses. By 5 a.m. the dogs and horses are loaded and Graves and Blackie are on their way over Fairview Mountain to the place where they will start the hunt.

I clean the kitchen and return to my bed to sleep another two hours. After a hurried breakfast I set out to explore the mountain the HOK house is built upon. The hillside is open—only a few small cedar or juniper trees to break the expanse. A steep hollow plunges from the hilltop to the level the barn is on. Some bushes along the edges might yield a twisted root or two. By now you may have discovered my passion is desert driftwood. I had an excellent source when we lived in the canyon where I grew up, and I had amassed such a collection that it took a twenty-foot gooseneck trailer to move it to the little ranch we had bought near Van Horn. But like any collector, I am always searching for another prize to add to my collection. Each piece is different and distinctive. As I traverse the open hillside I see **IT**—not a tree within three hundred yards, but there it sits: a juniper gnarl on a base about seven inches in diameter, swirling up to almost a point fourteen inches high—as perfectly sculpted as if it had been designed by a master craftsman, which it had—God working through the processes of nature.

I prowl the remainder of the hillside but do not find a stump or even a limb to indicate where my prize had originated. *"Pues quien sabe?"* The hunters return about 3 p.m. When I see their vehicles approaching I start to get their dinner ready. There is plenty of time because they will see to the needs of their horses and dogs before they come to the house for their own meal.

They tell me it was an unsuccessful day. The dogs cold-trailed a lion but the trail was too old to make any progress. They decide the lions have followed the deer, which have moved to better grass down the canyons. The hunt the next day will cover that area. The second day of the HOK hunt gets the usual early start. I climb the mountain just for the exercise and because I like to climb. There is nothing of special interest to me—just the typical open rocky, bare, treeless hillside of that elevation in New Mexico. Graves comes in to HOK Ranch alone. Today the dogs crossed a bear's trail. Bear hunting is very different than lion hunting. When the bear hears the dogs, he makes a run for the highest saddle on the biggest mountains. Bears that you see in a zoo may look like they are only capable of a clumsy shuffle, but in the wild they can run very fast, even uphill. When they stretch their legs to run they have a very long stride and can cover the ground rapidly. Graves' dogs have run bear before but Blackie's dogs are used to trailing by scent. Scent left by a bear is only when his feet touch the ground between these long leaps, so is not a continuous trail. Blackie's dogs are encouraged to keep up by the barking of Graves' dogs. The hunters ride like crazy to keep up with the chase, but they can only travel where there is some semblance of a deer trail.

As usual, the bear gets over the mountain and can roll into a ball, roll off the cliff, and land far down the mountain, be on his feet and immediately be running, leaving no trail of scent from the top of the

218

cliff to the bottom.  The dogs lose much time having to go around the cliff and trying to find the bear's trail.  This is why Blackie does not like bear hunting.  He likes to watch the dogs work out a trail by scent, see how the dogs cooperate as they move the trail.  This is not possible on a bear hunt.  Graves returns about 3 p.m. with two of his dogs.  He reports the bear got over the mountain.  Blackie waits for his and Graves' dogs.  They always return to the spot where they have been unloaded that morning.  Even if the pickup is no longer there, they wait.  Blackie feels very responsible for his dogs so he waits until night with nothing to eat since 4 a.m.  Only two of his dogs make it back to the pickup.  Three are still missing.  The men will be hunting dogs tomorrow.  They get the same early morning start with the horses in the trailer and any dogs that are not too sore-footed to hunt.  These New Mexico forested mountains are not as hard on dogs' feet as the bare rocky mountains of the Trans-Pecos area, so all the dogs are able to go.  They drive to the spot where they unloaded yesterday and find both of Graves' dogs and two of Blackie's.  They feed these dogs with the dog chow Blackie brings.  There is plenty of water in these running creeks.  Then they drive to a better lion hunting area where the dogs soon strike a lion's trail.  They watch with interest as the dogs move the trail, and with excitement as the trail leads to a tall pine tree where forty feet up the lion crouches on a bar limb.  One shot from a pistol, and the lion falls to the ground where the dogs "wool" him to show their mastery and make sure he is dead.

Graves and Blackie arrive at HOK about 2 p.m.  After a hurried lunch we break camp, for Blackie and I need to be home.  Graves offers to look for and ask about Blackie's young dog.  Maybe he will show up.  We arrive home at the Running W at 9 p.m., glad to be home after a typical New Mexico hunt.  Blackie sorrows for his lost dog, who had never been to New Mexico before; this was his first trip.

Some three months later, Blackie receives a postcard that says only, "I have your dog," and a man's name at Findlay, Texas, a community west of Sierra Blanca that had been a stop for water for steam locomotives. This was no longer needed with diesel engines; also the highway had bypassed Findlay. Only three or four houses remained for men who maintained the railroad. Blackie immediately set out for Findlay. Every hunting dog wears a collar with the owner's name and address on a plate. We did not have a telephone when these name plates were made. There is a joyful reunion for Blackie and his dog. Who knows what this young dog had experienced on his three month-long journey, where he had crossed the Rio Grande, travelled the sparsely- populated country east of the river, by-passed the large city of El Paso, and was almost to his 375-mile destination. He had only fifty miles, a railroad, and two highways to cross to get back home. If he could talk, what a saga he had to tell!

*Blackie and the country he hunted*

**This is a copy of the letter I wrote to my cousin, Ruben Evans, when his mother died:**

"Dear Rube,

Since the going home of your mother and my Aunt Gene, I have been thinking of how my life has been blessed and enriched by the close ties and association with both your parents. You know I lived all my childhood at the EV Ranch knowing and adoring Uncle Graves, your dad. He was good to us, but expected us to do our share of things. He had a Marmon car with smaller wheels than others, and he gave us an inner tube from it that worked like a life jacket and helped us learn to swim.

His choice of words instilled in me an appreciation for words to express the exact meaning of what you were saying. Some I remember learning from him were: superfluous, supercilious, idiosyncrasy, and indispensable—words my parents didn't use. We all loved and respected him, but were agreed we had rather get a whipping from our parents than a "bawling out" from Uncle Graves.

I was about 10 years old when he married Gene. She was such fun! She treated us as her peers and talked to us as such, while to most other adults we were just "kids." She was so spontaneous in showing her love for Graves. As he came in from riding looking after the cattle, she would run out the door to meet him, and they would come from the barn, arms around each other.

She taught us to make fudge candy—hers was so good and creamy. She was such a marvelous cook. The light bread she made was the best ever—tender, but you could make sandwiches with it and it didn't crumble or break. When we were going on hunts she always had food prepared for our entire stay. Even after I felt she wasn't physically able to do this and I begged her not to, said that I would do it, she would say, "No, this is my part of the hunt since I can't

221

go."

When she was at the HOK Ranch, of course I stayed with her and we would go in to T or C.  She would buy extras—candy, cigarettes [she didn't smoke] and food and take these items to old or needy people. Sometimes she would not let me go into their homes with her.  She would say, "Oh, honey, it is too bad for you to see."  It was never too bad for her to take time with them and bring them something they especially liked or needed and give them some sense of worth and caring.

She would say, "Now don't tell Graves."  Then Uncle Graves would tell us that Gene was a better person than he was because she took time for these old and needy people.  I could not agree with him because I knew of some things he did, like finding my mother suffering agony with an arthritic knee—bone scraping on bone—and he not only made contact setting things in motion to have her knee replaced, but paid for the surgery and hospital.  This was before Medicare.  All these twenty-something years, that replaced knee has never hurt her again.

Your parents were so kind and loving, each in his own way.  What a legacy they left!"

**In 1985 we made a trip to Columbus, New Mexico**, to visit friends, Dunc and Lucy Freeman. Blackie and Dunc were best hunting buddies. They had hunted mountain lions together when both worked with the Hoof and Mouth Disease Control program. Lucy and I had shared life on the river, good times and bad times. We looked forward to visiting while Blackie and Dunc took their dogs to hunt lions in nearby mountains.

Columbus is a very small town on the Mexico border. The neighboring town, Colonia, Mexico, had much more to offer—a restaurant, apothecary store with jars of strange herbs and seeds, a bar, and several small shops. After taking in all the sights except the bar, we went to the restaurant where we were met by waiters in black suits and ties, white shirts, and a spotless white napkin an arm, and very polite service. We each ate a typical Mexican meal. Not long after we returned to Columbus, we began to feel sick. By the time Blackie and Dunc returned from hunting, we were too sick to want to live. That was my first and last meal at a restaurant in Mexico. Montezuma had his revenge.

**A rancher south of Marfa, Texas, was losing a large number of calves to a mountain lion.** It seemed unbelievable the number of calves that had been killed. Blackie left home with his mule and dogs in the pickup and trailer in time to drive over a hundred miles and arrive before daylight to start hunting. There was a killed calf where the dogs picked up a lion trail. By mid-morning they had worked the trail to a rocky bluff on the point of a mountain. The dogs bayed a big male lion. After this lion was killed the dogs did not seem to be satisfied as at the end of the usual hunt.

Blackie soon realized his best dog was working on another lion's trail. All the dogs joined in and after trailing several miles, a second lion was treed on a rocky hillside. After this lion was sent to wherever calf-killing lions go, the dogs were still not satisfied.

Blackie let the dogs have their way and they picked up another trail. Was it just an old trail of one of these now-dead lions? No, the dogs will not trail a lion they know is dead. The trail was leading the dogs to a different area. It was a fresh, workable trail. Men and dogs were excited to a feverish pitch. Who had ever found the trails of three distinctly different lions on one hunt in one day? By mid-afternoon the dogs had worked the trail to a rocky mountain where the lion was. This was the third large adult lion to be trailed by the same pack of dogs and killed in one day. It was a record that has never been equaled. Sometimes a female and her two young lions have been caught, but never three mature lions found by three different trails. Blackie holds the record. The grateful rancher had a saddle made for Blackie by the famous saddle maker in Fort Worth, Wendy Ryon.

**A man who owned a ranch in Mexico contacted Blackie.** He and a native rancher were losing calves to predatory mountain lions. Not all mountain lions kill calves—deer are their usual meat—but once a lion kills a calf he becomes a devastating calf killer. Blackie was loathe to take his dogs into Mexico. He knew of one hunter who took his dogs hunting in Mexico and then the officials would not let him bring them back into the United States. He lost his dogs. This man, Mr. B, assured Blackie that would not happen to him. Blackie would be met at a river crossing where he and his dogs would be transferred by truck to the Mexican rancher's hacienda. Finally, Blackie agreed to this arrangement and they agreed on a price. This hacienda was about 100 miles beyond Chihuahua City. They drove for hours, Blackie and his four dogs and several vaqueros in the back of a bob-tail truck. After midnight the driver stopped. The peons jumped out and gathered wood and built a fire. Water was heated on this fire. When the water was hot they made instant coffee for everyone. The coffee pot and the men were loaded back into the truck. They drove about two miles and came to the hacienda.

The hunt started early that morning, though Blackie had only about three hours sleep. The ranchero led to an area where calves had been killed, but the dogs found no trails there. The next morning in another area of the rancho they were having no better luck. Blackie had noticed a mountain some distance from the mountains where they had been hunting. He told the ranchero he wanted to go there. Surely enough, the dogs picked up a hot trail and after an exciting chase the lion was cornered and dispensed with. It was a very large male lion. Blackie assured the ranchero this lion was the killer since they had found no other lion trails. He had been killing calves on these adjoining ranches.

The senora had learned Blackie was married and wanted to send me something. She brought several *mananitas* for Blackie to choose from. The one he chose is natural-colored beige and brown hand spun wool woven into a circle with slits for the hands to go through.

**Clayton Williams was concerned about a mountain lion** one of his ranch hands had seen on the Alpine, Texas, ranch. When he asked about someone to get rid of this lion, he was assured by everyone he asked that Blackie Woods was the man who could do the job. Clayton called Blackie that he had a lion on his Alpine ranch that he wanted caught. They set a date and Blackie drove to Clayton's ranch the afternoon before with his dogs and riding gear. After a supper of dry cereal in the kitchen, they visited in the living room—Clayton with a decanter close at hand. He drank his neat. Blackie did not join him in that, for he did not drink any alcoholic beverage, not even a "social drink."

Early the next morning they mounted their horses and rode out on this beautiful ranch. The dogs soon struck a good lion trail. After an exciting chase the lion was cornered on a high cliff and Clayton disposed of him. They found no more lion trails or sign—obviously there was only one lion.

Several months later we received an invitation to a barbeque at Clayton's Alpine ranch. We thought it would be a novel experience—it was. His ranch was only 100 miles from our Running W. When we arrived on the date, there were armed guards at the gate who inspected our invitation. We were admitted and drove on to the area of the barbeque. There were already about 200 people there and others arriving in cars and also helicopters and private planes on Clayton's landing strip on top of the hills. We got in line for the barbeque supper, but it was all gone. There must have been food prepared for only 100 or 150 people. We knew the cook, who was embarrassed, but that was all he had been furnished to work with. It was evident that barbeque was not the main focus. There were pressurized beer kegs in a grid of about 30 feet apart all over the expanse under scattered trees—several acres of them. Clayton's house and the band stand were on an elevation above an amphitheater where people could bring their chairs or sit on the grass. There were only a few chairs down front. Clayton, over a mike, made a welcoming speech. His patriotic vocabulary was interjected liberally with four-letter words, especially "damns." There were too many of these damns to count. It must have been the only adjective he knew.

Merle Haggard's band provided the music. Merle must have been coached by Clayton, for his speech was also punctuated by the same four-letter words. We decided we had seen enough and departed. When we exited, there were no armed guards at the open gate. We arrived home early. We were thankful that man was not successful in his bid for governor of Texas.

I looked up "damn" in my dictionary, and he wasn't even using the right word for his meaning when he said, "We have the best damn country, best damn state, etc. He was actually, according to the dictionary, saying, "doom to hell, cause the damnation of, or may God damn." Damn may be used as verb, noun, adjective, or adverb.

Also means condemn or censure. In his patriotic speech he was saying, "cause the damnation of our country, our state, etc., e.g.: cause eternal punishment in hell."

**Hunting can be hazardous for dogs in many different ways.** One ever-present danger is rattlesnake bite. Dogs usually are quick to sense a rattlesnake and give the snake a wide berth, for they are very afraid of snakes. Sometimes in the dog's concentration on the chase the snake is encountered too quickly for the dog to be aware of the danger in time to avoid it. Such was the case when the dogs had a lion bayed at the top of a high cliff. They were baying and leaping up trying to get closer to the lion. One dog, Blue, happened to be in a rattlesnake's territory. As Blue leaped and fell back to the ground, this rattlesnake bit him each time on his hind legs. When Blackie discovered this, the lion was allowed to go free as the snake was killed and the dogs called off their prey. Blackie carried the snake-bitten dog in front of him on the saddle to the pickup. The drive home took an hour or so. Blue was in very bad shape by then—sick, swollen, and in intense pain.

As soon as Blackie told me of the problem, I removed the antivenin kit from the refrigerator, injected the syringe-full of serum into the vial of powdered venom, shook it to dissolve it, drew it back into the syringe, and went to Blackie and Blue. Blackie quickly injected this mixture into Blue's hip. Blackie was adept at this from years of vaccinating calves for Blackleg. Within ten minutes after this injection you could see that Blue was in less pain. He was already responding to the antivenin which was counteracting the poison. Blue did recover, though it took a long time before he was able to hunt.

Other animals can be a danger. Blackie was hunting on a ranch south of Marfa in the vicinity where he had trailed and caught three adult lions in one day—an unequalled record. His dogs encountered

a pack of *javelinas*.  The dogs had never before seen these animals.
At that time there were no *javelinas* in our area, but they had
migrated to the Big Bend and Marfa area in their steady infiltration
of Texas.  *Javelinas* are vicious fighters and are well-equipped to
harm with their sharp, curved tusks.  The dogs were no match for
these cruel animals.  Several dogs received cuts and one dog's flank
was ripped open.  Thankfully, the membrane enclosing the intestines
was not broken, but a large seven-inch v-shaped portion of flesh and
skin was torn loose and needed to be sewn back in place.   The
nearest veterinarian was one hundred miles away, and at times he
was away from his clinic on a call to a ranch.  The dog's wound was
not bleeding now, so Blackie decided we could suture it.  I brought a
spool of upholstery thread, a curved needle, and a leather needle,
which I sterilized.  I cleaned the wound with peroxide before we
started.  The leather needle proved to be the most efficient.  The dog
was a good patient even without anesthesia.  He seemed to know we
were trying to help him.  The wound healed with no infection, but
the dog had a particular hatred for *javelinas*.

*Javelinas* are very treacherous—not ever to be trusted.  Blackie had
a friend on whose ranch he had caught many lions on the east side of
Gomez Peak near Kent, Texas.  This friend, Len, had a lucrative
source of income from taking paying hunters who wanted to shoot a
*javelina*.  He encouraged the propagation of javelinas and even fed
them grain cubes around his corrals.  There were always some of the
animals around his house and corrals.  Blackie had not been able to
contact Len by telephone—his telephone service was not always
functioning—so Blackie drove to Len's ranch to arrange a time to
hunt lions.  Blackie stopped his pickup at Len's front gate as Len
came out to greet him.  Blackie stood in the opened door of his
pickup while talking to Len.  There were *javelinas*, including a sow
with piglets, nearby; but neither man paid much attention to them.
This group of *javelinas* circled in front of Blackie's pickup and from
the opposite side came under the pickup and struck Blackie at the

back of his knees, knocking him face-down to the ground. They were immediately upon him, biting him in spite of his efforts to rise, and Len's attempts to beat them off. Len is a big, strong man, but he was not able to dislodge the *javelinas*. He called to his son to bring a bucket of feed and with that enticement and Len's continued kicking of the *javelinas*, they left Blackie alone so he could stand up. They had not cut through his jacket and Levi's enough to tear his flesh, but he was bruised and sore. What a harrowing experience! I am convinced that had Blackie been alone, the *javelinas* would have started eating him while he was still alive. But had Len not been home, Blackie would not have left his pickup, so we will never know about that.

Len was a very good friend. One spring when we had not had rain he let Blackie bring forty head of cows with calves to one of his pastures that he did not use, in payment and appreciation of Blackie's catching many mountain lions that preyed on deer and calves and even *javelinas*. Len's ranch had not had much rain either, but it was fresh space. We drove the seventy miles to this pasture to feed the cattle cottonseed cake and the return trip of seventy miles twice a week until we had good rains that summer. This saved that calf crop and was a real financial boost for us.

**Blackie needed some young dogs**. His brother, Thomas, told him a man in south Texas had two dogs descended from Thomas' dogs that he would sell. The man was contacted and a deal made. One cold early morning we left our ranch at 2 a.m. to drive to Floresville, Texas, south of San Antonio. When we reached Alpine, one hundred miles away, the road was icy, with snow on the hills. As we came to the lower altitude at Marathon the snow was gone. We arrived at the dog man's house about 2 p.m. His wife called him but he said he could not leave his feed store. His wife knew which two dogs were for Blackie. As we neared the dog pens and the dogs saw that woman they panicked. I have never seen any animals that were as afraid as those dogs were of that woman.  I can't imagine what she had done to cause them to be so terrified of her.  They would run away from her to the other side of the large enclosure and hit the fence, only to run across the pen to the other side—more frightened than any wild animal I have ever seen.  Blackie finally managed to catch the two dogs she pointed out.  He loaded them into the trunk of our car and we started home.  Late that afternoon Blackie started to look for an old motel that might have a shed out back where he could put the dogs.  Wishful thinking!  There was nothing like that to be had, so he kept driving.  At 3 a.m. the next day we arrived home after that killer trip of 25 hours.

Another time Blackie was needing young dogs.  He very rarely hunted female dogs—they had to be exceptional for him to keep them.  He had to depend on other sources for replacements.  Again, his brother knew of some of his strain of dogs owned by a man in Phoenix.  Phoenix was considered a day's drive from Van Horn at the then-current speed limits.  We left home at 3 a.m., arriving at Phoenix around 2 p.m.  It was hot.  The people who had the dogs had a good air conditioner which we enjoyed while we waited to leave shortly before sundown, thinking it would be cooler driving in the evening.  That is the case in Texas, but not in Arizona, as we learned.  When we stopped at Casa Grande to eat supper, our car was shaking.  Blackie quickly opened the trunk to see these dogs were panting enough to shake the whole car.  They were almost done for.  What could he do?

Dogs have a very inadequate way of cooling their bodies—only through their tongues and the pads of their feet.  I told him to go to the convenience store across the street and get some bags of ice.  He quickly did that and we packed those two dogs in ice.  It was not long until their panting slowed down and then stopped.  We continued our journey, stopping occasionally to check on the dogs' condition.  We arrived at our Running W Ranch about 3 a.m. the next day, after a typical dog trip.

**Weather is not that much of a factor in hunting.** It is a year-round sport. Lion hunting in New Mexico was being restricted, so my Uncle Graves Evans wanted to hunt with Blackie in Texas. He came to our ranch in June. The first morning out the dogs struck a fresh trail and had an interesting race to where the lion was cornered and disposed of before the afternoon temperature high. The next day dawned without the usual cool temperatures. The hunters soon decided to abort the hunt, as the dogs had not found a trail. As they were returning to their vehicles the dogs crossed a fresh trail of a lion and started moving it. It was soon evident the running dogs were in trouble. They could not bark and pant and the pads of their feet were touching the hot ground. Soon the lead dogs were gasping for breath. Blackie and Graves rode hard to overtake and stop them, but not in time. Three dogs were so hot they could not breathe. It is a terrible thing to see a dog die of suffocation, even if it is a quick death. Blackie carried a gallon canteen of water in his pickup, but it was miles away. They were too late to save those three dogs and two more were going down. With the lead, and best, dogs no longer barking, the remaining dogs gave up the chase. They were getting overheated too, but survived. There were two sad hunters as they returned to the pickups and brought the remaining dogs and the five empty collars home. Three of Graves' dogs and two of Blackie's were lost that day—a real tragedy.

**Blackie was ever looking for a better or replacement mule.** A man in the Brownwood area had a mule advertised for sale, so we drove in the car to Brownwood, something over 300 miles from our house. I called the man for directions, but found the mule had sold or somehow was no longer available. It was Sale Day at Brownwood, so we went to the livestock auction. From the catwalk Blackie had seen these two mules in one of the pens, but they looked to be too small for his use. When the sale was nearly over, they came through the sale ring. They were good stout young mules, brother and sister, one year apart in age. They were black, the male with stocking legs. The mare mule had a white rump and tail, a rather startling marking. Blackie bid on them and bought them as a pair for $605.00. They were both gentle and even good in the mountains. He was told they had come from New Mexico. After spending that night with our daughter in Dublin, we returned home to come back with pickup and trailer for the mules. Blackie got a lot of good riding out of them for several years. Then he decided to sell the male. A rich man who owned the Eagle Mountain Ranch wanted to buy him and asked how much Blackie wanted for the mule. Blackie said $750. Mr. Richie answered, "That's not enough for that mule. He is worth a thousand," and gave Blackie a check for $1,000.

Sue Frank, who hunted with her husband and Blackie, named the mare mule. Sue liked to ride directly behind Blackie when they started to hunt because she could always see that white tail before daylight. She called the mule "Taillight."

As you may have noticed, I did the telephone calling making the arrangements for lion hunts. I had talked to Mr. Richie several times before I met him. When he learned Blackie and I had been married 55 years, he confessed he had told his wife I must be a second wife—I suppose because my voice was strong, he thought I must be a lot younger than Blackie, whom he knew.

Later when Blackie decided to sell the mare mule, Taillight, I called Mr. Richie and asked if he still wanted her. He asked how much Blackie wanted for her. I told him she was about like the one he had bought. He said, "I will send you a check for $1,000." Blackie didn't come out that well on other mule deals.

**Rattlesnakes are probably the most feared creatures** in the United States, though actually they bite very few people proportionate to the total population. Since they are found in the area where I lived, I felt I should learn all I could about them. I checked out every book our library had pertaining to reptiles, particularly snakes, though it gives me a creepy feeling just to see a picture of a snake. I found that outside of what is observed in reptile gardens, little is known about snakes in the wild except that they are unpredictable, which I already knew. Rattlesnakes are pit vipers, so called because of a small indentation near the eye. They do not lay eggs as non-poisonous snakes do—their young are born live, and she may have from 12 to 37 at one time. The young come equipped with fangs and rattles and a mean disposition when they are born. I have seen one only five inches long, and he behaved just like one five feet long, only on a smaller scale. The female of the species is larger than the male. They eat insects, lizards, other snakes, rats, mice, and rabbits, which they swallow whole. The jaws are hinged so they are able to swallow these creatures, and their bodies are flexible enough to accommodate an object much larger around than they are.

Once, the meter reader knocked on my door. He wanted to show me something. He had noticed a very wide snake track that crossed our front yard. It was at least seven inches wide. We trailed it across our road and toward a large mesquite bush. He acted like he did not really want to find that snake. I learned later that he had been bitten by a rattlesnake. Blackie, who was an expert at tracking all creatures, tried to trail this snake when he returned home that afternoon, but the wind and sun had obliterated the track on the hard ground almost completely. We never found a snake large enough to have made a track that wide. Later I found where that snake had made her bed against the sun-warmed cinder blocks of our yard fence. I am sure she was full of cottontail rabbit because snakes don't get that big in our area as they do in the South and other parts of Texas. A snake five feet long with a body diameter of three inches is a very large snake for our area. There have been some larger, but that is rare.

Rattlesnakes, as all snakes, shed their skin as they grow. They rub against rocks or bushes to help loosen their present skin, which is shed intact. With this loose skin the snake is really fierce-looking. The skin is shed from the head first as the snake literally crawls out of its old skin. It is broken off at the rattles—other snakes shed the entire skin to the point of the tail.

**A windstorm had broken off a large limb** of our big peach tree just outside of our back yard. Blackie had thrown this limb over the barb wire fence prior to hauling it away. As I looked over the back yard fence I saw a rattlesnake lying straight and still next to the trunk of the peach tree. I knew I was safe inside our back yard, so I went into the house for my .410 shotgun. Before I could shoot, this snake began moving backward in a straight line. Then I realized another snake hidden by the leaves of the broken limb was pulling her backward. They were mating. I shot, but the snake disappeared into the peach limbs. What to do now? I was not strong enough to lift that big limb and be ready to shoot, too. While I was debating my dilemma a Border Patrol vehicle drove up. It was a friend making a routine check for wets. I quickly told him of the situation. He was strong enough to move the limb. He used my .410 shotgun and killed both snakes. They were no longer joined as in mating.

**I have heard many rattlesnake stories**, but I think my experience is unique. One night as I was sewing I noticed some pieces of lint in the corner of my sewing room. I thought, "Oh, I have a mouse in my house." When you are the only house in a large area, this happens. We had a box trap that captured the mouse alive. I got it and put it in the corner where I had seen the lint. Several nights later I heard movement in the trap and knew I had caught the mouse. It was necessary to immerse this trap in water to drown the mouse before emptying it out. Since it was night I didn't attend to this then. When I did carry the trap outside it seemed rather heavy. I was busy so the trap stayed under the water for several days. There was a door at one end of the trap to empty it of the mouse. As I opened the door I saw not a mouse, but a rattlesnake. I threw that trap as far as I could, although I was sure that snake was dead. I must have made some startled sound or cry because the dogs became alarmed and began to bark as against some danger. They did not bark without some unusual cause. Upon examination we found a small hole where the floor did not meet the wall and was open to the crawl space under the house, but the carpet had covered it. You can be sure that when Blackie mixed the concrete to stop up the hole, we poured and pushed concrete into that hole until no more could be packed in. I looked the house over carefully to be certain there were no more holes covered by the carpet.

**When we lived at EV Ranch and had sheep** Blackie kept steel traps set under the fence line for the coyotes. When he checked his trap line he found one trap thrown, but instead of a coyote he had a big rattlesnake that was heavy enough to trip that trap. Once as I was driving to Van Horn, about halfway to Highway 90 I saw a rattlesnake by the side of the road. What should I do? I had no way to kill the snake, and he was too close to my house to leave him. I was directly in front of our neighbor's house about ¼ mile from this county road. I could hear him and his sons talking so I began to honk the car's horn. When I stopped my car the snake had assumed a striking position. Since I did not get out of my car he stayed where he was. Finally the neighbors heard my car horn and thought I had car trouble. The man drove to my location, where I showed him the snake, which he shot and killed. He held the snake up to show me how "pretty" it was. He said he would skin the snake and make a belt for himself, which his wife would not let him bring into the house. I thought he would have to stretch the snake skin a lot to make a belt for himself. I wasn't that long a snake—about 24 inches.

**At Runaway Bay at Bridgeport, Texas**, just last summer (2008) one of my grandsons, Bob Woods, was to spend the night with his brother, Britt. It was not a dark night when he went out of the house to get something out of his pickup. He sensed, rather than actually saw, a snake slither between his legs. They turned on car lights and porch light and began the hunt for a snake. This yard was where Britt's young children played. No one had a flashlight but they found and killed the rattlesnake, which was 57 inches long and had 20 rattles. The next morning everyone went shopping for flashlights.

**After we had bought our ranch** but before we moved there I had tomato plants needing to be planted into a garden. I planted them in the yard of our new home. Several days later Blackie, JP and I took a load of household goods to our new home. I went to check on my tomato plants and saw a snake under a plant. I immediately called, "Snake!" but before Blackie and JP got to the yard I had a better look at this snake—he was spotted. I called, "It looks like a rattlesnake but I have never before seen a spotted one." They killed the snake, and it was like no other snake we had ever seen—thick-bodied for its length, rather blunt tail, and pointed-shaped head with a hard shiny nose with a short horn on the end of it. Blackie said it was a Hog-nosed Adder. The snakes were not listed as poisonous, but they coiled and struck like rattlesnakes, so we treated them as poisonous.

Once, as I went out my front door I saw a bull snake scooping out a depression in the sand with a loop of her body and realized she was preparing a place to lay her eggs. I quickly chased her out into the pasture. The last thing I wanted was a bunch of little bull snakes in my front yard.

**In El Paso I spent most of one afternoon** selecting various household items at Gibson's, at that time a good place to shop.

Blackie bought dog food there—a ton or more at a time. When I checked out, the girl would not accept my out-of-town check for about $300. I was indignant—after all the checks I had written to that store with no questions asked—not even a driver's license request. I had never before had a check turned down. I was insulted and asked to see the store manager. "Sorry, he was out." I was getting more frustrated and indignant. The cashier was no help. I left the store getting angrier with each step toward my car. I had spent all my time shopping there and I needed somehow to take what I had purchased home with me. It was too late to shop anywhere else. I should get started home, 150 miles away. With each step my rage increased.

No, the assistant manager was not in either. I was not sure what to do next. A nice man wearing a patch over one eye approached me. "Lady, maybe I can help you." He was the store detective, who had witnessed my dilemma. We called my bank in Fort Davis and verified the check. I thanked him profusely. He showed me a stack of checks two inches thick that he was trying to collect. He told me, "When you came back into the store, I knew your check was good."

**My hobby of hunting and collecting sun-purpled** or amethystine glassware was begun with two identical pickle bottles that Blackie found and brought to me. They were found where in years past someone had a picnic by the river. Their trash had become treasures. Over the years the heat and rays of the sun had turned them from prosaic clear to a beautiful pale amethyst. I have ever been fascinated by glass and all the things that can be done with it, from utilitarian window panes to intricately-shaped and cut glass. The challenge of finding a glass item that was made before 1914 and has survived intact despite its fragility is amazing and rewarding.

Various chemicals were added to the glass mixture to color it or make it more transparent. One ingredient added particularly to cheap glass to make it transparent was magnesium permanganate. This chemical was a poison used as an antiseptic. The cowboys used it to doctor animals with screw worms. A common name for it was gentian violet. It made a deep purple permanent stain on everything it touched. This magnesium permanganate was used in varying amounts to make the glass clear or transparent. With exposure to heat or the sun's rays, glass containing it will turn various shades of purple or amethystine, depending on the amount added to the glass mixture. The more added, the deeper the shade of purple. For some reason I don't understand, broken pieces of glass turn a deeper color than intact pieces. Many pint whiskey flasks will turn a deep purple color, as will the big fifths. Since my family were all teetotalers I never found a whiskey bottle on EV Ranch. A multi-great grandfather founded the first temperance society in the United States.

My collection consisted of items from medicine and whiskey bottles I found in old trash piles to pressed and cut glass bowls, cruets, pitcher, and sugar-and-creamer sets I bought in antique shops or junk stores. You might never know where you would find an amethystine treasure. Some glassware I bought as clear turned to amethyst. A boat-shaped cut class bowl bought when clear, I set in an east window because I liked to see the sun make it sparkle. It turned a beautiful amethyst. A small art cut glass dish that had been my grandmother's turned purple while I had it. Art cut glass is pressed glass that has had the design cut deeper. I had several art cut pieces.

My glassware collection grew to include Depression glass—that made between 1920 and 1940. I had a good start on that because many of our wedding presents were Depression glass—bowls, platters, cake plates, sherbets and cups and saucers. I knew they were the real Depression glass because we had received them when they were popular during the depression. They grew more valuable and cherished as the years passed. I had a few pieces—candlesticks, cream pitchers—small items that turned yellow. A cream pitcher that had belonged to my maternal great-grandmother was now yellow. I bought two pairs of yellow candlesticks. There was a celery dish and a handled, covered sugar bowl—all transparent yellow glass. Also found was a telegraph insulator half-buried in dirt. The half exposed to the sun was yellow, and the buried half was still clear. I still have six deep purple telegraph line insulators.

Cobalt added to glass mixtures makes it blue—from the deep blue hand-blown Mexico glass to various light shades of blue. I inherited a five-gallon water bottle that turned blue while my mother had it. My daughter, Judy, now has it. My other daughter, Chance, has a cut glass rose bowl which was clear when her mother-in-law gave it to her. It is now a deep shade of blue. A hundred twenty-plus purple bottles became too much of a chore to dust. I put them in the local museum in the Evans-Powell room that I had furnished with our family's pictures, relics and antiques.

**About 1984 I bought a Bernina sewing machine** and was delighted at how smoothly it sewed. Such a joy to sew on it! I had never liked the Singer machine I was using. The presser foot jumped up with every stitch, so you had to be very careful to hold some tension on what you were sewing or the seam wobbled. At best it did not make a smooth seam. This Bernina sewed very precisely with a beautiful straight seam and very quietly—just a low hum of the motor.

Quilts had always fascinated me, especially designing the patterns. Through the years I had saved patterns for children's quilts. Now this Bernina machine made the narrow seams necessary for accuracy in quilts very simple. I began making quilts in earnest. I made quilts with bears, kittens, or cowboys appliquéd on them. I made a quilt for each of my great-grandchildren and I sold some. I designed a Texas themed quilt for a joint effort of Twentieth Century Club to make and raffle off.  Ruetta, who won it, said it was the only quilt she had ever wanted, so we were glad she won it.

I had saved the larger scraps and remnants from clothing I had made so I had a plentiful supply of fabric suitable for making quilts.  It was an enjoyable challenge deciding which colors and patterns to combine into the quilts' designs.  A child's color book furnished dinosaur patterns for a quilt.  In another quilt I used imaginary critters as aliens from outer space for the theme.  They made up into interesting quilts.

I had made various dolls and stuffed animals that could be played with, but also some dolls depicting personalities that were not playthings.  Then I saw the picture of a doll made in the image of Albert Einstein, showing his facial features, even wrinkles; and I realized that was the kind of doll making I wanted to do.  I found that as I fashioned each doll, it would reveal to me its "personality" and how it should look.  I got a lot of enjoyment making these dolls.

**One of my very earliest memories** is of the washtubs of peaches brought from the EV orchard to the cool hallway of my grandparents' house.  There at age two or three years I could have my choice of any nice ripe peach I wanted to eat.  No matter how many I had eaten, when I was asked my answer was always "two," so my parents told me.  These tubs full of peaches were to be canned for out-of-season enjoyment.  The men of the family set in to peel these peaches with their razor-sharp pocket knives.  The women packed the peeled peaches in glass quart Mason jars, filled the jars with sugar syrup, affixed the lids with rubber seals, and placed these jars in a very large kettle full of water.  After a required time, the kerosene stove which heated this kettle was turned off and the entire kettle and contents wrapped in an old quilt and left until the next morning.  Since glass of that time was prone to break with abrupt temperature changes, these jars of peaches had to be cooled gradually, lest they break. This large oblong kettle must have held twenty quart jars.

One summer when we were visiting Blackie's parents at Breckenridge, Blackie's mother, Eva, heard of an orchard at De Leon where you could pick all the peaches you wanted for a small fee. Eva, Blackie's sisters Mary and Fay, and Blackie and I went to De Leon for peaches. The boxes we had brought were soon filled and we started just putting peaches in the bed of our pickup. When Eva, Mary and Fay had taken what peaches they wanted, the bed of our pickup was still covered with peaches. Blackie and I came home the next day with our load of peaches. We were living at EV Ranch with my parents, Paul and Wertie Evans, at this time, about 1944.

At the sight of all those peaches, Dad sharpened his pocket knife, but I had discovered that by a quick dip in scalding hot water the peel would slip easily off the peach. The glass jars were more stable and did not break with changes in temperature. We had large aluminum pressure cookers to process the jars of peaches that were heated on a stove fueled by butane gas. These modern appliances made canning foods much faster and easier. We worked feverishly to get these peaches canned. It was surprising how few peaches were wasted, despite their long hot ride in the pickup bed.

About 1953 on one of our trips I had bought some very good peaches at a roadside stand. After I had prepared them for us to eat, I dug a trench in a flower bed and buried the seeds and peels. The next spring many little peach trees had started to grow in the flower bed. Blackie fenced an area with a gentle slope east of our house at the Neal Ranch and dug rows of holes connected by ditches. We set out these fragile-looking little plants you could hardly call trees and watered them faithfully. We were fortunate to have a strong source of water from a windmill and supply tank up the slope from the house. Almost all of these transplants survived and we ended up with twenty-three possible peach trees. Peaches bear fruit at a young age. When these trees began to bear, we discovered we had five distinctly different types of peaches. Two were clingstones and the other three were various sizes of Elberta-type freestones.

1961 produced a bumper crop, and methods of preserving fruit were by freezing. I bought plastic pint and quart containers with a square shape that fit in the freezer shelves with no waste space. The peaches were quickly peeled and packed in syrup in these containers, the lids fastened, labeled, and put in the freezer. Preserving the fruit had evolved into an art instead of a drudgery. I completely filled one large freezer for us to enjoy through the coming months. The tree with the best and largest peaches was watered by the drain of my automatic washing machine.

Along with canning peaches and other fruits I made jellies from whatever fruit was available. *Alzerita* or *agrito* (little sours) made excellent jelly. The *Alzerita* bush is made up entirely of grey three-pointed leaves with a needle-sharp spine on each point. In spring they are covered with yellow flowers that are very attractive to bees, followed by small berries barely one-eighth to one-fourth inch in diameter and very tart. To gather these berries a tarp or plastic sheet is placed on the ground under and all around the bush, which is usually about five feet high. Then the bush is threshed with a stick to knock the berries off onto the tarp. These berries are cleaned of leaves and stems and trash, washed and cooked in water to extract the flavorful juice for the jelly, which is delicious. I also made jelly from prickly pear apples. The cacti with the large purple pears were best for jelly. You needed to singe the small red spines off before boiling the pears in water. They made a pale pink jelly with a mild flavor. I tried using mesquite beans; but though I used the best red streaked beans, when cooked the juice smelled like mice so I did not make it into jelly, but threw it away.

242

When I was a child at EV Ranch we gathered wild mulberries in the Wildcat pasture, but I guess they did not survive the drought of the 1930s, as we did not find them later. Red haws grew around the springs of water at the Cowden Ranch on Gomez Peak but did not survive the drought of the 1950s when some of the springs dried up.

**Chance has many strong points**, but mathematics is not one of them. 1990-91 had been a hard year for me. Unknown to me, my children planned to give a birthday party for me. For several years Tim had hosted a barbeque on July 4 for family and friends. They decided to have this surprise birthday party in conjunction with Tim's barbeque. Blackie and I had not attended these barbeques before. We were urged to come for this one. I am sure they told Blackie their plans, but I was in the dark.

Despite the summer heat we drove to Tim's, north of Fort Worth. During the barbeque dinner they brought out this beautifully decorated cake with "Happy 75th" on it, and gave me a lovely amethyst ring. I was really surprised. We would have all been surprised if I had been one to keep track of ages. I never think of age as pertaining to myself. When filling out papers calling for age, I have to do some subtraction. I do know the year I was born. The next year our children were together and talk turned to ages and birth years. Tim, who is good at math realized and stated, "Mother wasn't 75 last year. She was only 74." We have all laughed about that 75th surprise birthday party.

**Growing old has many disadvantages and disillusionments.** I am fortunate to be loved, respected and treated as the personality I still am by my family and friends. I am thankful that my memory and mentality are still fairly good. My looks I do the best I can with despite the ravages of time. I try to dress as neatly as possible. On a recent trip with my daughter, Chance, we checked in at a nice motel. Two young girls were working the front desk. As the one who waited on us got the information and papers prepared, I gave her my credit card. She ran it through and then pointedly asked Chance, "Can she sign it?" I was so stunned at such outright blatant rudeness that I could not say anything. I was offended, insulted, and felt as if I had been slapped in the face. I signed in a firm, decisive manner and exited the lobby. I would hate to be remembered as I remember that insultingly disrespectful girl. Oh well, she may be old someday.

**Mexico Mission Trip 1989**   A group from my church planned a trip to Cuauhtémoc, Mexico, to help people in church there hold Vacation Bible Schools. Our pastor was bilingual and knew the pastor at Cuauhtémoc. I thought that would be an interesting experience, though my Spanish was limited. I had helped with a group of Mexican ladies who did not speak English. We taught them to sew bags and pillows out of upholstery fabric donated by a company in Waco. These ladies were clean, in clean starched and ironed dresses, but they had not yet learned of underarm deodorants. I had made some trips to villages across the Rio Grande River in Mexico teaching the women and girls to sew tote bags. This was something they could use. These people had so little of material things.

Cuauhtémoc is a city of about 100,000 people in the foothills of a mountainous region, with high mountains rising to the west of it. It is 7,000 feet in altitude at Cuauhtémoc. It is some seventy miles southwest of Chihuahua City. Though such a large city, there were not many paved streets. In the outer fringes of the city the pot holes and mounds of trash made driving hazardous. The paved streets surrounded only the central plaza and downtown business district consisting of a few two or three-story buildings.

We were to take sleeping bags. The women in the group would unroll their sleeping bags on the church pews; the men on the floor in the halls or other rooms. The women of the church would prepare our meals in the church kitchen. We would give them money to purchase the ingredients. We drove in our church bus, an old school bus, to Presidio, the Port of Entry. There was quite a delay there, as the Spanish Bibles and Vacation Bible literature we were taking had to be transferred to the pickups of Presidio natives. Mexico was under strong communist leadership at that time. No Bibles or Christian literature could be taken through Customs. After the usual wait of checking our birth certificates through Customs, we were issued *touristas* visas. We then drove to a house in Ojinaga and picked up our boxes of Spanish literature and Bibles. They were not inspected at checkpoints farther on. We were merely "*touristas*" in a bus with First Baptist Church painted on the sides. As we neared Chihuahua City the communist logos on telephone and highline poles and walls became more numerous. It looked like we might have been in Russia except for the Spanish captions. I began to understand why my husband had not wanted me to go on this trip to Mexico.

The church at Cuauhtémoc had sent two young men to escort us from Ojinaga to Cuauhtémoc. As it was getting to be supper time as we came to Chihuahua City, we asked if they knew of a good place to eat. We envisioned a quaint Mexican café. They guided us through many winding streets and turns to a very American Kentucky Fried Chicken. They probably wondered why we laughed so heartily.

A young couple waiting with the rest of the congregation insisted that an older woman, a frail-looking woman, and I stay at their apartment. I asked if they had "dos camas." "Oh, *sí,*" they assured me. I didn't know how to say "extra beds" in Spanish. I asked again, "*dos camas?*" and they replied, "*Sí, sí.*" They were correct. The older woman who was not feeling well was shown to one bedroom. The frail woman and I were shown to the other bedroom.

The apartment and linens were spotlessly clean. The young couple and their three-year-old daughter slept on a blanket on the living room floor. Such hospitality! I had never had anyone give their bed to me and sleep on the floor. They were most gracious. There was a large white-tiled bathroom at least 10 feet square, complete with a shower, but no hot water. Brrr! Even in July, at 7,000 feet altitude that water was cold. It didn't take long to shower. They were saving money to buy a water heater.

There I tasted my first mangos. They had a large box of mangos in the kitchen. I could never decide if I really liked their taste. Certainly not well enough to pay the price they are here in the States. When they learned it was my birthday they sang *"Feliz Cumpleaños"* and recorded it on tape for me.

At the church each morning we were divided into two groups to go to outlying communities to hold Vacation Bible Schools. A woman from the church told the Bible story. We helped with crafts and refreshments of cookies and Kool-Aid. The children were eager to learn, as were the women who crowded around. We returned to the church for lunch the women had prepared. The food was good but extremely hot with chili. Our pastor explained that we were not used to such hot chili and they tried to tame it down, but it was still very hot.

The bathroom at the church was typical of many foreign countries. It had a shower for cold water and a six-inch hole in the floor to the sewer with no P-trap. A place you did not visit except in absolute necessity.

Some of the group discovered within two blocks of the church there was a Baskin Robbins ice cream parlor. We all had to check that out. The ice cream was brightly-colored and extremely sweet. One afternoon we visited the Mercado. It was a duplicate of the one in

*Cuidad* Juarez, except it was larger and had a balcony of shops surrounding the main floor. They had the same brightly-colored woven blankets and serapes, pottery, jewelry, and leather goods and Mexican curios. I visited a shop that had only cut glass—beautiful, sparkling cut glass. The group was not interested and was ready to leave before I bought any cut glass. I thought I would have another opportunity, but I regret that I didn't.

We visited a large Mennonite settlement near Cuauhtémoc. These Mennonites are German and still speak the German language and have their schools in German. The boys are allowed to learn Spanish but the girls are not supposed to know Spanish. From the way these pretty little girls smiled when we asked them questions in Spanish, I think they knew what we said. The language prohibition is supposed to prevent inter-marriage with the Mexicans. We had several round-faced, blonde or red-headed children in our Vacation Bible groups. These Mennonites had very thrifty and productive farms and orchards. They had John Deere tractors for farm work. Their buggies and family wagons were pulled by horses, with an occasional one pulled by tractor. These family wagons were enclosed wooden box-like carriages with seats inside. The men wore straight-brimmed felt or straw hats to town. The women wore sailor-style wide-brimmed hats. The married women's hats had wide black ribbon bands and streamers in the back. The unmarried girls wore the same style hats but with white ribbons and streamers. We saw some women in Chihuahua City wearing long navy flower-printed dresses and little lacy white caps holding their hair at the backs of their heads.

We went through their cheese factory. I bought a two-pound wooden box of cheese but it had a flavor too strong for my taste. The pastor of our church and another man each bought buggies which were made by these Mennonites. These buggies were shipped to them at Van Horn. This colony had a thriving business of manufacturing buggies for the Amish and Mennonites. There are also some Mormon colonies in northern Mexico. The best high school principal—and later superintendent—at Van Horn was from the Mormon colony of Las Colonias.

Each evening we had preaching at the church, in Spanish of course. Their a cappella singing was beautiful. They had no piano. We sang the familiar hymns in English while they sang in Spanish. Truly in Christ we are one.

It was sorrowfully that we bade these warm and friendly people *"Adios."* On the trip back to Ojinaga we were delayed at one checkpoint. I think the soldiers were wanting some *"peloncillo"* to cross their palms. To be back in Presidio made me thankful that I lived in Texas in the good old USA.

# HATS I HAVE WORN

## For Love

1. Daughter (niece, sister, aunt)
2. Teacher
3. Wife
4. Mother
5. Grandmother
6. Great grandmother
7. Housekeeper
8. Gardener
9. Floral Arranger
10. Furniture Refinisher
11. Upholsterer
12. Chef – special occasions
13. Laundress
14. Hostess

15. Bookkeeper

16. Painter
17. Carpenter
18. Chauffeur—15 miles to school bus
19. Go-getter for parts
20. Club Woman – Pres. (every office but treasurer)
21. Windmill Assistant
22. Assistant Cattle Feeder
23. Assistant Cattle Worker

## For Pay

1. House Cleaner
2. Laundress
3. Alterations Specialist
4. Designer
5. Shirt Maker
6. Sales for Skin Care
7. Market Director
8. Skin Specialist
9. Color Analyst
10. Wardrobe Advisor
11. Quilt Maker
12. Doll Maker
13. Knitter
14. 1990 Courier, Special Agent for Census
15. 2000 Crew Leader for 4th largest county in Texas

24. Vet's Assistant
25. Manager
26. Purchasing Agent
27. Firefighter
28. Wallpaperer
29. Public Speaker – Class (certificate Christian Leaders    &
　　　　　　　　Speakers seminar)
30. Author

**Blackie was scheduled for cataract surgery** in El Paso, so we drove to Chance's home the afternoon before. On that Sunday there had been a young teenager at the church she attended who said his folks were away and that he had no place to go. The pastor took this teen home for lunch, but the pastor himself had to go to another city and could not keep this boy. Chance volunteered to take him to her home, where he stayed that night. The next day Chance took him to work with her and showed him how to play Solitaire on the computer. This boy was still at her home when we arrived that evening. While we were eating supper, he came to the door and said he was going out and would be back in a while. After supper I thought of something I wanted from our car. When I went outside to get it, our car was gone from the driveway. This kid had stolen it. Upon checking my purse, my car keys and the money in my wallet were gone too. We phoned the police and reported the car stolen, giving them the description and license number. The current fate of cars stolen in El Paso was that they were driven across the bridge to Juarez and promptly dismantled to be sold for parts in the United States, as well as Mexico. I felt so sorry for Chance as she cried because she felt she was to blame for this happening. The next morning she took us for Blackie's eye surgery. That afternoon the police called that they had found our car. Such good news! That boy and his girlfriend were driving it around in Horizon City, a suburb of El Paso. We could pick it up at a certain wrecking yard where it was unhurt, but had been towed. All we had to do was pay the towing charge to get it. The young boy had been taken to the Juvenile Detention Center where he was well-known. At age fifteen he was a professional thief. In the trunk of our car there was a man's dress jacket, a cocktail glass, and a red rose. Evidently this young couple had partied on my money.

**Once during our church service**, an usher called my husband, Blackie, to the telephone. I had some anxious moments while he was gone. Who but one of our children would know to call there?

251

And they would call there only in an emergency.  He sat down when he returned, so I knew it had not been bad news.  After church he told me the sheriff had called to tell him to stay in town until further notified.  The deputies were chasing someone who had stolen a saddle and a Volkswagen from our neighbor, the doctor, and was heading toward our house.  They were afraid he might "hole up" in our house and they did not want us coming into such danger.  I thought it was quite a commendation of Blackie's character and habits that the sheriff knew where to find him between 11 a.m. and noon on Sunday morning.

**My Evans family and friends enjoyed doing things together—** movies, stage shows, and such in El Paso where my brother Paulie and wife, Myrtle, lived.  We were not sports fans but enjoyed many other activities.  When these entertainments were over, Paul and Myrtle would invite us all to their home for mealtime.  Myrtle had the amazing ability to go into the kitchen and, with the contents of the refrigerator and freezer and supplies on hand, in a short time have not just a meal, but a feast, prepared.  She was an accomplished artist at this.  Myrtle had one of those hard-sided Samsonite suitcases that a heavy man could stand on without denting it.  When the crowd exceeded the number of their chairs, she would say, "Of course we have enough chairs.  Paulie, get the suitcase."  This suitcase, when stood on its end, made a sturdy seat.

**My sister, Frances, and her husband, Charles Carpenter**, bought their first motor home about 1978.  This was just a boxed-in truck with empty space behind their seats where they could put their bed.  I rode to Dallas with them, sitting on a folding chair behind their seats.  On curves this chair would slide with the curve.  It was a wild ride.  They progressed from this to real motor homes with kitchen and bath.  They really enjoyed traveling.  They went to Alaska on the Alcan Highway while it was being built, the first of several trips to Alaska.  They visited all forty-nine continental states.  They also visited Hawaii, the fiftieth state, but of course not in the motor home. Charles was a carpenter by ability as well as by name, so they went on many trips where they helped build churches as members of Campers on Missions.

**Blackie's mother, Eva Woods, was in the hospital** in Breckenridge, Texas, and was to have major surgery the next morning. The weather was bad when we left EV Ranch to go to Breckenridge, over 500 miles away. We came to ice-covered bushes at Kent, and from there the weather and the highway worsened. At Colorado City the snow was getting deeper. There was almost no traffic. Blackie was an excellent driver, so we kept going to Abilene where we usually exited I20 to go to Albany and Breckenridge on Highway 351. Highway 351 to Albany was covered with snow about seven inches deep, with not a car track or anything to define the highway. That was too risky to attempt to travel that deserted stretch of road covered in that much snow. We returned to I20 and planned to exit at Cisco and go north on Highway 576 to Breckenridge. Before we reached Cisco we saw a snow-covered car out in the middle of a field south of I20. The tracks showed this car had been westbound and had skidded across the median and the eastbound lanes and come to rest in that field 200 yards from I20 without turning over. What a ride that must have been! A car full of people had passed us at about Sweetwater and then drove very conservatively ahead of us. The road was icy underneath the snow and very slick. After we had followed this car at least 150 miles of steady driving, as the driver started up the rise of an overpass his car skidded and came to rest balanced on the guardrail of the overpass. These people jumped out of the car and looked underneath it. They were unhurt but very concerned about their car. Since they were unhurt, Blackie did not try to stop lest he go into a skid too. How that car stopped exactly balanced on the guardrail with the rear wheels not touching the road and the front wheels hanging out in space atop the overpass was a miracle. It had looked to us that the car would careen off the overpass and fall onto the crossroad below. It was a big heavy car but it did not collapse the guardrail. It was snaky, terror-stricken driving on that snow-covered icy road to Cisco and on to Breckenridge. Not even DPS patrolmen were on the road. Breckenridge was iced in but Blackie made the drive successfully.

Several years later I had scheduled a skin care demonstration with a woman and her daughters in Kent, Texas. The weather was cold that afternoon but didn't look threatening as I drove to Kent. I drove the 42 miles to Kent, conducted the demonstration, visited with these friends and prepared to leave. Imagine my surprise to see my car covered with snow, and the roads all looked like level ground with the snow. It had been quietly snowing all the time I had been in this friend's house. I needed to be home, so I started driving through this trackless snow. Thankfully, it was a divided highway and there were no other cars on it. I had only the occasional posts marking the culverts to steer by. After the very scary driving through the hills, the highway straightened out and I could see one set of taillights in the distance ahead. I was driving a Chrysler New Yorker, a big heavy car that held the road well. The snow was deep but it was not icy underneath. I carefully drove on, keeping in sight of those taillights. That is all I had to steer by, for the snow covered the tracks between my car and those taillights. It was hairy driving. Not a track had been made through the snow when I exited I20 to Highway 90, a two lane highway. I drove as carefully as I knew how and prayed for protection and guidance. I was the first car to travel that expanse of road to our home. What a relief when I safely reached the carport at our home.

Driving in a bad dust storm is almost on a par with driving in snow and ice for danger. Your visibility can be restricted to less than the length of the hood of your car. It must be like flying blind. Upon leaving the paved areas of El Paso there were only sand dunes along the two-lane Highway 80. It felt as though giant shovels threw yards of sand over my car with great force. I did not dare stop lest someone behind me see my taillights, assume that I was moving and drive into my car. There was nothing to do but inch along the road as best I could. Driving was somewhat better after I left the area of sand dunes at Ft. Hancock. After I passed Sierra Blanca the road made a dip into a low place. Immediately ahead looked to be a semi truck. I put on my brakes to avoid running into it. Then I could see there was no truck; there was only the exact image left through the thick dust where the truck had pushed away the dust. It was an eerie sight. Weather can be a formidable foe, in our driving experience.

**Census 1990 was advertising for workers**. I thought that might be something interesting to do now that we lived close enough to town to take part in things. I took the test and passed; the tester got her quota before she got to me. That **W** again?

The Field Office Supervisor was a very uptight, harried, nervous man. Before the test I had heard him say that he needed someone to drive him. He had a very large sector—from Pecos to Alpine to Marfa, Presidio and Van Horn—about a 400 mile circuit. Since I had not been selected for enumerator but had passed the test, I asked him if he really meant what he said about needing a driver. He said, Come into this office and let's talk." I seemed to meet his needs, so he hired me. I think he got into trouble with the El Paso office for that, but they made a place for me and I served in various capacities. Census 1990 was not the strictly structured organization it was in 2000. He was very proper about this. He had me drive to Pecos for a meeting at his house and to meet his wife. He made a point to meet my husband. His wife told me that he had told her, "I have hired me a sophisticated lady." Perhaps because for anything in town I dressed a little more professionally than what I wore for house work.

I furnished my car but was paid mileage. I drove him many,

many miles. He slept a lot, especially at first. I really think I may have saved his life. The agitated state he was in, the way he was so distracted by his responsibilities, he was almost sure to have had a wreck had he driven himself.

I was called to find a man in Sierra Blanca that the enumerators had not been able to locate. Arriving in Sierra Blanca, I went to the kitchen of the main café. The Mexican women who work in kitchens know everything. Sure enough, they told me where to find him—at the town dump. He was most cordial and helpful, insisting that I get out. He smelled very strongly of alcohol, so I declined and conducted the interview from the security of my car. He informed me that his address was the Sierra Blanca Sanitary Landfill. I learned later that incident gave me quite a reputation in the El Paso office. I was just doing what they asked me to do. I had a number of special assignments like that. When called to Presidio to find some people, I went first to the City water office. I figured they would know the location of these addresses.

Presidio was booming—new buildings, newly bladed-off streets—and almost no street signs. A highway from the interior of Mexico to Ojinaga, the sister city to Presidio, was almost finished. The U.S. was building a new concrete bridge across the river with new Port-of-Entry buildings. People had come, I guess, from all over Mexico to these job opportunities. It was wild trying to locate any place. There was only the one paved street, a continuation of the highway from Marfa through two or three blocks of downtown businesses. Presidio had been just a sleepy little border town; now it was the fastest-growing Port-of-Entry on the Mexico border, thanks to NAFTA.

I knocked on one door; the woman who answered quickly led me through her kitchen and hallway to her living room. I had come to her back door. These people were very helpful. Though they spoke no English and I knew very little Spanish, we managed to communicate. They were very polite and respectful. There were no house numbers on the new dwellings. There would be a house, like a giant octopus, with long extension cords and water hoses running from it to mobile homes, little shacks, and new houses, all sharing utilities. The man from the Water Office was an invaluable help.

I served as Courier, driving the 100 miles to Pecos, picking up the paperwork from the Crew Leader, returning to Van Horn, another 100 miles, to meet the Courier from Marfa to turn this paperwork over to the Courier from El Paso 120 miles away. Distance is a factor in West Texas. We did not have the services of FedEx then.

A position with the Census is an appointment, and a person cannot be fired. The situation can become such that the person will resign. There was a Crew Leader in Alpine who thought she knew the area better than the ones preparing the maps for zoning the area. She proceeded to redo the maps. This could not be tolerated, for her unit was not getting on with enumerating. The U.S. Census Bureau is a full-time functioning organization. Their workers work full-time year-round, every year. The maps are from aerial photographs. They are very accurate and detailed. The map of our ranch showed not only the house, but the barns, sheds, pump house, roads, ditches, and cow trails—any little indentation. It was necessary to have this woman resign.

My FOS called me to meet him at a certain restaurant in Alpine at noon. The waitress brought his meal just as this woman arrived. The FOS started eating with gusto while asking her about things she had not done that she should have. She got very flustered. The FOS said, "If you walk out, that's it." As she got more upset, she walked away, but returned. The FOS kept telling her that if she walked out that would be all. She would be through with the Census. Finally she did walk out. The FOS told me goodbye.

As soon as I got home from the 100-mile drive from Alpine, the telephone rang. My FOS told me to write all I had seen and heard in Alpine and send it to the main office in El Paso. That I did, and was later called to come to El Paso and give that report to the man in charge there. I was glad I had kept a copy of that report, because I was called from the office in Dallas to give that report. This woman had appealed to OSHA but evidently didn't get anywhere because I was not called to testify in person.

**My husband, Beary (Blackie) Woods, was the healthiest person I have ever known.** He was never sick. He was physically strong and able to work long hours of hard work, day after day. In April 1993 at age 85, he detected blood in a stool and went to our family doctor in Van Horn. Dr. Lipsey sent him to a doctor of internal medicine in El Paso. This doctor discovered a malignant tumor which had almost blocked the colon. He wanted to operate the next day. Blackie persuaded him that he needed a few days to arrange for the care of his hunting dogs, mules and cattle. The surgery was scheduled for the first week in May.

All five of our children came to El Paso to be with us. This was the most shattering thing that had ever happened to our family. Our stalwart cowboy husband and father was in a condition leading to death. Everyone has a dread of the diagnosis of cancer, especially when it is far advanced. Friends and relatives and our pastor came to the hospital the day of the surgery to support us with their love and prayers. The surgeon reported he had removed the tumor and nine inches of the colon, but the cancer had spread to the entire lymph system. On a scale of 1 to 4, with 4 the stage preceding death, Blackie's condition was rated stage 3.

With cancer you don't know what to do. You are at the discretion of the doctors. We were told Blackie's oncologist would be Dr. Blank. This doctor set up a schedule of chemotherapy of an injection of a very toxic substance every day for a week, then once a week for a year. With so many injections to be done, doctors advised implanting a portacath—a device surgically inserted into the chest above the heart with a tube draining directly into the heart. A diaphragm at skin level was for the needles to be inserted for dispensing the toxic chemical through a tube directly into the heart. Besides these injections, Blackie was to take some pills before each treatment. These pills were the same chemical that is used to treat animals for grubs of the heel fly and other parasites by pouring a small amount on the animal back. It penetrates through the skin and all through the animal's body. These pills must have been too toxic for us to keep on hand. The pharmacist in El Paso would deliver them the day or night before use. Obviously the profit on those four pills was great enough for them to be delivered to our ranch, a 300 mile trip.

We followed this routine for about 4 months. Blackie was getting worse instead of better. Everyone in the area around Van Horn who had chemotherapy or radiation was now dead—not a good prognosis. I knew a woman who had breast cancer who was still alive. I visited her to find where she went for treatment. She told me she went to Baylor Medical Hospital in Dallas. You can't just go to Baylor Medical and say, "I want to see a doctor." But when she said Dallas, I knew a cardiologist in Dallas to give us a referral. I called him and learned that he used new alternative methods of treatment in his practice and treated cancer with great survival success. We went to Dallas.

This fine Christian doctor used methods and substances to build up the body's own immune system so that your own body overcame the cancer. Blackie started on this regimen and soon began to feel better. He had stopped the chemotherapy that was making him worse. Our family doctor advised us to stop the chemo.

As a check on his condition, once a month a vial of his blood was sent to a laboratory in Boston which used a very accurate method of testing for cancer. This blood sample had to be frozen by the laboratory in Van Horn and packed in dry ice to be shipped to Boston. It could not be used for an accurate test if it was thawed when it reached the lab in Boston. Sometimes UPS overnight delivery was delayed and the blood was thawed. We would have to try again. The lab technician in Van Horn was very helpful—an expert technician and a fine Christian man.

Blackie continued to feel better and stronger. After about four or five months of this doctor's regimen several of the blood tests showed *no cancer*. I had noticed a strong odor about Blackie's body and told this doctor. His response, "Could it be dead cancer cells?" Evidently it was that, for when the cancer was gone, so was the odor. Blackie continued following this doctor's regimen and was completely cancer-free for the twelve remaining years of his life. He did not die of cancer.

**Census 2000 was advertising for workers** in Culberson County. My experience in Census 1990 had been an interesting and pleasant one; so I applied, passed the test, and was told the training sessions would be in Pecos the next week. I drove the 200 miles to Pecos and home each day. I hate the loneliness of hotels. There was only one other woman, also from Van Horn, in the class. We were issued manuals. I soon realized the leader was reading from the manual. I thought he was not well-prepared, but found out that was what he was supposed to do. You are taught to follow this well-prepared manual literally—no ad-libbing. When the training session was over, I was told that I would be the Crew Leader and the other woman would be my enumerator. My car trunk was filled with boxes of maps of Culberson County and sections of two adjacent counties, Jeff Davis and Hudspeth. That was my sector. My office and assembly room was in the Convention Center, the nicest public building in Van Horn. I was soon assigned several more enumerators. I felt at a loss because I had not been trained for Crew Leader. I knew that one woman in my crew had been trained in El Paso as Crew Leader. She was a good friend, so I asked if she had a crew Leader's manual. She did, and graciously let me borrow it. Studying that manual was my training for Crew Leader.

Culberson County, though sparsely populated, is the fourth largest county in Texas in area. There are only two towns in the county— Van Horn, the county seat, and Kent, a small community with a sub-post office, filling station, and general store. Everything except the post office is owned by the Long X Ranch. Any children were bused to Van Horn for school. Part of Guadalupe National Park is in Culberson County.

The Field Office Supervisor (FOS) was a competent young man and an invaluable help to me. He knew how to fix it if I messed up. My crew consisted of a Hispanic school teacher who was a very productive enumerator. She worked after school hours and weekends and equaled or bettered full time workers.

There were two married couples—one man a retired Border Patrol officer who knew the county well, and his pleasant and skilled wife. As for the other couple, he had been a navigator in the Navy. The maps he drew looked as precise as blueprints. Everyone else's were rude sketches. His wife was a tireless worker and would tackle any situation and do it well. She had worked for Census 1990. There was a town woman who had some trouble staying in her assigned area. Then there was Maria. Maria could not remember which corner of her map to start enumerating. She would encounter these people who said they had already been counted; and they had. Maria had started on the wrong side of the street and was working an area that someone else had already done. But Maria's accounts of her experiences kept us all laughing. Someone would volunteer to go with her the next morning and get her started off right.

A unit from El Paso was sent to help us. They were really no help. Several years before, an organization, probably the Chamber of Commerce, had erected signs at all street intersections throughout Van Horn. These signs were easily lifted off the posts. Many of these signs now decorated teenagers' rooms or were just vandalized. This was not a handicap to natives of Van Horn who not only knew where each citizen lived, but also everyone else who had lived at that place. For these people from El Paso it was utterly demoralizing. This put them at a total loss as to how to find a location. I didn't even try sending them out of the city limits.

If a structure had windows and a door but now one lived there, it was listed on the census. The enumerators found many vacancies, so many, in fact, we were instructed to re-canvass some areas. My enumerators were correct; there were that many vacancies.

Census appointees are sworn not to talk about any information given them by the people they interviewed. After the census was completed this information was categorized and the totals made available to government agencies and businesses for long-range planning purposes. Information of individuals is not released until after 37 years have elapsed.

After we finished enumerating in my sector, I was sent to Fort Stockton in Pecos County to help with the census there. I was required to attend several training sessions in El Paso for clean-up work. This consisted of double-checking to verify facts or make sure no one was counted twice.

My crew encountered some people who claimed they had been counted in February. Census did not begin in Culberson County until the latter part of March 2000. I found these people were correct. Advance census workers travel over areas to confirm certain things. They are full-time employees of the Census Bureau. They work every year preparing for the census every ten years. The census is such an expensive undertaking they told us it would not be done in this manner again. I think it will be done by computers and Social Security numbers. *Quien sabe?*

I worked through January 2001, when I was terminated January 31, 2001. An unforgettable experience.

**In 2004, Tommy Lee Jones,** movie star and producer, filmed parts of several movies in the Van Horn-Trans Pecos area—Lonesome Dove and its prequel, etc. When he was filming "The Three Burials" in Van Horn, word around town was that they wanted elderly women to be in the filming. That was something I felt I could qualify for, so I applied, as did about every other woman in Van Horn who was past middle age and would admit it.

I was impressed by the attractive, friendly and efficient young people working in the office and in all other capacities. They took my statistics and my picture and said, "Don't call us; we will call you." They called and took another picture and again, "Don't call— we will call." To my surprise they called me to be on location at 7:30 the next morning.

On location the wardrobe girl checked the changes of clothes I had been instructed to bring, okayed the clothes I had worn, and told me to wait. I found there is a lot of waiting in making a movie while the filming and other crews get the lighting, sound and cameras set up. We waited in the supply room at the back of the grocery store where the filming was to take place. One young man's sole job was to stand with Tommy Lee and hold two six-packs. These he handed to Tommy Lee when the filming started, and Tommy Lee carried them to the cash register, then handed them back to the young man.

I was the grandmother shopping for supplies to make a birthday cake. As the camera ran, I pushed the shopping cart to the checkout area. For a second take I walked slowly from the aisle to the front of the store. All of the waiting and the few seconds of filming took over three hours. I was paid minimum wage for an eight-hour day.

Alas, since there was no sex or dirty words in the scenes I was in, they were not used in the movie.

**Shopping in a modern supermarket** such as I found after moving to Lubbock in 2005 is an overwhelming experience for me. I am awed and confused at such an abundance of products. My previous shopping experience has not prepared me for these immense supermarkets. In the small towns that were my only shopping source, there would be perhaps two grocery stores with five or six short aisles of products. Shopping in either store was easy, as there would be only one brand of any product. Occasionally the larger store might have a choice of, say white flour or wheat flour. The choices were limited and thus simplified. If they had one kind of a product, you got it—if they didn't, he had to do something else. If oatmeal was on your list you might have to decide on Quaker's quick-cooking or regular. Then Surefine products became available and you had to be careful, for Surefine had a duplicate of each other product. You had to make a choice of which was a better product or a better buy.

In the small community where my husband grew up, a man had a little store of staple foods, but if he had only one of any item he wouldn't sell it. He would say, "If I sold you that I would be plumb without." You were out of luck if you didn't have any sugar at home. He would not sell his last sack of sugar, or whatever.

My son in Dallas had a story to tell his friends when I said I needed ice trays but I could buy only one because that was all they had in the store. The other store in town didn't have even one. He got a lot of mileage out of telling that story to his Dallas friends.

I find that I am a very visual shopper. I do not remember brand names well. I look for an item by how the package looks—its color and decoration. This can foul me up when the packaging is changed in order to "new—improve it," or when a different product is offered in a similar package. Also, items above my eye level pose a problem. Recently I have needed to limit my sugar intake to raise my pH level by drinking lemon juice in water. To make this more palatable without using sugar, I thought about the product, Splenda, which I had heard about. I began to look for it in this huge supermarket. I was lucky. It was only five aisles away and at the other end of the second aisle. On a high shelf I spied Splenda. I reached up and got a small package I thought would fill my need and dropped it into the basket. At home I opened the package, pulled out and opened the pencil-sized packet, and poured it into the lemon water. Just as I noticed it made the lemon water look milky, I read on the packet, "flavored with French vanilla creamer." Who would have ever thought of flavored Splenda? It sure made the lemonade taste funny.

**"I'm taking you down for an MRI,"** announced the young man. So here is another uncomfortable transfer from my bed to his speed wagon. Out we go through miles of hallways at top speed, despite the speed bumps. They forgot to equip hospital beds with shock absorbers. Finally, we reach the elevators to the nether regions where the latest torture machines are. We go to the basement where, like the dungeons of old, the machines of the worst torture are.

Now, the preparation for this endurance contest. Unlike other endurance contests, there is no training for buildup of stamina. This test comes after a miserable, restless, sleepless night. The technician explains this machine is somewhat noisy and puts earplugs in my ears. "Somewhat noisy" is the understatement of all time. My head is fitted with a football facemask-like device with (thankfully) more padding over my ears. It is impossible to move my head in this helmet contraption. They slide me headfirst into this monster's belly—my face a mere four inches below his cruel upper mouth. Being in these close quarters is almost claustrophobic for me. I have never liked to be in close places. Even the Cave at Bloys took a lot of nerve for me to go through.

There was an empty metal water tank mounted on a wagon at EV Ranch that had in the past been used to haul water to the cattle. It was about 3 feet in diameter and 8 feet long with an opening in the center top just big enough for a child to squeeze through. When my many cousins visited, one of the daring activities was for everyone to enter this hole and crowd into the empty water tank. Since I lived at EV Ranch, I would "let" the others go in first. With eight or nine cousins, it became crowded in the tank. I always made some excuse to keep from going in until last so that I would be closest to the exit. If I could, I would fudge a little and not go completely inside—leave my head or upper body out the exit hole. Only to keep from being "chicken" could I even begin to enter the tank. I think of that water tank now, and my excuses don't work. I start to plan how I will write about this MRI experience.

Deadly quiet—then the riveters start. Rosie had nothing to compare with these for speed, velocity, and power. They do enough riveting to put three battleships together. After a lull the jackhammers take over, tearing up acres of concrete directly below me. Now it is the electric hammer's turn. It sure is not Woody Woodpecker. They stole his idea and multiplied it—whamity, whamity, whamity to 50,000 times per minute.

The cannons begin—no mere 17 gun salvo this—they do not have to wait to reload. The cannons in the 1812 Overture are by comparison toy pop guns. The decibels and vibrations continue until, thankfully, the machine has run through its full cycle.

Back from the MRI just before breakfast is brought, the bone doctor arrives to examine my knee. With his wicked needle-equipped vial he drains what seems like a half-gallon of nasty-looking goop. From this he decides I must have surgery for him to drain and wash out the knee joint. So it is NPO—no breakfast or even water that day. My mouth already feels like it is full of cotton balls. So much for the awaited cup of hot coffee . . .

Hospital gowns are noted for their discomfort and lack of fit. The ones I was expected to wear would have fit the household refrigerator better than my size 4 petite frame. But the most uncomfortable feature was the fabric itself. In my past hospital stays the gowns were of smooth cotton fabric. Not so at Covenant. Now I have a good idea of the sackcloth of the Bible—the roughness of the weave against the human skin. That, in fact, would be a symbol of your grief or repentance. When I could no longer abide the abrasive cloth against my old and tender skin, and the many lumps and wads of excess fabric under and around me, I would slip the gown off and cover with the sheet. The aides especially were concerned that I did not wear a gown. When my daughter brought my sleepwear, one of the aides lifted a garment from the bag and exclaimed, "No wonder she don't like our gowns. Hers are silk!"

**Blackie was not your usual cowboy**, known for never walking except to his horse. There was even a lot of walking with his hunting, from where he would have to leave his mule and walk and climb to where his dogs had a lion cornered. He continued to walk the one-fourth mile from our house down the lane to the county road and back up the slope to the house, a total distance of one-half mile, at least once a day even after he had sold his mule and no longer rode. His once eagle-eyed eyesight had been impaired by macular

267

degeneration.  He carried a cane when he walked—the cane that had served him for catching sheep by the neck with the curved end of the cane, as shepherds had done for thousands of years.  But he did not use it for walking; he carried the 37-inch cane under one arm.  One morning he noticed something at the side of the road where he walked that looked out of place. He punched the object with the tip of his cane.  When it coiled he realized it was a rattlesnake.  That cane was the only weapon available to vanquish the snake.  He started striking the snake with his cane until the snake no longer moved and was left for dead.  Blackie continued his walk.  Later that morning our son, Beary, drove up the lane and, seeing the dead rattlesnake by the roadside, stopped to investigate.  This very dead snake had a gash six inches long in his length, obviously made with an object applied with great force.

After seventy years of courtship and marriage to this remarkable cowboy and rancher, Blackie Woods, he passed from this life into eternity.  Now in 2014 his family has five generations living under God's protective care.  Mine has indeed been a wonderful life.

# Assorted Stories

## TWO BEARS
### By Bill Vanderpool

When I answered the phone one evening last spring, I knew immediately who it was by the resounding, "FBI, Bill!" Jim Moore is one of the top lion guides in the country and guided Ted Rowe, SIGARMS' President, and me on a great trip back in '94 in West Texas. But it wasn't long-tails on Jim's mind that evening, but bears . . . black bears. "I've got a friend in Cloudcroft who is one of the top bear guides in New Mexico," Jim told me. "Glenn Hopkins has a great pack of bear dogs. He keeps asking me to come out and to bring a friend. Interested"

Does a ten-pound sack of flour make a big biscuit? Of course I was interested. Over the next couple of months all the details were ironed out except one. Which gun to use? Eventually, Jim and I started thinking about the .357 Sig. Jim had been so impressed with that gun's performance during our lion hunt that he acquired one. But would it be enough gun? I asked around and got advice from, "you'd be way under-gunned" to "should do the trick, as long as you can place the bullets." I knew I would need a deep penetrating bullet, preferably a hollow point, which meant the heaviest bullet available. With that I talked with Dave Embry, Hornady's chief ballistician. He recommended Hornady's 147 grain XPT. I ordered some and once they arrived I checked the zero on my personal 229 and found the heavier bullet printed only an inch or so high at 25 yards. Close enough for government work.

269

In October, Jim's bright smile greeted me as I got off the plane in El Paso. Before dark we were in Cloudcroft, hunting licenses in hand. Glenn Hopkins turned out to be a quiet, unassuming young man, except when he was poking fun at his good friend Jim, and vice versa. The entire trip was an outdoor version of the Odd Couple with no good-natured jab left undone.

Up at 4:00 a.m., "0:Dark Thirty" in Cloudcroft. Coffee and soggy sausage and biscuit sandwiches and a full day of trying to pick up fresh bear sign. Glenn's pickup was equipped with a steel dog box on back with a four-wheel ATV perched on top. Attached to the front bumper was an open dog box where three of his best dogs rode to check for scent along the mountain roads. Plenty of nibbles but nothing hot. We spent more time hunting dogs than bears. The scenery helped make up for the lack of bears. The quaking aspens were in full good and made a nice contrast to the stands of pines.

Up at four a.m. again the next day and back up those mountain roads in the dark. At one point we could look down on the lights of Alamogordo, the gateway to White Sands Missile Range. I had been stationed there as a young GI and this trip brought back lots of memories. During that time I had gotten hooked up with a rancher whose spread was north of Silver City and rode for him every chance I got. After discharge, I worked a ranch for him over on the Arizona-New Mexico border, near Duncan. Great memories? Yes. But a hard way to make a living.

Just about dawn we struck a hot trail. Glenn turned the dogs loose and they disappeared down the mountain in a barking frenzy. For the next hour or so we could follow their progress down the mountain, then lost the sound of their baying as they dipped into some deep canyon. Finally, way off, we heard them barking "treed." Now some folks doubt a hound can tell you when he hits pay dirt, but all I can say is that doubter has never been on a good lion or bear hunt. There is a difference when they get the critter stopped.

Glenn headed down and Jim and I followed shortly. After a rough half-hour of hiking we found Glenn and the dogs. And the bear. Perched about forty-five feet up the pine, it was dark brown, weighing perhaps 160 pounds. Not anywhere near a record but it was my first bear.

Glenn told me where to aim. I decided to take my own advice, given over many years to FBI trainees at Quantico. "If it's worth shooting, it's worth shooting twice." I double-tapped that bear right behind the shoulder and it came down hard, rolled a few yards and stopped . . . dead. Not a flicker. Again I was impressed with the stopping power of the .357 Sig. A nice trophy and even worth the long climb back up the mountain to the truck. I was a happy man.

Up the next morning, four a.m. of course. It was getting to be a habit. This time we were to try for Jim's bear. Glenn drove us in another direction, passing apple orchards and sheer cliffs in the dark. The headlights lit up the three dogs riding in front. They would bounce along, leaning over the side so they could pick up any scent from the road. Glenn was telling us, "The woman who owns that apple orchard we just passed has had trouble with a big bear raiding her farm. It has been tearing down limbs to get to the ripe apples. Perhaps we can help her out."

Less than ten minutes later we hit sign, fresh bear droppings on the dirt road. The dogs went wild. Glenn quickly turned them loose and they clamored up the mountain and kept going. Within a half-hour we couldn't hear them, nor could Glenn get a signal on his directional finder from their transmitter collars. Finally we drove through the canyon and around to the other side of the mountain range, checking as we went. Mid-morning found us up a rough road near one corner of the Mescalero Apache Reservation. Glenn picked up a faint signal, way up into a spectacular canyon. We unloaded the ATV. "I'll drive up as far as I can and see what I can find," he said. He disappeared up the rocky trail and Jim and I settled down to wait, and to catch up on lost sleep. An hour later Glenn was back. "I think they have something treed. They're way up a side canyon."

Jim and I hopped on the ATV with Glenn as best we could and started up. Jim is an ex-rodeo cowboy and that early occupation helped him on that wild ride up. We both managed to stay on but it was exciting. When the trail stopped, we climbed stiffly off and checked gear. Our holsters, from El Paso Saddlery, were designed for security, not speed, so we still had our pistols after that crazy ride. In the distance we could barely hear the dogs. Glenn started up the canyon, Jim and I following through the thick brush.

As we got closer, the dogs' baying seemed to become even more urgent. Glenn pulled ahead, worried about his pack of hounds. And for good reason, for as I pushed up the leaf-filled draw I stopped. Lying dead in the path was Freckles, one of Glenn's best trackers. He looked like he had been hit with 00 Buckshot, but they weren't bullet holes. They were bear bites, and by a big bear.

Winded, I pushed to the dogs. They had surrounded a tall pine, leaping six or more feet up the trunk in their exuberance. I looked up...and up. Sixty feet up was a huge black mass. As my eyes adjusted against the sky I saw the bear, lying over a limb while he watched the dogs below. We watched him for a while, taking pictures. Glenn tied up the dogs nearby and we held a woodland conference.

Glenn told us that was a big bear, the biggest he had treed this year, and it had already killed one of his dogs. "That bear has to come out of that tree dead," he said. It was agreed I would back Jim up, only in the event the bear wasn't hit hard. We got ready, guns up, watching, and Jim said he was ready. His shot rang out, followed by two more. My finger eased on the trigger as I saw that bruin start falling. He hit the ground with a thump and the dogs went wild. Jim and I covered the blackie with our pistols as it raised up, then dropped into the leaves. We watched him closely and then slowly approached. It was dead and I was awestruck. I had never seen a bear so big outside a zoo. His paws were as big as saucers—that is, if saucers had two-inch claws. The head was massive. Glenn estimated he was 375 pounds and we found little fat on him as we started skinning him. "He would hit close to five hundred just before hibernation," Glenn guessed. He looked at the pistol in Jim's holster. "That's some hard hitting gun. I'm impressed."

We buried the unfortunate hound and headed down, the huge pelt draped over Glenn's shoulders like a caveman's fur coat. Jim and I were two happy hunters and Glenn was pleased that his close friend had been so successful. The ATV ride down was even wilder, sharing the vehicle ride with that bear hide. We loaded the pickup, collected the dogs and headed back to Cloudcroft. As we drove down the twisting dirt road, Glenn commented, "Well, we saved a lot of bears' lives this morning." I looked at him in surprise. "How do you figure?" He told us that a bear that size, a male, would fight and try to kill any other male in the area and would also try to kill any cubs he encountered. "Did you see the scars on his head? That bear has been in a lot of fights."

We enjoyed a celebration dinner that evening and early the next morning (but not 4 a.m.) Jim and I headed south. We checked our bears in with the game department in Las Cruces and then continued to El Paso. The taxidermist there put a perfect ending to the trip. He measured the skull through the hide and estimated it would go over twenty inches. It looked like Jim had killed a bear for the Boone and Crockett record book. Two bears with pistols. Not bad for a couple of beat-up old cowboys.

**Remote Control Hunting**   A friend of Blackie's built his home on the banks of Barrilla Creek, a lower extension of Limpia Canyon. This home had an open porch where friend Len had his bed and liked to sleep rear round.  One January night while his teenaged sons were watching television he was awakened by feeling something unusual.  He opened his eyes to see a mountain lion by his bed and looking him in the face.  He called out as he jumped up.   The mountain lion quickly exited to the creek.  Len called friend Jim who had dogs and hunted mountains lions.  Jim and his daughter Holly were on their way home from seeing the El Paso Rodeo and were about an hour's drive from their home and dogs in Balmorhea.  Jim assured Len that he would come and bring his dogs as soon as he could get there.

Len ran after the lion who seemed in no hurry as she prowled leisurely up the creek.  When Jim arrived his dogs quickly picked up the scent and overtook the lion who had climbed a tall dead cedar tree. Jim said to his daughter, "Holly, go back to the pickup and bring my tranquilized gun.  We will take this lion alive."   The teenaged boys had left watching TV and joined the chase.  Someone, seeing an object in one boy's hand, asked, "Is that a pistol?"  No, it was the remote control for the television, still in his hand.

**TV Cow   A friend I have known all his adult life told me of this incident.**  He is a steady, level-headed rancher, honest and hard-working.   The cattle on his ranch were being rounded up.   A Mexican ranch hand came racing his horse full speed to the roundup, his eyes wide with terror—so scared he could only say, "TV cow, TV cow."  This was at a time when the news was full of accounts of killed and mutilated cattle on western farms and ranches.  This was thought to be the work of pagan cults which were prevalent then. After the cattle work was done, the ranch owner rode over to investigate.  He found one of his pregnant 2 year old heifers dead. She was lying in a circle of scorched-looking grass.  Her female

274

organs and lips had been removed. Otherwise she was untouched. There was no blood on the heifer or the surrounding ground. There were no footprints or car tracks around the area. As he monitored the scene, he found that the dead heifer did not decompose as the usual dead animal. The grass did not grow back on that scorched area. The coyotes and other scavengers, even the buzzards, did not eat from the carcass. *Quien sabe?*

## My First Lion Hunt

*As told to Lottie Woods by Jim Moore*

"Although I grew up in a small town in the Trans-Pecos area of Texas riding horses and mules on my uncles' ranches, and I had hunted mule deer, I did not know anything about hunting mountain lions with dogs. Friends of mine told me that they had seen a mountain lion close to their home at the Boy Scout Ranch deep in the Davis Mountains of far west Texas. They feared for the safety of their young child, since the lion had come so near their dwelling. They did not want a wild animal, a predator, to be so familiar with where they lived.

I had heard of Blackie Woods' reputation as a mountain lion hunter of the very highest caliber, and had been introduced to him by a mutual friend. Blackie's reputation was such that if you wanted a mountain lion caught, he was the hunter who could deliver the goods. A telephone call to Blackie brought his assent to come the next morning and bring his dogs. "Yes, I'll meet you at the gate to the Boy Scout Camp at 4:30 a.m. Bring me a mule to ride, as mine is barefoot and it is too late to shoe him tonight."

I always had a corral full of mules, so I picked a good gentle one for him. Blackie was about 72 years old at that time but could ride all day in rough mountains without lunch or even a drink of water. He had trained himself in his work of cowboying to drink 3 or 4 big glasses of water in the morning before he left the house, and that had to suffice; for most of the time there was nowhere to get a drink of water all day. He did not drink out of the stock tanks where the cattle did. He said he never thought about eating or drinking water (his only drink) while riding in the rough mountains without lunch or even a drink of water. His thoughts were on the dogs as they worked a trail. He would not be tired when he got home from hunting. This was usually after arising at or before 3:00 a.m. and driving his pickup anywhere from 50 to 200 miles to the place where he was to hunt. Then, it was that same distance back home.

The established procedure for hunting mountain lions with dogs is to arrive at a place as far as pickups can go 'way before daylight; leave the pickups and trailers, mount the saddled mules and ride on those dim mountain trails in the dark (no street lights) while the dogs spread out seeking the lion's scent as they had been bred and trained to do. That morning we followed that procedure to the place where the lion had been seen.

Blackie was riding first in line right after the dogs. An unwritten law of hunting with dogs is that no one ever rides ahead of the man with the dogs. Two other men were along this morning and I was bringing up the rear. The dogs started barking, indicating they had found the lion's fresh trail. These dogs don't bark until they have something to say. Our riding pace livened up. The sound of the dogs barking in the early dawn, echoing in the mountain canyons, was a new experience for me. I was a bronc rider and competed in rodeos and bronc riding contests. That was my forte. But I liked the music the dogs made. The harmony of each individual dog's voice blended into a sort of symphony which to the experienced hunter's ears told him what was happening.

Things were really happening that morning. The tone and tempo of the dogs' barking changed. At that time I didn't know what it meant. With his very subtle sense of humor, Blackie called back to me, "Jim, do you want to shoot this fox?" I looked ahead to where the dogs were excitedly clustered around a very tall tree. High up in the tree was a sizeable long tail hanging about three feet below a limb occupied by a very large animal. It was not yet good daylight, but I could tell it was too large for a fox. "That's no damn fox," I yelled as I dismounted, unsheathing my 30-30 rifle as I hurried to the scene of action. A well-placed shot brought the lion crashing down from the tree limb to the ground, where the dogs "wooled" him around, making sure their job was done and there was no more life left in the lion.

I hunted many more times with Blackie, learning about lions' habits, how to look for their "sign," how to know what the dogs are telling you—all clues to being a lion hunter. Although it was about two years from that time until I got some dogs of my own, front that first hunt I was hooked on lion hunting. It gets in the blood and you never get over it."

## Lion in a Crack

*As told to Lottie Woods by Jim Moore*

On a lion hunt with Blackie Woods the dogs had trailed a young mountain lion and bayed him in a crevice of a high rocky escarpment. Blackie decided we could take this lion alive and use him to train some young dogs.

The lion was backed up in a narrow crevice about 50 feet from the bottom of the bluff and about 20 feet from the top where Blackie and I were standing. There was a narrow ledge about a foot or so wide in front of the crevice where the lion was. It looked possible for a man to climb down to that ledge and get close enough to see the lion back in his safe hiding place.

277

I climbed down to this 2 foot wide ledge where I could see the lion. Blackie handed me his rope from off his saddle and said, "Here, get this rope on that lion." Well, I knew that when I attempted to rope that lion he would come out the only exit, and that was where I was standing. There wasn't room on that ledge for both of us. I didn't want to be the one falling off that 50 foot cliff to the rocks below. I handed the rope back to Blackie saying, "Rope him yourself if you want him alive." Blackie then handed me his .22 pistol. A .22 pistol was all he ever carried to shoot lions. I shot the lion, then noticed that was the last shell in that automatic pistol. "Blackie," I called, "there was only one shell in this pistol." "Well," replied Blackie, "there was only one lion, wasn't there?"

## HOW TO COOK STEAKS
*A friend I shall call Dan told me this story:*

Ranchers were and are the most dedicated conservationists. Long before these misguided people who call themselves "conservationists" took up the cause, ranchers were managing their land to husband it. If you take care of the land, it will take care of you. The government stepped in, and to make jobs for the new graduates in agricultural engineering, created an agency to tell the ranchers how to use their land. If you made some improvements according to their specifications and approval, they might pay some of the costs.

Rancher Dan had already been making a lot of improvements, diversion dams and tanks, pasture rotation, and thought maybe he could get some help with the costs. Such work with bulldozers is very expensive. The officials in this agency wanted to inspect his work. A field day was set up—the date set. Several carloads of men would come for a tour of his ranch. Dan would furnish a meal for them. Dan contacted a colorful character called Chicken Charley who had a café of that name about 100 miles away. He did some catering. Yes, he would fix a barbecue and bring it to Dan's ranch.

On the appointed day, Chicken Charley prepared the barbecue in his large portable pit he could pull behind his pickup, and started to Dan's ranch. When he arrived in Van Horn about 25 miles from Dan's ranch, black smoke pouring from his barbecue trailer told him the tragic story. As he drove along the Interstate, a draft was created in his barbecue pit that fanned the coals to a hot fire and his barbecue was a mass of blackened cinders. He called Dan, "I can't come. My meat is all burned up."

What was Dan to do? There are no delicatessens in that area. Dan told Charley, "Go to this grocer's store and pick up the steaks he will have ready for you. You can cook the steaks on my grill." Then Dan called the grocer and told him to cut 25 of the best steaks he had and put them on Dan's account and that Chicken Charley would pick them up.

Charley drove on to Dan's ranch where Dan had some hot coals under his grill. Chicken Charley laid the steaks on the grill; but the steaks were not all Charley had picked up in Van Horn. He had laid in an ample supply of beer, for he knew he would not find any beer at Dan's.

As the steaks began to cook, Chicken Charley would open a beer, take a looong drink, shake the can vigorously and spray the rest of the beer on the steaks. This was repeated—open a beer, take a looong drink, shake the can and spray it on the steaks. When the six-pack was empty, the steaks were done.

The officials returned just as the meal was ready. They ate with great gusto, declaring those were the best steaks they had ever eaten.

*"[Pecos Higgins was] an old cowboy in Arizona 72 years old, been in the penitentiary twice, married five times, drank barrels of whisky, rode in the 101 Miller Bros. Wild West Show, went to England and rode for the King, lived for the devil and made him a hand for more than 70 years, converted through the influence of the cowboy camp meetings."* —Joe M. Evans, El Paso, Texas

# Looking For Work

*By Pecos Higgins*

Dear Lord up in Heaven, will you listen a bit?
I am talking to you from below.
There is quite a few things I don't understand
And a whole lot more I don't know
When I look back over my wild rugged life
And the things I used to do,
I could never have lived to be as old as I am
If it had not been for you.

I have worked for the Devil most of my life.
Lord, I made him a hand.
But now I come over to your side of the range
And it was not because I got canned.
I have rode bad horses in three western states
That was plenty mean and tough,
And worked wild cattle in mountain range
That was plenty brushey and rough.

There was many times in life, Dear Lord,
The jackpots I was in,
I never dreamed you protected me
Or cared about my sin.
Since I have found You, Dear Lord,

280

# Memories of a Ranch Wife

I know how I got thru.
You helped me out in every way;
All the credit goes to you.

I have pulled many boneheads in my life
Life many old cowboys do.
But I have rode gentle ponies, lived better life
Since I been working for you.
Satan, I reckon, misses me now,
For I could stir up a whole lot of sin.
I never failed him on any job,
No difference what shape I was in.

But laying all other jokes aside,
Understanding is what I crave.
I don't mind leaving this old body of mine
Down here in a six-foot grave.
My spirit is what I am thinking about,
Since I am trying to get it clean.
I never cuss or drink any more,
And never think anything mean.

I have cowboy friends to went someplace,
And some relations, too.
I pray, Dear Lord, You gathered them in
And they are all there with you.
When you get ready to put out my light,
I pray your favor I have won,
That You will let me hang out at your Headquarter Ranch
When my work on earth is done.

# Rock Creek Round Up

*By Pecos Higgins*
*Nutrioso, Arizona*
*Aug. 4, 1956*

Heavenly Father, will write you a letter.
We are out on a big round up.

Old Marney is doing the cutting.
Joe Evans is holding the cut.
Ralph Hall is running the wagon,
Tom Myers is leading the drive.
Stanberries and Clarks on day herd.
Lord this outfit is alive.

The Mavericks I think are plenty.
One tough one slipped in for salt.
If we don't rope him and brand him,
It surely won't be our fault.
The cooks are putting out their best.
We are all praying in cahoots.
The only trouble I am having
Is getting used to these cowboy boots.

# THE DIFFERENCE—MY TESTIMONY

Does what you believe make a difference in your life? I would like to share the difference Christ has made in my life. I was born the first child of Christian parents and into a loving home. My earliest memories are of Mother reading the Bible to Dad and to us, and singing hymns in her lovely, clear soprano voice, often with Dad accompanying on the guitar; of Bible stories and Sunday School in our ranch home. I knew that I was loved, but as I entered my teens, there was confusion and emptiness inside of my being. There was much talk at that time about the end of the world, with some people setting dates for its coming. In August of the year I was fourteen the Trans-Pecos area suffered a terrible earthquake—6+ on the Richter scale. It was centered in the Valentine area and included our ranch. Many lesser quakes continued for more than a year. Now, an earthquake just before good daylight in a canyon with steep mountains on three sides is a fearful experience. The unforgettable rumbling sound of the earthquake itself and of huge rocks rolling and sliding and bounding down the mountains hitting other rocks, the dust and smell of hot minerals as rocks struck each other and broke into pieces with sparks flying made you think of fire and brimstone—and of the end of the world. It was truly an earth-shaking event! I realized that I was not ready for the end of the world. I knew I was not prepared to meet God. Still, I did not realize the vital need of personally meeting Christ. After all, I was a member of a good Christian family—Christian parents, grandparents, and great-grandparents for generations back. Persecution for their beliefs in God was the reason for my forefathers coming to America in the 1700s. I had read the Bible my grandmother gave me, had memorized verses from the Bible for as long as I could remember. I loved attending church services at Bloys Campmeeting, which was the only church I knew then. Wasn't that supposed to make me a Christian too? Was everyone as confused and dissatisfied inside as I was?

Then at Bloys Campmeeting one night after church, my mother came to the tent where my sister and I had our bedrolls on the ground. She talked to me about the importance of knowing Jesus personally as my Savior. The next evening as the preacher gave the invitation for those who wanted to make their decision for Christ to come forward, I could not wait to explain to the boy who had walked with me to church why I was going forward. I had made my decision to be on His side on earth and with Him in heaven, and I quickly went forward to make that decision public and to claim His promises. "For whosoever shall confess me before men, him will Christ confess before His Father in heaven."

Did this make a difference in me? Yes, it did. I did not suddenly change, but I had a "peace that passes all understanding" in my inner being—my soul. I knew that I now belonged in God's family. That was a long time ago. Has it made a difference in my life since then? Yes, I can truthfully say that it has. Christ has changed me from a self-centered, selfish person to one who loves and cares about other people. If I have befriended you or treated you fairly in business, it is because of the love and compassion Christ has shown to me when He gave me new life in Him, abundant life not only at some future time in heaven, but now this life is mine through Him. That is another difference Christ makes. He makes life so wonderful here as well as hereafter.

Not to say that I have been protected or spared from the tragedies and crises of this life. We have had shattering crises in our family, things that have broken our hearts. And God led us to a deeper understanding of His love and gave us compassion for other hurting people. I know what it is to hurt and grieve for loved ones and for myself. But God's love and care is always there and is sufficient for all our needs in good times and bad times. He does make the difference in whether these tragedies beat us down and make us bitter, or whether with His help we rise above them to make our lives and the lives of other better. He cares about His family. He cares about each person, no matter what the situation. "For it is not His will that any should perish, but that all should come into the kingdom of God."

# Evans Family Story

*George W. and Kate Evans*

The most beautiful piece of jewelry I have ever seen was my paternal grandmother's cameo.

As a child Kate Isobel Means lived near McAnnelly's Bend of the winding Colorado River of Texas. She was interested in all phases of frontier ranch life. Her older brother, John Zack, and his cowboy friend, George Wesley Evans, were helping work cattle at one of the pens near the Means ranch house. Eight-year-old Kate climbed the corral fence to watch. When the cow work was finished, George rode to the fence, lifted Kate onto his horse, and she rode to the house in front of him. As they neared the house George told her, "Take good care of yourself and when you grow up I'll come back

286

and marry you."

Kate continued to attend school and to learn from her mother, Berlinda Means, the many things necessary for a woman to know to adapt to this newly developing state of Texas. They no longer had the many Negro slaves that Berlinda had been used to as a young girl. Berlinda was a fastidious and very proper woman. But it was Berlinda who was called upon when one of the field hands got hurt or sick or a woman was having difficulty giving birth. She was very knowledgeable of what to do in these emergencies.

George Wesley Evans was born at LaGrange, Texas, the second son of William Musgrove and Annie Maule Evans. He was twelve years old when his father went to fight in the Civil War. His older brother, Samuel, had already gone to join in the war effort. This left George to be the man of the family of his mother and two sisters and his brother, Tom. The Evans family moved close to Camp Wood on the Nueces River, probably for protection. They had a hard time finding enough to eat. They robbed bee hives in rocks and trees for honey and killed turkeys, and occasionally deer for meat. George had killed two turkeys and was very proud of himself. They would have meat to eat. On the way home that afternoon he began to sense something following him. When he looked back, there was a panther following him by smelling the drops of blood from the turkeys. He was so scared that he dropped the turkeys and ran home without any fresh meat.

Times were unsettled and danger was always near. There were bands of Indians roaming through the country and outlaws looking for anything they might find unprotected. George remembered seeing his mother stand guard with a shotgun to protect her family.

When his father, William, returned from the Civil War times were a little better. George obtained a horse to ride to look after the cattle his father had amassed. It was his responsibility to ride herd on these cattle to keep them from straying too far. There were no fences. George really enjoyed this task. He liked the solitude of being out on the open range. In this work he met a young man, John Zack Means, with the similar task of watching his family's cattle. They liked this lifestyle and became good friends. George and John Z led a carefree life riding in the Hill Country between the Means' holdings at Bend and the cattle owned by the Evans' at Uvalde. They hunted the hills and fished and swam the rivers of that wild area. Though very different in physical build and personalities, they were as close as brothers. John Z was of medium height and tended to be rotund, was affable and gregarious. George was reserved and a deep thinker, a gangly six feet two inches, with black hair and blue eyes inherited from his Welsh ancestry. Their complimentary personalities and love of the ranch style of life drew them into a friendship that lasted the rest of their lives.

The Mexicans made a raid into Texas and drove many cattle back to Mexico, including the Evans' cattle at Uvalde. A posse was formed to recover the cattle. George W and his seventeen-year-old brother, Tom, led this group to the Rio Grande River where they crossed the river, surrounded the stolen cattle, and drove them back across the Rio Grande to Texas. After the ensuing battle Tom was not among those bringing the cattle back to Texas. He had been shot in Mexico and badly wounded. When George missed his brother he prepared to re-cross the Rio Grande, despite the pleadings of the other men. "They will shoot you too." George replied, "I must go. I cannot return home and tell my mother I left Tom to die in Mexico."

As his companions stood watch, George rode across the Rio Grande River, picked up his dying brother, and brought him back to Texas. At such courage the Mexicans held their fire until George's mission was completed and Tom was carried on George's horse back to

Texas, where he died the next morning, September 28, 1870, and was buried on Texas soil.

George W and John Z met often in their work of caring for their families' cattle. They became adept with ropes and captured some of the unbranded wild cattle. They could put their brands on these cattle they roped and thereby lay claim to them. These wild cattle had to be necked to gentle cattle until they were subdued enough to stay with the domestic cattle. In this way George and John each acquired a small herd of cattle.

John Z had met a tall steadfast young woman that he was very attracted to. She liked him but did not respond to his courtship because of his wild cowboy ways, and said she would not marry a man who was not a Christian. John Z began to be more interested in the Means business at headquarters. He remembered his mother's Christian teaching. He realized being a Christian was the right thing to do with his life. Exa Weir then agreed to marry him.

At the wedding of Exa Weir and John Zack means, George Evans took notice of John's little sister, Kate, now a lovely young woman of sixteen years. He liked her petite stature of five feet two inches, her light brown hair and blue eyes, and her modest and gentle ways. George began courting her on his visits to the Means ranch, visits which now became more frequent. Kate also was attracted to this tall, quiet, protective cow man. Their admiration and respect grew into love for each other. George Wesley Evans and Kate I. Means were married July 24, 1878. They began their life together near Lampasas, Texas. Their church was a brush arbor where meetings were held when a minister came to the community.

It was necessary to do some farming as well as have the cattle George had acquired. Hogs and chickens helped provide food. George was not content with their small place at Lampasas. He wanted to expand his holdings—but where? He liked the Hill Country, but it was being populated by German immigrants and people from other European countries. There was no place for him there. Some men even hitched their wives to the plow to ready the land for planting. George wanted none of that. His respect and high esteem for women made such a life unthinkable. His thoughts turned to new frontiers with lots of space.

News filtered back through travelers and newspapers from the west where there was lots of land available. The Indians were being driven out of that area. The railroad was being built westward. George was now a family man. The first son of George and Kate Evans was born in 1880 and named William Franklin. He was followed by another son, Joe McClain, born in 1882. The birth of these sons increased George's desire for a better way to provide for his family and share with his neighbors. That fall he killed a hog and his neighbors helped him butcher it. He gave each one some fresh pork. Three days later he went to get meat for Kate to prepare. It was all gone except for one leg and foot. He brought it in to Kate, laid it on the table, and said, "Kate, pack our things. We are going west where there are not so many people. I won't live where I can't neighbor and have enough for my family too."

"Going west—what would that be like?" Kate wondered. Away from her family and friends. Away from her familiar life style, away even from the preaching services under the brush arbor that were so important to her. How would she cope without a house to shelter her little sons until they could get a house built? Kate trusted her stalwart husband. He had lived out in the Hill Country without even a tent for shelter. And she had promised to love, honor and obey him until death did them part. She would go where he led.

Planning began for the journey west. George and John Z had been talking about the opportunities in West Texas. They both liked the idea of settling in a new area with plenty of space for expansion. John and Exa Means had started their family too with the birth of a daughter, Elma, and a son, Samuel Franklin. Kate and her sister-in-law Exa shared the excitement and enthusiasm of their husbands, even with some trepidation of making their homes in this new and different country. It was an opportune time. The last battle with the Indians was fought in Victoria Canyon January 29, 1881, in the Diablo Mountains, ridding the whole Western area of Indians, who were driven into Mexico to stay. There would be no more threat of Indian raids. The railroads were pushing westward and had reached Van Horn, Texas, west of the Pecos River, in January 1882. Now there was a way of travel and of shipping supplies via the railroads. They could be assured of being able to get food and the supplies they needed.

George began to amass what they would require for the long journey west and to start their ranch. He bought wagons and mules. One wagon pulled by mules was for Kate to drive with their two sons and their household goods. One wagon would be used to haul tools and equipment and any newborn calves while they were too wobbly and young to travel. The calves would be unloaded each evening to nurse the mother cows and had to be caught and reloaded into the wagon the next morning. George had these wagons made waterproof so they would not leak when they crossed the rivers.

It was a busy time for Kate, too, as she would need a good supply of sewing equipment—needles, thread, fabric to make clothes for her growing boys, as well as for George and herself. Hers was the responsibility to decide what food supplies they would need.

Excitement and anticipation ran high for everyone—everyone, that is, except for Kate's mother, Berlinda Means. Berlinda was horrified that George would plan to take her fragile and dainty Kate and her precious grandsons to that wild and dangerous West Texas, away from the decency and safety of Lampasas. Not only Kate and her children, but John's family planned to go west, too. How could she bear the separation and missing out on seeing her grandchildren grow up? Berlinda raged, ranted, and fumed against these plans. It did her no good. Kate was adamant that she was going with her husband. Finally, in resignation, Berlinda wrote out detailed instructions for coping with illness or accidents and births so that Kate would be prepared for these emergencies. Berlinda's knowledge of these things was almost like a doctor's of that time.

Several other families planned to go at this time to points west. George knew Perry Bean, who had gone west in 1880 and established a ranch northwest of Van Horn. Now he was returning with his wife and children. The Means, Evans, and Bean families planned to travel together so they could drive their combined herd of cattle and help with other tasks. Someone was needed to drive the calf wagon. The men would be busy with driving the cattle. Finally a rather dim-witted young man was located. He knew how to handle a wagon and team and he wanted to go west and be a cowboy. He was hired to drive the calf wagon with the big barrel for water fastened on its side so they would have water for human use when they had to make a dry camp—a camp away from a stream or any source of water.

In the early morning half-light on the day of departure everyone gathered for a farewell service held by a young minister, Rev. L. R. Millican, invoking God's blessing on this trip west. He chose as his text Psalm 1: "(1) Blessed is the man who walketh not in the counsel of the ungodly, nor standeth in the way of sinners, nor sitteth in the seat of the scornful; (2) But his delight is in the law of the Lord, and in his law doth he meditate day and night; (3) He shall be like a tree planted by the rivers of water that bringeth forth his fruit in his season, and whatsoever he doeth shall prosper. (4) The ungodly are not so, but are like the chaff which the wind driveth away.

(5)Therefore the ungodly shall not stand in the judgment, nor sinners in the congregation of the righteous. (6) For the Lord knoweth the way of the righteous, but the way of the ungodly shall perish."The Evans' adopted this First Psalm as their family psalm which it remains to this day.

All was in readiness, save for the fond and loving farewells to the families staying behind. Who knew when or if they would see each other again? But the decisions had been made and the time of departure had come. George hoisted four-year-old William onto the wagon seat, lifted Kate to a place beside him, and placed two-year-old Joe in Kate's lap. Kate untied the reins from the brake and gave the mules a gentle slap of the reins. The wagon rolled forward, the other wagons took their places in line—Exa's wagon was pulled by two high-horned Georgia steers—the bawling cattle began to move.

May 13, 1884. As the sun began to lighten the eastern sky, the long trek to West Texas had begun. Kate followed the familiar way along the Colorado River to San Saba. She had been over this route to visit relatives and friends. The cavalcade was to follow rivers and streams wherever possible to be assured of water for the livestock and the people. They made their first camp near the Colorado River. The baby calves had been unloaded from the calf wagon and were full and nestled by their mothers. The weary cattle contentedly bedded down after grazing on the lush grass along the river bank and watering in the river. They would require little watching that night. Campfires were built for supper to be cooked in the Dutch ovens— bread in one and venison fried in the other. This evening there were poke greens gathered along the way for the meal's vegetables.

In San Saba they spent time visiting relatives and friends and purchasing additional supplies. More families joined the westward travelers. They continued along the Colorado River where they saw many birds of different kinds and small animals. They gathered berries to eat and edible plants for vegetables.

The journey continued, six days of travel and a Sunday of rest for the livestock and the people. This day of rest prevented the livestock from becoming sore-footed. It was an acknowledgment of thanks to God for his care and guidance of this trip. It also gave people, especially those who walked and drove their oxen, a welcome rest. The wagons and equipment could be checked and repairs made if necessary. Some travelers that started with the cavalcade did not take this Sunday rest, but pushed ahead in their haste to arrive before the others and claim the best land. Kate was glad for this extra time to read her Bible and enjoy playing with her young sons. Also she could cook a roast as a change from the steady diet of quickly fried meat.

The day came when they reached the Concho River where it joined the Colorado. The Concho flowed from the west, so the travelers now followed the Concho River. Westward was the direction they wanted to go. After days of travel along the Concho, they were glad to arrive at Fort Concho where there was fellowship with the soldiers stationed there and news of other wagon trains, as well as supplies they could purchase.

John Zack was a great asset in scouting out the best route because several years before this time he had been over this way with his small herd of cattle and other westward travelers. They were within 200 miles of their destination when they reached Comanche Springs, the present site of Fort Stockton, Texas. They made their camp at these strong springs, feeling all was well. The next morning when they awakened they saw they were surrounded by Indians. They felt they were goners for sure, but the Indians indicated by signs and gestures and a few words that they only wanted the cattle. In exchange for the cattle they would not harm the people. John Z said it was the easiest decision he ever made. The disappointed pioneers returned home unharmed. At San Saba John Z worked to build up another herd of cattle. He was filled with enthusiasm for the opportunity this new land of West Texas afforded and was eager to return in 1884.

After days of travel the Concho River was left behind. From now on they would have to depend on creeks and water holes for their water supply. George W and John Z rode on ahead scouting out the best route for the wagon train to follow and locating sources of water. The wind blew from the west for sometimes several days without stopping. This made the people and the livestock edgy. Kate missed the trees that had afforded shade for their rest stops. Here there were only hills and plains of endless grass. Sometimes George would take Will or Joe on his horse, holding whichever boy on his saddle in front of him. Then the boys felt like real cowboys.

Kate grew weary and longed for a leisurely hot bath as she had enjoyed at her home in Lampasas. Now with water in short supply baths were hastily performed with limited water, often unheated. The sun seemed hotter with the absence of trees. Kate was grateful for the sheltering sunbonnet that protected her face and neck and the gloves that covered her hands as she held the reins.

They encountered the first herds of antelope with their fluffy white rumps and bouncing gait. The curious antelope would come toward the wagons before they became startled and bolted swiftly away. The travelers were assured of a bountiful supply of meat and considered the antelope meat better than venison.

Some people who had started with this wagon train did not stop for a Sunday of rest. As the Means and Evans group journeyed on westward they passed these people stranded along the way. Their livestock would be too sore-footed to travel; a wagon wheel had broken and couldn't be repaired, or some of the people had become sick or too weary to continue. They could go no further; their greed had not gained them any benefit. The days passed as the Evans and Means wagons pushed steadily westward for six days and rested on the seventh. They passed Fort McKavett, almost the last outpost of civilization.

There came a time when John Z or George W had found no source of water within a day's drive. They would have to make a dry camp. Kate was thankful for the big barrel of water on the calf wagon. The thirsty cattle were restless and bawling. They would need extra guards this night to avert a stampede. Kate took her bucket to get water from the barrel on the calf wagon to wash her hands and start supper. As she filled the bucket she saw that the water looked murky and then she noticed a very unpleasant odor. What had happened to their only water supply? She took her dilemma to George. He agreed the water was too foul to use, but why? He questioned Jack, the driver of the calf wagon. "Oh, Mr. Evans, the mud was so deep at the last watering it came over the tops of my brogans and got my socks muddy. I had to wash my socks because I don't have another pair, and the barrel was the only water I could find." This stop was *really* a dry camp.

At last the pioneers reached the Pecos River which had to be crossed. It was at flood stage and out of bounds from spring rains on its watershed. The muddy water was widespread and looked menacing. Kate, although she had spent childhood along the Colorado River, had never seen a river of muddy water and she was frightened by it. George W had packed among the supplies a very long well rope. As he was a powerful swimmer, he swam across the Pecos River pulling the well rope which he had tied to Kate's wagon. The waterproofed wagon beds floated like boats. With this well rope he pulled the floating wagons across the river one by one. The livestock reluctantly swam the river after much urging by the men on horseback. No person or any livestock were lost in the crossing.  They had passed one hazardous milestone without accident.

From the Pecos River it was a long dreary stretch through limestone hills to the Butterfield Stage Stop and thence to Comanche Springs, but from there they could see mountains and the promise of water and trees. Fifty miles farther they camped at San Solomon Springs at the very foot of the Davis Mountains. This is the present site of Balmorhea State Park and the noted spring-fed swimming pool. They traveled around the northern end of Gomez Peak to Tatum Springs just west of the present junction of I20 and Interstate 10. At this strong spring of good soft water they stayed several days and washed all of their bedding and clothes.

The mouth of a wide grassy canyon lured the Means and Evans families southward toward the mountains. The Bean family proceeded westward some sixty miles to the ranch Perry had founded earlier. A winding creek of running water snaked up the broad canyon now known as 'Dobie House Canyon, land once owned by the Reynolds Long X Cattle Company, and scenic route of State Highway 118 to Fort Davis, Texas.

July 24, 1884, George and Kate's sixth wedding anniversary, near the head of 'Dobie House Canyon, they turned east up a steep hill to a broad mesa and Cherry Creek Canyon which follows a steep brushy course down the mountainside eastward past present Balmorhea, Texas. Here they made camp at last. John unyoked Exa's steers and dropped the yoke on the ground to leave it for 27 years, when he returned and recovered it to hang on the wall of his dining room at Y6 ranch.

After over sixty days of travel, plus Sundays of rest, it was good to be in camp where they could pitch their tents and cease their travels. The summer was cool and pleasant. There were wild cherry trees whose small cherries made delicious jelly. Wild grape vines also grew in the vicinity and the grapes made very good jelly. For shade and firewood there were oak and pinon trees. George W and John Z explored these mountains in every direction from their camp. Deer were plentiful and there was evidence of bear in this area. Later in the fall when the bear were fat they would kill a bear to render the fat for lard for frying, and which was said to make excellent biscuits. They found many acorns and food that would be good for hogs. They planned to buy good quality hogs and turn them loose to make their own way. The grass was good and the cattle were fat.

Kate and Exa kept busy with the usual women's work of cooking and cleaning along with sewing clothes for their growing children. All clothing had to be made with only a needle and thread—they had no sewing machine.

On July 3, 1885, Kate bore her third son, Lee Stinton, with only her sister-in-law, Exa, to assist at the birth and her mother, Berlinda's, written instructions.

The water in Cherry Creek began to dry up. It was necessary to find a place with a better water supply. They again moved and trailed the cattle down 'Dobie House Canyon and around the northern perimeter of the Davis Mountains to the western slope of Boracho Peak where there were two springs of water not far apart. George and Kate camped at one spring and John and Exa at the other. There was an abundance of grass but no trees. These springs of water were not strong springs. It was soon evident that the two herds of cattle were too many for the amount of water.

John Z was very discouraged, even to the point of planning to return to the San Saba country. He told George, "I think I will go back to San Saba where water is not a problem. There is always plenty in the rivers and creeks."

"Now, John," countered George, "Do you want to go back there and farm? Or do you want to raise cattle? This is cattle country. Think how fat the cattle get to be by fall. This grass has a lot of food value because it cures out instead of growing fast and then drying up when the rain stops like it does in Central Texas. Cattle in this western country stay strong through the winter because this grass is good. There must be underground streams of water in these mountains. We can dig wells for water."

John Z was persuaded to stay and look for other country. He found a partner to help him buy a ranch about 20 miles west of Fort Davis, Texas, in the southern section of the Davis Mountains.

1886: George and Kate moved their camp south to the mouth of a canyon near large water holes. (The hitching post was still standing there in 1977.) As winter was coming, they desired a more protected place to live, so they moved farther up into this box canyon that George had explored. Here the mountains on three sides would shelter them. The creek along this canyon would provide water. There was room on a bench at the foot of the north mountain for a house, corrals, and orchard. They started hand-digging a well for permanent water. As the dirt and rocks were dug loose, the keg containing this debris was winched up and emptied, then lowered for the next load or to haul the ones doing the digging out of the well.

At a depth of sixty feet they encountered a rock too large to dig out. They set a charge of dynamite and went to Kate's tent for lunch. While they were eating the dynamite exploded. When the blast cleared they heard the wonderful sound of rushing water pouring off this rock into the well. What rejoicing! Now with permanent water a house could be built and they could have a home. No more moving to hunt water. George and Kate had found the end of the trail.

These were exciting times. With a permanent water supply they could build a house. Plans were quickly made and lumber and supplies were ordered to be shipped by train to Boracho Station, unloaded and brought to EV Ranch by wagons. Kate would have a house at last. Now with a dependable source of water, trees for an orchard were sent for—several varieties of peaches, plums and grapes. A plow to be pulled by mules was ordered so that ground for a garden could be readied. Furniture for the new house must be decided on and purchased.

In the early days of open range George had branded his cattle with his wife's name—KATE with an open "A" all across the animal's side. This big brand was unmistakable and made it almost impossible for cattle rustlers to rework the brand. Now with a permanent location to live there was no need for such a large brand. George started branding the cattle a large EV for his Evans Ranch shortened to EV. The cattle did well on the mountain pasture bounded on the north and west by the rim-rocks to keep the cattle from straying that way. The rim rock served as a fence—there were no fences. It was only necessary to ride the eastern perimeter to keep them from grazing too far eastward.

Joe and Will were now old enough to ride herd since Will was seven coming eight and Joe was past five years old. They could go with their dad. One evening as they were returning home from this mountain pasture and starting down the trail off the north mountain, they met four Indian braves coming up the trail. George had some anxious moments as he realized how vulnerable he and his little boys were, unarmed. George had never packed a gun. The Indians were peaceable. They had travelled back to this area in search of plants and herbs necessary for their culture that did not grow where they now lived in Mexico. Since that occasion that trail has been known as the Indian Trail.

The creek that arose on Boracho Peak and ran down by the headquarters had water during the summer rains and there were big cisterns in the rocks before the creek plunged off the mountain. Only in dry winters and for the cattle ranging to the south did water have to be drawn from the new well. This was done with the keg that had been used to haul the dirt and rocks that had been dug up out of the well. To do this one end of the rope was tied to the keg and the other tied to the saddle horn of Will or Joe's horse. With the rope over a support the keg could be pulled to the top of the well where George would empty it into a trough hollowed out of a log. It took a lot of trips pulling the keg of water to the surface to water very many cattle.

Soon a device was obtained that could be operated by a mule walking around it in a circle. With an arrangement of gears the water was brought to the surface through a pipe. The mule was harnessed to a beam that turned a big ring gear that turned a pinion gear that ran the shaft that worked the pump jack. This mule-powered water pump worked on the same principle as the mule-powered hay baler that was later purchased and used to bale the prairie grass hay. One mule would be worked until noon, then exchanged for a fresh mule to work the rest of the day.

They first had only a moving machine pulled by mules and brought the loose hay to the headquarters in wagons to make a very large haystack. Corrals were built around the haystack and to work the cattle when the calves were branded. It was beginning to look like a ranch headquarters.

Before long a new invention was heard of—a windmill. The wind turned a large wheel on top of a tower. This wheel was geared somewhat like the mule-powered pump, except the gears were on top of this tower. These gears changed the rotating motion of the wheel to an up-and-down motion of the sucker rods in the pipe in the well, bringing the water to the surface at the top of the pipe. This windmill would pump water whenever the wind blew. One of these windmills was purchased and installed. Tanks were dug out of the dirt to hold the water as it was pumped out of the well. From the tank, water flowed through a pipe to a trough where the cattle could drink. This windmill was so successful that another well was dug about 100 feet south of the first well. It too was a good strong well and was equipped with a Samson windmill. By 1894 a third well had been dug and equipped, but it was not on the main underground stream of water and was later abandoned.

Materials for the house had come promptly, and construction was underway. Kate was excited to have the spacious four-bedroom house with a roomy kitchen-and dining-living room. The roofed porch along the front of the house would be an enjoyable place to sit and see the new barn, corrals and growing orchard.

Kate and her children rode the train to Lampasas since she needed to select furniture for the new house. This was the first time she had been away from George since their marriage. George wrote her this letter:

"Nov. the 12, 1886
Kate Dear Wife, I am still at Mr. Perkins. He will hunt 3 more days longer. Mr. Johnson has sold his catel and is going to Ft. Davis after his money today. It thought as I had a chanse I would drop you a few lines. We have found soum 20 head of our cows. I see the hogs here. They are offal fat. I am nearly crasey to see you and the children but I don't want you to start hom by yourself. I will cum after you if posiably can. I dont think that eneything but death will ever separate us this far again. I thought that I could stand it beter than I can. We(ll) there is no use of grieving for we cant get together for a wile.

Yet your loving Husband G. W. Evans
Kiss the children for me."

Kate was especially thankful to select the new dining table and chairs. Until this time wherever they were camped the overturned wagon bed had served as their dining table. When they had visitors the wagon bed was covered with one of Kate's white linen table cloths and set with her good dishes.

The fourth son of George and Kate was born October 5, 1887, in the almost-finished house. He was named George Wesley Jr. Kate felt that this might be the last opportunity to be sure of having a son to carry on his father's full name. Kate was kept busy sewing clothes for her growing boys. Almost every minute not spent in cooking and cleaning found her sewing a small shirt or pants or mending torn clothing.

The hound dogs George had brought from Lampasas were a help to keep the raccoons and foxes from the chickens. They really proved an asset when a hungry and daring panther, or mountain lion, jumped into the milk pen, killed the milk calf, and carried her over the fence and up the steep hillside to have his feast. The hound dogs took the panther's trail and bayed him up in the rock bluffs so George could kill this fierce predator. George soon realized this canyon was a favored area for these panthers. He and his hounds had many exciting hunts for the panthers. So numerous were these panthers that in a matter of ten years or so twenty-four panthers had been trailed and killed. Henceforth this canyon was named "Panther Canyon."

Kate and her sister-in-law Exa Means had wished for a brush arbor meeting in this new country like they had known at the Lampasas-San Saba area where they could worship and hear God's word preached. Kate especially prayed for this because her husband

George, a fine, honest, upright man, had not made a public profession of accepting Christ as Savior.  Kate felt a brush arbor meeting would give him the opportunity to do that.

A Presbyterian minister, the Rev. William B. Bloys, was sent to Ft. Davis, Texas, for his health.  As the high, dry climate brought about his improved health, he began to travel with his horse-drawn buggy to visit the new ranch families.  At each ranch he would hold a worship service in the home.  When he reached the Means Ranch at Crows Nest about twenty miles west of Ft. Davis, he was welcomed and asked to spend that night.  After the worship service as they visited, Exa Means shared with Rev. Bloys how she and Kate Evans had wished for a brush arbor meeting where ranchers could meet for preaching services as they had at Lampasas.  Rev. Bloys thought that an excellent suggestion.  John Z offered to scout out a centrally located area he had in mind as a place to meet.

Several days later as Rev. Bloys reached the EV Ranch in Panther Canyon he was heartily welcomed.  That night after the worship service as Kate voiced her great desire for a brush arbor meeting she was told that the Means' had shared that desire with Rev. Bloys.  After visiting with other ranchers who approved this plan, a date for the meeting was set for October 10—13, 1890, to be at Skillman Grove sixteen miles west of Ft. Davis.  Skillman Grove was several beautiful clusters of oak and pinon trees on the slope of a rocky hill to the east.  At one time Indians had ambushed the stage driver, Henry Skillman, in a one-sided battle here.  After a volley of arrows came rattling about the stage, Henry raced to a cluster of oak trees. He was armed with a brand new Sharps rifle with a range of 1,000 feet.  As his weapon was too cumbersome to hold and fire effectively, he lodged the barrel in the crotch of a tree.  Then he drew a bead on a hideously painted Indian who had dismounted and was seeking protection behind his horse.  Sighting carefully, Henry pulled the trigger, giving the warrior the full impact of the rifle's charge. One shot was sufficient and his battle was won. On seeing the frontiersman's bullet knock their comrade a full ten feet, the other Apaches jumped on their ponies and fled in disorder toward the safety of the hills.

Since there was a doctor now in Pecos, Texas, Kate wished to avail herself of his services for the birth of her fifth child. Kate and George rode the train from Boracho Station where George had flagged it to a stop, to Pecos. There a place was procured to stay until the birth of the expected baby. Kate's fifth son as born February 25, 1890, and named Ruben Musgrove Evans. She and George were raising a houseful of sons.

Plans were made to attend the brush arbor meeting October 10. Since the EV Ranch was some eighty-five or more miles distant, George and Kate's family would have to camp there those three days. A trunk for clothes and bedrolls for sleeping, as well as camp cooking utensils, were readied and packed in the wagon several days before October 10. The trip would take the better part of three days. On the ninth of October, George and Kate pitched their tent in Skillman Grove to be ready for the next day's brush arbor meeting. George and Kate Evans and their five sons were the only ones who camped at Skillman Grove for the first meeting. Everyone else lived near enough to come for each day, bringing copious baskets of food. Early the Sunday morning of October 10, ranchers and their families and people from Ft. Davis began arriving in buggies, wagons, and on horseback.

Rev. Bloys announced time for each service by calling, "Come to church." The first service was held under a large oak tree and everyone came when Rev. Bloys called, "Come to church." Men and their wives and children, several unmarried cowboys—a total of about 48 people attended. Rev. Bloys' first pulpit was an Arbuckle Coffee crate stood on its end. This meeting was so successful that plans were made to meet the next year in July.

**The names of those attending that first Sunday, October 10, 1890, were:**

The Rev. William B. Bloys

Dr. and Mrs. D. T. Finley and their four children, Otis, Lee, Don and Scotty

Mr. and Mrs. George Medley and their seven children, Tony, Oscar, Maude, Pearl,

Herbert, Gaddis, and Arthur

Mr. and Mrs. John Z. Means and their five children, Elma, Sam, Huling, Barbara,

and baby Graves

Mr. and Mrs. George W. Evans and their five children, Will, Joe, Lee, G.W. Jr., and Ruben

Mr. and Mrs. W. T. Jones

Mr. and Mrs. Claude A. Smith

William Farmwalt and his two sons, Will and Johnnie

Miss Lovie Chadborn

Miss Viola Pruitt

Miss Ora Pruitt

J. P. Weatherby

J. W. Merrill

A. G. Prude

Albert Carpenter

E. L. Jones

A. Roland

Will Pruitt

Charlie Farmwalt

There were a total of 25 adults and 23 children. Everyone returned to their homes that evening to come back each day except the Evans family who were camped there.

There was an abundance of stirrup-high grass for people's horses and mules and a large water hole for water with plenty of shade trees to tie their horses or mules under. Everyone was pleased with the quiet and beautiful location.

*An excerpt from "Border Skylines" by Will F. Evans* said, "At the appointed time in 1891 people in hacks and buggies, on horseback, and in covered wagons began heading for Skillman Grove. The horses and mules, after their long hard trips, were turned loose to graze. A great fire had been built by the assembled campers. Dead oak wood was the fuel with its tantalizing aroma. Tall flames were wavering and flickering toward the evening sky. When the flames began to settle into live coals, pioneer women well used to cooking over open fires busied themselves in preparing a meal of regular ranch chuck, which then consisted of wild mountain game. To these men and women, ravenous with that hunger only an outdoor appetite can give, the rude provender seemed a sumptuous feast indeed.

"Picturesque was that gathering in its primitive setting. Bearded and mustached were the men and clad in homespun and jeans; the women in calico and homespun, their simple gowns of the "Mother Hubbard" pattern. Barefooted were most of the children, even those up to 15 years of age. Among all there was gladness, and rollicking laughter rang out as they regaled themselves with humorous incidents or tales.

"This was the second annual gathering, and the campground began to assume some aspect of permanency. Soon an arbor of poles and brush was under construction. Brush for the purpose, hitched by ropes to the horns of their saddles, was dragged to its site by Tony Medley, A. Roland, and John Means. In order to roof this crude structure, other men toiled willingly in pitching this brush atop of the frame. Brother Bloys, a rather handy carpenter, supervised the work of building the seats for the meetings. These were just some heavy 2 x 6's that were laid on 6 x 6 timbers set upon blocks. For some of these rough seats, the little minister devised some crude lean-backs; the seats with backs to them were prized luxuries at that early day camp meeting.

"It was at this second meeting in the Cow Country that the much loved Doctor Finley was converted, the first man to come to God on the Bloys Campmeeting ground. In itself, this was an important thing in those days, when words from a doctor's lips were as falling from those of an oracle.

"The doctor was then a gray-haired man who had grown old in the service of healing and ministering to the physical ills of the Mountain People. Being a doctor at that time meant something in those pioneer days. It meant long, hard rides on horseback, with perhaps all the available medicines in that part of the country stowed in one's saddle bags. And owing to the scarcity of doctors and the trouble of getting them, usually they were not sent for until the good women of the Cow Country had exhausted their own primitive knowledge of all the home cures. For years, day or night, whenever a panting, white-faced horseman brought him a hurry-call, good Doctor Finley at once set forth on an errand of mercy, riding on horseback in answer to the summons, across the wildest regions of the Davis Range.

"These gatherings of cowboys of the Mountain Country, for social intercourse and religious edification, present a cross-section of life in the making in Texas. History, generally, as read and taught—once considered infallible and almost sacred—often fails to record the real meat of the story.

"Historical occurrences, sacred and impious, as a matter of fact, are closely allied. The history of the Bloys Cowboy Camp-Meetings presents an enlightening panorama of the varied activities of the people in the earlier days in West Texas of their religious observances, their amusements, their manner of living, their general interests, and their jokes.

"When the Founders and those who joined with them met at Skillman's Grove for their third camp meeting in 1892 they felt fortified because of the success of the two preceding meetings, and it was with great gladness that they assembled.

"This year, Rev. Bloys for the first time had an assistant preacher— the Rev. Henry Little, of Denton, Texas. He and Brother Bloys had known each other well down in Coleman County, and there was harmony in the pulpit between these two warm friends. It was E. L. Jones who met this good man in Marfa and brought him in a hack to the camp ground. To his coming is attributed much of the success of the Bloys Camp-Meeting as an institution. His wit, his wisdom, his keen judgment of human nature, incited words that reached into the hearts of hitherto unresponsive men. Perry Bean was one of those converted at this meeting. His taking the step gladdened his many friends."

Kate and George Evans were there with their six sons. Eldridge Bean Evans, the sixth son, had been born June 17, 1892, in Pecos, Texas. Kate had a second time traveled to Pecos where there was a doctor to deliver her baby. But this time Pecos in June was hot. It was a different heat from June in the mountains, almost unbearable with no way of relieving the heat. She was glad to be in the cool atmosphere of Bloys Campground.

To this third meeting came Professor C. B. Smith of the Pecos public school. He was one of the first leaders of the men's prayer meeting. The fourth of these gatherings witnessed the beginning of the group plan. This was due to the large crowd that assembled for the session in 1893. There were entirely too many people attending for them to be able to camp in one spot and too many for the women to cook for. So it was decided that separate camps should be formed. The founding families and their guests would pitch their camp in a spot while another group would have their campfire some distance away. This started the different cook sheds. Kate Evans was pleased to have a cook for the Means-Evans group. She had not yet completely regained her strength from the birth of her sixth son in June.

The first Campmeeting cook for the Means-Evans group was Cladio Parra. Much of the morale and well-being of ranch life depends on the cook. The camp cook is an artist at preparing meals under various conditions—many of them adverse to readying a meal. The cook holds a special place in the echelon of ranch life. He will prepare your food and wash your dishes, but he is servant to no one. This was borne out when on one occasion a pompous and overbearing cattle buyer seated himself on a bedroll and commanded rather brusquely to Cladio, "Gimme a cup of coffee." The cook did not take orders from anyone but his boss. The man's bullying tone made the old Mexican resentful; so he replied, not irritably but in all the softness of his Latin intonations, "Copes in de boax, coaffee in de pote." And there was not a move on his part to comply with the request.

Cladio was the first permanent cook ever hired by the Means-Evans camp on the grounds of the Bloys Camp meetings. He began to cook for them in 1893 and held the job for over forty years, until his death. Cladio was employed by the Means family at their ranch off and on during his entire life as boy and man. His only failing was his fondness for liquor. Sometimes he would ride into Valentine on his pony and there get on a debilitating drunk while at the ranch a whole crowd would be waiting for him to prepare breakfast. Then he would be fired but always he would be hired back again, for he helped Exa with her extensive garden of vegetables and flowers.

Kate Evans had taught a young Mexican man of Indian descent to cook in her kitchen. He proved to be adept at camp cooking also. He was a good gardener too. He, Alexandrio Valdez, was head cook at Means-Evans cook shed at Bloys for many years while he worked at EV Ranch.

In 1895 Kate was expecting another baby. She was proud of her six sons and loved each one dearly, but she longed for a daughter in this masculine household. She embroidered little bibs with the name "Grace" on them. But it was not to be. Paul Means Evans was born June 15, 1895, her seventh son. He was taken to his first Bloys Camp Meeting in July when he was one month old.

Seven sons and the oldest fifteen years old. There would be plenty of help with the chores on the ranch and the cattle work on the range. Lacking daughters, Kate taught her boys to cook, clean house, and do laundry as they grew old enough to do such work. The boys would rotate these chores so that each one became adept at every type of work around the household, as well as learning to handle horses and work cattle.

The cattle were multiplying and the fruit trees in the orchard were blooming. Kate rejoiced at the prospect of having fruit this summer. There was still a large haystack from the prairie grass cut the summer before. Life was good. Since there was no market for heifer calves the cattle were rapidly multiplying. As approximately half of the calves were heifers, there were many EV cows on the open range. At roundup time each calf was branded whatever brand the mother cow had. The spring roundups were for branding the calves. In the fall of the year the roundups were for the purpose of gathering the 2, 3, and 4-year-old steers to be shipped to market and sold, usually in Fort Worth, Texas. George or one of the older boys, after the steers were loaded into the railroad cattle cars, would ride in the caboose of the cattle train. This was to make sure at each place the train stopped he could see that there were no steers down in the cattle cars to be trampled on by the other steers. Although sand was spread on the floor of the cars, footing could become treacherous with the shifting of the train on curves and in stopping and starting.

In Fort Worth, George or the son old enough for this responsibility saw that the steers were unloaded into the stock pens and supplied with water and hay. When the steers were sold he collected the money and rode on a passenger train to Boracho to be met by someone from EV Ranch. That money was the entire income for the coming year.

In 1898 Kate was expecting another baby about the last of May. She told George, "I don't think I can bear to go to Pecos again when it is so terribly hot to wait for this baby." George, ever concerned for the well-being of his beloved Kate, caught the train at Boracho, rode it to Pecos, and talked to the doctor. The doctor arranged to take his vacation that week and came with George on the train to Boracho. There they were met by one of the Evans sons and taken by horse and buggy to EV Ranch. The doctor enjoyed the cooler mountain climate as a respite from the Pecos heat. On May 29, 1898, he delivered a healthy baby girl who was named Gracie Kate Evans. Kate had her long-awaited daughter. Paul, three years old, was not thrilled at relinquishing his status as baby of the family. When he was brought in to see his baby sister his comment was, "Looks like a little 'Meccan' (Mexican) to me."

In 1900 more room was needed for the EV cattle, so George W purchased from Jim Nunn the Cherry Creek ranch where they had first settled in 1884. This ranch was some 30 or 35 miles over in the Davis Mountains from the EV headquarters. Two log cabins and corrals and a large dirt tank had been built there. Enough cattle to stock this ranch were driven from EV Ranch.

This mountain ranch was a game paradise, with mule and whitetail deer, panthers, and many black bear. The bear and panthers were harmful predators of the cattle. Although it was necessary to hunt and kill them to protect the cattle and horses, hunting them with dogs proved to be great sport. These predatory animals had every advantage in these mountains where they lived. It took much hard riding in the thick brush and steep mountains to reach where the dogs had the animals cornered. The bear were hunted mainly in the fall of the year when they were fat, for the rendered fat made an excellent substitute for lard. The meat-eating bear were not as fat as those that ate acorns, pinon nuts, and berries and plants. They needed to be eradicated as soon as possible to avoid their killing more cattle.

The winter of 1902 saw the Evans and Means families moving to San Antonio to send their children to school. Until this time the children had been taught by governesses who lived with the family during the school term. Now the older boys needed the advantage of higher education. Some of them attended Peacock Military Academy. It was necessary to ship their horses and buggies by train from Valentine to San Antonio because there were no automobiles yet in this western area. Kate and George returned to EV Ranch when the school term was over. The Means family came back to their ranch. This routine was followed for several years, for it was important that they be at the ranches to work the cattle, and especially to attend the Bloys Cowboy Campmeeting.

In 1904, Kate was expecting another baby. She was thankful to be in San Antonio where a doctor's services were available. November 21, 1904, Kate's eighth son and ninth child was born and named Amos Graves Evans. Her family was complete.

Bloys Campmeeting 1902 was a great year for those who for over a decade had been attending these meetings in Skillman Grove. In that year the Bloys Campmeeting Association was formed and chartered and the section of land on which the gatherings had been held each year became the property of the Association. That year the founders of this cowboy undertaking resolved to buy outright the land on which they had been meeting. Paying cash, they bought one section of land from E. P. Hill for $1,500.

To raise the money the following Presbyterians subscribed: George T. Reynolds $100; W. Keesey $100, D. O. Finley $100; Geo. W. Medley $100; M. U. Finley $50; J. W. Merrill $50; V. M. Ward $50; Dr. D. T. Finley $50; E. L. Jones $50; W. T. Jones $50; J. C. Powell $50; Medley Bros. $50; R. P. Bean $25; H. M. Truehart $25; O. Z. Finley $25; Lee Prude $25; J. A. Espy $25; E. G. Haddock and Gus Thomas $25; Oscar Medley $420, Bean Bros $20; Henry Mayfield $15; Earnest Beardsell $10; C. A. Merrill $10; John B. Finley $10; A. G. Hart $10; C. A. Smith $10; J. E. Nunn $10; Dr. Martin Merrill $10; and Sam Selman $10, or a total of $1,080.

Baptists: G. W. Evans Sr. $100; John Z. Means $100; Lacy Duncan $50; A. L. Means $25; B. L. Hues $25; James F. Everett $25; J. C. Bird $25; Evans Bros $20; Means Bros $20; R. D. McAnelly $10; and E. R. Millican $10, a total of $410.
Methodists: Arthur Mitchell $10; L. B. Woolford $10; Haynes Mixon $1; and Vincent Mixon $1, a total of $22.

These men together with Bro. Bloys became the charter members of the Association. Brother Bloys wrote out the charter which was put on record in Austin, and is still in force.

in 1902 everyone rejoiced that Bloys Campmeeting was held on its own land. There was a feeling that they were attending a beloved institution whose permanency was assured. The gospel tent which took the place of the brush arbor that dripped water on those under it even after the rain had stopped was a matter of great satisfaction.

The year 1904 found the annual gathering still growing. A Secretary's book had been bought to keep a record of the business meetings of the Bloys Association. A new gospel tent had been secured to take the place of the smaller first one. Growing crowds made the first tent far too small.

"The magnitude of the task of stretching this big canvas tent will remain impressed indelibly in the memories of those who helped to set it in place, its great weight to be sustained by three tall poles. These poles were laid in proper position before the mass of heavy sheeting was laid out above them. Several men and boys then had to crawl in under the smothering canvas to right the long poles into position, being obliged at the same time to lift their combined weight. The job was by no means an easy one, and if one pole fell it would jerk the other two down. So there was great relief on the part of those who had to erect and hold up the poles when those busy boys on the outside finally managed to tie the buy-ropes to convenient trees and to stakes which had been driven into the ground. Brother Bloys darted about from stake to stake, and every one of them must driven in exactly the right place to suit him or up it would come.

"This tent was a big old three-pole circus appurtenance which was large enough to seat several hundred persons. It was lighted by gasoline torches. These were metal affairs that were hooked up on hails in the poles. They gave a very poor light and were nothing to speak of when it came to trying to read by them. The gentlest breeze would cause their flames to flicker and many times to be snuffed out altogether.

"Doctor Little was still preaching at Bloys after fifteen years of loyal service. Doctor Little probably did more than any other one man to lead the people of the Davis Mountain region to the ways of the Lord. He and Brother Bloys made a great and successful team. The little minister would gather the strays up from the by-ways of life and Doctor Little would explain the gospel to them in a way they would understand.

"Brother Bloys was a great hand at reaching out for sinners in unexpected places. It was this sort of thing that assured the little minister a place in the hearts of all in the western country. He and a former cowman of the vicinity who moved to El Paso were great friends. When the little preacher visited that city he was always the guest of the old pioneer.

"El Paso in those days was somewhat wild and wooly and a pretty tough spot. On each of its streets there were several saloons. On one occasion as Brother Bloys was walking along these streets with his friend and another preacher, the trio were halted frequently by men coming from the "gin places" who would hail Brother Bloys, begin talking with him, and seek to hear news of the boys back home. Usually they were men from the mountain regions whom Bloys had known. Brother Bloys' pious companion evidently disapproved of this procedure. Finally, seeming much embarrassed he said, "I believe I will just walk on a ways."

"Go right on, young man," said Brother Bloys. "These are the very kind of fellows I am hunting."

"Dr. Little was a man of the pulpit and the city, a man of eloquence who never failed to carry his point with wit and pleading. But Bro. Bloys and Br. L. R. Millican were men of the range in heart and spirit. Bro. Millican was a cowboy preacher, a circuit-rider, who had been coming to Bloys meetings for several years. He was not eloquent, but his utterances were genuine and to the point. His prayers touched chords in many lives that had been dormant for years."

*—excerpted from "Border Skylines" by Will F. Evans*

In 1905 the rains had been plentiful and the cattle were fat and bringing a good price on the market. God had blessed and prospered George Wesley Evans and his wife with eight healthy sons and one lovely daughter. George and Kate had been married 27 years. George loved and admired Kate so deeply for who she was and for the grace and fortitude with which she had borne the vicissitudes of frontier life through drought and lean times as well as times of prosperity, from bearing sons with only the attendance of her sister-in-law Exa Means to hosting and presiding at festive dinners in San Antonio society. He wanted to give her something special for their anniversary. He consulted with a jeweler in San Antonio who helped him design a fitting gift—a pink cameo with a surrounding gold ring set with 27 one-fourth carat diamonds.

Kate was thrilled upon receiving this beautiful pin, which she wore everyday for the rest of her life. It looked just right not only on her Sunday best dresses, but also pinned at the throat of her cotton housedresses.

After her husband, George's, death she never stayed in the bedroom she and George had shared, but chose to stay in another bedroom in the EV house. She would ask me, her 7-year-old granddaughter, to spend the nights with her so she would not be alone in the big house. I remember each morning when she arose she washed her face, combed her hair into a bun at the back of her head, and, dressed in her cotton housedress, pinned the diamond-surrounded cameo at her throat, where it looked just right.

Upon Kate's death the cameo passed to her only daughter, Grace, who never wore it or enjoyed it. Grace said it was too ornate, and she kept it in her safety deposit box. Somehow it had never looked too ornate on Kate's housedresses. Before Gracie's death, in her sense of fairness, she decided to have the diamonds removed and reset in various rings and bracelets for her two daughters and two granddaughters. Before she had this done she did have the original cameo surrounded with the 27 diamonds photographed.

Upon Gracie's death the plain cameo was bequeathed to her older daughter, Josephine Cowden Marek, whose husband, Bruce Marek, promptly had 27 diamonds replaced surrounding the cameo. These diamonds are set adjacent to the cameo instead of on a surrounding gold ring. It is still a beautiful locket owned by Josephine's only child, Janice Marek Gensler, who has no children. What will become of this cherished family heirloom cameo pin?

*Kate Evans' cameo with 27 diamonds*

# PIONEER PEOPLE
## Memoirs of Paul Evan

Recollections of Paul Means Evans

Written in the early 1970's. Special thanks go to Chance Hart for transcribing the original handwritten manuscript, and to Lottie Woods for preserving it until it could be typed into the computer by Judy Roach and printed in 1997.

Paul Evans has been described as a "Frontier Man of God." Born in Panther Canyon on June 15, 1895, the seventh of nine children of George Wesley and Kate Evans, Evans knew from birth something of the strict Christian discipline instituted in the family circle.

His parents had a hand in launching the original Bloys Encampment and in developing ranching empires in Texas and New Mexico. Paul Evans was scarcely three months old when his parents took him to his first session of the Bloys Campmeeting. He served on the executive committee and was a member and underwriter of Cowboy Camp Meetings, Inc., composed of twelve camps conducted in Arizona, Wyoming, Colorado, Nebraska, Texas, and New Mexico. Mr. Evans recalls how they brought their own camping equipment and slept in a tent, cooking over an open fire.

He recalls getting most of his schooling on the ranch. He graduated from high school at Valentine, then took a business course in Pecos so he could take over management of two ranches comprising 125 sections owned by his father. The spread accommodated about 3,000 head of cattle; and when ready for market, they were driven to Kent, Valentine, and Van Horn for shipping.

Mr. Evans knew the Big Bend country well, as he participated in six-week roundups all the way from Pecos to the Rio Grande. Without fences, Paul recalls cattle drifting all the way from the Plains to the Texas border in search of water. One year, the Evans crew worked with the Means outfit, then their own, and then with the X-Ranch Reynolds Cattle Company from September until Christmas, branding some 13,000 calves.

Married to the former Susan Wertie Powell, Paul Evans lived in Panther Canyon where he was born and ranched for many years until his retirement. Mr. and Mrs. Evans had five children: Lottie

Virginia Woods, Frances Elaine Carpenter, and Paul M. Evans, Jr., all still living; and Mary Sue and Yvonne, who died in childhood.

He was once a member of the Evans Boys Polo Team, consisting of himself, Graves Evans, Truett Evans, and Robert Everett. They played for six years all over West Texas, against Fort Bliss cavalry, Marfa cavalry, three Big Bend teams, Lamesa, San Angelo, Midland, and others.

He was a long-time member and supporter of the First Baptist Church in Van Horn, Texas, holding numerous positions in the congregation as well as in the Big Bend Baptist Association. He was a Mason and a member of the Order of the Eastern Star.

Mr. Evans died November 23, 1975, and is fondly remembered by a host of family and friends.

# COMING WEST

I am including in my writings historical information dating back more than one hundred years. These are all true stories told to me first-hand by people that lived at that time, and until I was in my early thirties, at which time they began to die, one at a time, until they were all gone. But I was at the listening age when they told me about the old days, even before the Civil War began. My father was twelve years old when the war broke out, and my uncle, Sam Evans, was old enough to go through the war and come out alive.

My father was George Wesley Evans and my grandfather was William Evans. My grandfather was a rancher in the Big Bend country of Texas from Victoria to Uvalde, with lots of cattle and horses. They were all driven across the Rio Grande by Mexicans, and that broke up his ranching. The claims were put in for all of this loss. But it was turned over to the governments of Texas and Mexico for settlement, and eighty years later, we got very little out of the settlement.

Two of my father's uncles, Robert and Sam, went down in the Alamo at San Antonio. You can see their names there on the wall with the rest of the men that were killed by the Mexicans.

All of the men except the real old men and the boys went to the Civil War. This left no one to care for the women and children except the old and the very young. My father was twelve years old at this time and, of course, remembered everything that happened. He said they had a hard time finding enough to eat. They robbed bee hives for the honey and killed deer and turkeys for meat. He said he had killed two turkeys one night and was really proud of himself. He began to sense something was following him, and when he looked back, there was a panther following him, smelling of the drops of blood from the turkeys. He dropped the turkeys and ran home without any fresh meat.

My father and Uncle John Means were very close friends when they worked cattle together down in Central Texas while they were growing boys. One day, they were penning some cattle when a small girl came out to watch them, and to see her brother John. She was John's sister, Kate Means. Papa liked the looks of John's little sister, and when they got the cattle penned, he put her on his horse and let her ride to the house with him. When he was ready to leave, he told Kate he would be back for her as soon as she was old enough. He did come back for her, and they were married and started the Evans family.

In all, there were eight boys and one girl born to this union: namely, Will Franklin, Joe M., Lee S., George Wesley, Jr., Rube Musgrove, Ell Bean, Paul Means, Katie Grace, and Amos Graves. They were all good Christian people, and made a good mark in this world. At one time we had one thousand sections of land all stocked with cattle in West Texas and New Mexico. I helped work it all at times.

My father was a good provider and he always shared with his neighbors. He killed a hog, and some of his neighbors came by and helped him butcher it. Of course, he gave them all some meat. About three days later, he went out to get some meat, and it was all gone except one leg—just the bone and foot. He brought it in and threw it down on the table and said to Mama, "Pack up your things. I am going West where there is not any people. I won't live where I can't neighbor." Like always, he meant what he said. He started gathering his cattle to come West.

The trip West was long and it was a dry drive. Many who started never did make it. You will find dry bones and old wagon parts in the Castle Gap only a short distance from the Pecos River. Our people took everything in consideration. They made their drive during the rainy season in July, so they could make the long stretch between the Colorado River and the Pecos River. The drive consisted of the Means, Evans, and Bean families, with their herds of cattle which were small at this time. When it came time for them to start the drive, Reverend L. R. Millican, a young preacher at that time, called them all together and read some Scripture. He chose to read Psalm 1:

"Blessed is the man who walketh not in the counsel of the ungodly, nor standeth in the way of sinners, nor sitteth in the seat of the scornful: But his delight is in the law of the Lord; and in his law doth he meditate day and night. He shall be like a tree planted by the rivers of water, that bringeth forth his fruit in his season; his leaf also shall not wither; and whatsoever he doeth shall prosper. The ungodly are not so, but are like the chaff which the wind driveth away. Therefore the ungodly shall not stand in the judgment, nor sinners in the congregation of the righteous; for the Lord knoweth the way of the righteous: but the way of the ungodly shall perish."

They had prayer that God would give them a safe trip west. The travelers took God at his word, and rested the herd every Sunday; and, believe it or not, they got to their destination before the ones that drove their cattle hard so as to get there first and locate on the best country.

When they reached the Pecos River, it was out of banks, and they had to swim their cattle across. Papa had a well rope in the wagon, so he swam the river and floated the wagons across. He was a powerful swimmer. He had ordered the wagon beds made water-tight so they could be floated across a river safely without getting the contents wet. Mother had never seen any muddy water before, and she was really frightened of the water. But, they made it across all right.

324

There was a young man with them to help drive the cattle. At one dry camp (an over-night stop where there was no water) this young man washed his socks in the only water they had along to drink and cook with.

They reached their destination on July 28, 1884, and settled in the head of Cherry Canyon. They stayed there about three years before the water began to play out and they had to move. They moved over to the west side of the Davis Mountains where there were some pot holes of water and some small springs.

The Evans camped at one spring and the Means camped at the other one. They were about three hundred feet apart. It wasn't long until they had more cattle than they did water. Uncle John Means told Papa that he was going back east where there was plenty of water. Papa had a hard time talking him out of going back.

Something had to be done, so the Means moved over on the south side of the Davis Mountains to the Crow's Nest Ranch, and lived there until John Means and George Medley bought the Moon Ranch and stocked it together. Later, Uncle John bought the Tally Ranch, which is now known as the famous Y-SIX Ranch.

The Evans families remained at the EV Ranch after finding a good well of water up in Panther Canyon. This is where I was born June 15, 1895. If you ever want to know how old I am, just add five years to the calendar and you will have it!

After they got water in the well, they watered the cattle by drawing the water with the same keg they had been drawing the dirt out with. They (Joe and Will) were big enough to pull the water out by tying the rope to the saddle horn and pulling it out with a horse. Papa would dump it in a trough hewn out of a log to water the starving cattle, until they could get a horse power pulled by a mule going round in a circle.  The mule was hooked to a beam that turned a big ring gear that turned a pinion gear that ran the shaft that worked the pump jack.  This mule-powered water pump worked on the same principle as the mule-powered hay baler that was used to bale the *tobosa* grass hay on the EV Ranch when I was growing up.

We would work one mule until noon and then we would change and put in a fresh mule to work the rest of the day.  We pumped water for years before we got engines to pump with.  We dug two more wells on the same stream and put up three windmills; then we had lots of water.  The only thing —it was all in one place, so all the cattle had to water there.  It was 1910 before we found another well two miles below the ranch.  But it only pumped 5-1/2 gallons per minute, and wouldn't water near all the cattle.  In 1912, we got another well and began to pipe water out three miles from this well. We kept drilling until we got nine wells and put in 30 miles of pipeline before we got it all watered.

The EV Ranch consisted of seventy sections of land and the ranch we bought over in the mountains had fifty-five sections in it, with very little water.  We owned it until 1925, when we sold it.  It was a great place to hunt all kind of game.

When our folks landed in the Davis Mountains, the country had never been tamed by the white man.  It was full of all kinds of wild game.  The bear and lion and lobo wolves were everywhere, and of course, all kinds of wild game abounded.  Quail were so plenteous that we drove them into nets.  I remember one time we caught eighty-four quail in one catch; they nearly flew off with the net.  You could see antelope by the hundreds before the state land was sold to the "nesters."

We would see bear when we were riding the range.  But we didn't kill any until fall, so we could get the lard from them to cook with.

If you have never eaten deer meat fried in bear oil, you have missed the best! And the bread made from the bear lard was the best ever.

When we skinned a bear, we left all the fat on the hide and when we got back to camp, we threw it over a big round log, hair down, and split the fat down the middle of the back. Two men on each side would soon skin the fat off the hide. Then we would lay it out flat on a big table, and next morning, it would be firm enough to cut into cubes about one inch square. Then we would put it in a big wash pot and render it out to get the grease.

In my lifetime, I have been to the killing of at least 500 bear and 200 lion. We didn't keep count in those days. I did keep count of some lion that I caught with one pack of dogs. I killed fifty-six lions in seven years. Joe caught one hundred five bear with one pack of dogs. "Old Blue" was the lead dog. Papa's count with "Old Brownie" was the biggest. Then, Dub (G.W. Jr.) with his two Brownies was very big also. In most cases, I was along. From the time Papa would have to lift me onto my horse, I went along. I stayed with Joe when he made his big catch. Then, I went with Dub on his big hunts. I became famous as a big game hunter all over West Texas and the Organ Mountains, Eagle Mountains, and the Black Range of New Mexico.

We had dogs that didn't come back when they got after a bear or a lion. You just had to hunt until you found them, or go back the next day after them. The best dog for big game is a bloodhound with a little black and tan, or blue tick blood mixed. Some had some red bone blood mixed in. Every lion trail has a hard place in it, and if you don't have dogs with enough nose to work it out, the lion gets away!

# HOW THE PIONEERS SURVIVED

We bought a ranch over in the heart of the Davis Mountains from Mr. Jim Nunn in 1900 near where our folks first settled, and it was a hunter's paradise. Both white-tailed deer and the big mule deer were thick. Panther and bear were everywhere. It was a timbered country and lots of acorns and pinons and wild cherries and berries of every kind grew there—a really good place for bear. The mountains were full of them. They had never been killed out at this time. We had lots of fun running bear for 25 years that we owned this ranch. It was also good for hogs, so we turned loose hogs and raised about one hundred pigs every year. Of course, the bear and lion killed some of them, but we would catch the killer with the hounds.

Each year, we would kill 20 to 25 hogs, and make tubs full of sausage. Some years, the hogs would be fat enough to kill, and some years, we would have to feed them corn for a while before we killed them. Every time the weather turned cold in the fall, it would be hog killing time. We always had some on feed ready to kill. For the younger people that have never see hogs killed, scraped, and cut up, I will tell you how we did it.

We had big wash pots we heated the water in to scald the hair off the hogs by laying the hog on a big board and covering him with tow sacks, and then we would pour buckets of boiling water on the sacks. It would loosen the hair so you could scrape it off with big butcher knives. We would put a stick in his hind legs and hang him up and dress him—this means taking all his insides out. We would then lay him on a big table and cut him up. I have cut up hundred of hogs in my lifetime.

You lay him on his back and saw down on each side of his backbone. Then, you take out his ribs and cut off his shoulders and hams and head. This leaves the big slab of fat after taking out the bacon. You cut the fat up into cubes to be rendered out into lard. You also take out the backbone and saw it up into pieces about six inches long and when you boil them up, they are the best eating ever! For years I wondered where pork chops came from on the hog—until I realized you can't have pork chops and Evans backbone too.

After you have him cut up, you spread the meat out on a big table and put lots of salt on it while it is still warm, so the salt will go into the meat and draw out all of the liquid. This is the first stage of curing the meat. After a few days, you put it in barrels and soak it in brine made of salt, brown sugar, and saltpeter for three weeks. You take it out after three weeks and rinse it off and hang it up to be smoked. The way we hung it was to cut some stays about like fence stays to go across the rafters of the smokehouse. We used Spanish daggers for strings. You can throw the blades on the fire until they blister and pop. This makes them soft so you can tear them into strips about 1/4 inch wide to use for strings to hang your meat up around the poles. The women would make some small sacks to hold the sausage

We didn't have any refrigeration, so we had to dry the beef, deer, and antelope meat. We would cut it in strips about one inch wide and about a foot long, then salt it down in a container until the salt would draw all the fluid out of the meat. Then you hang it out on a wire to dry. It soon dried enough to put it in a flour sack and it would keep until you ate it all up. You have never eaten good gravy until you have eaten it made of dried meat. You can also make chili gravy which is the best ever. We would carry some of the dried meat in our leggin pocket to eat when we didn't get home for dinner. You can eat it when it is raw. When it is dry, we called it jerky. You can live on it a long time, if you have to.

We learned many things from the older people. They had gone

through many hard times, which taught them how to survive under any of the worst kind of circumstances. My Uncle Same Evans went through the Civil War and  came out alive, and spent the last years of his life with us on the ranches.  He taught me many things.  He would skin a cow and tie her hide to his horse's tail and drag the hide to the ranch—something we had never seen before. We thought we would see him get bucked off, but a green hide is so heavy a horse soon settles down and drags the hide in to the ranch.  He would stretch the hide out, hair down, and stake it to the ground and salt it good and leave it until it was about half dry.  Then he would take his knife and go around it, leaving the legs and neck on the ground.  He would cut it in an oval shape like an egg.  He cut a strip about one inch wide, round and round and round until the hide was all cut up.  He would stretch it out between two trees.  It would be more than one hundred feet long and when it got firm, he would take a real sharp knife and scrape all the hair off.  He could make twisted ropes or plaited ropes, quirts, hobbles, bullwhips—everything you needed—out of rawhide.  He showed me how to do all these things, and many more.  A rawhide rope is good when it rains.  You can always catch horses with it, as it does not get hard like a grass rope.

My daddy taught me how to shoot a gun.  You never load a gun until you are ready to shoot; and on all of our hunts, he would not let anyone carry a loaded gun.  In all our hunting years, no one was ever shot with a loaded gun.  That was one of the rules—never carry a gun loaded.  He also showed me never to bring a gun down like most folks do; always come up from the ground until you get to the point you want to hit.

We fed an average of fifteen people on the ranch, thirty miles from a grocery store, and we had no automobile.  I will tell you how we did this.  You didn't buy groceries in paper bags in those days.  You had to plan a long way in advance.  As I have already told you, we had our own meat and lard.  Our biggest problems were flour, salt, sugar

330

and coffee. We would make out a list of groceries and send to Pecos to have the groceries shipped to Boracho by freight. On a certain day, we would meet the train and load our wagon full of groceries. Just to give you an idea of what we bought, here is a list of some of the things I remember:

Two barrels of flour
50 pounds of green coffee beans
200 pounds of sugar
200 pounds of corn meal
200 pounds of salt
4 cases dried prunes
4 cases dried peaches
4 cases dried apples
10 pounds baking powder
10 pounds soda
5 gallons honey
200 pounds Irish potatoes
200 pounds sweet potatoes
200 pounds *frijole* beans
6 gallons molasses

We also had all of our own milk, butter, and eggs at the ranch. We built a cellar big enough to hold all this and more, and covered it with about a foot of dirt, which made a good storeroom for everything but flour. We made a flour bin 3 x 3 x 8 feet. It would hold two barrels of flour. We made it out of tongue and groove flooring and put quarter round in all the corners and the lid was so tight that there never was a rat or even a weevil in the flour.

We all had to roast the green coffee beans in the oven like you do peanuts. No one ever ground their coffee at night. They all ground it before breakfast. That was the alarm clock. When you heard someone grinding the coffee, it meant the coffee would soon be ready.

We lived so far apart in those days were always glad to see some of our neighbors come. People were so different in those days from what they are now. We all pulled together. We had to in order to survive. We helped each other do everything from building houses to working cattle. No one lived to themselves like they do now. The more people become independent, the sorrier they get to be as neighbors.

God has a way of bringing His people back together. Before the depression, the people of our part got real independent, as they had prospered for many years. But when they lost their money and then the drought of the 30's came along, we didn't raise enough calves to pay the interest on the land we bought from Mother and the rest of the heirs. We almost lost the ranch before it started raining again.

When I look back over the hard times we had while we were raising our families, I can see why God kept us humble. It was a blessing to our children that we didn't have money to spoil them with. They all turned out real good.

I had a neighbor that was a real close friend to me. Although he lived about 20 miles from us, every time a panther started killing his calves, I would take my hounds and kill the panther. This went on for years, and we would help each other work cattle. When I moved to Valentine to send my children to school, he would bring in a load of wood and unload half at my house and half at his house. We didn't have any way to wash our clothes, so we would go use his washer. This man was John M. Moore....one of the greatest that ever lived.

I mentioned earlier in this history about why my father moved west, because the people were too thick. After he came west, he still neighbored with everybody. He shared everything that he had and he was a good provider. I remember when we would cut hay, he would give all his neighbors some. He not only would give it to them, he would take it to them; and when someone dried out, he would take care of their cattle until they got rain. This went on all his life until he got too old to live at the ranch. He bought a big two-story house in El Paso, so all of us could come home when we could. At Christmas time we would all gather there for a big reunion. I would kill a big beef and a hog or two and take them. The boys from New Mexico would bring turkeys and quail. When we got all of this together, Papa would have me saw up some big roasts of beef and pork. We would fill the old Buick full of meat and get the chief of police to take us around to the people that lived in the slum areas of El Paso, and who would otherwise be hungry at Christmas time. We would give each of these families a big roast for Christmas. When we got back to the house, he would give a big sigh of relief and say, "Now I can enjoy my dinner."

After we got those three good wells of water at the ranch, we planted out one hundred fruit trees of all kinds. We put up jelly by the tubs full, and filled a great big pantry with jelly and preserves of all kinds. Papa gave a lot of that to his neighbors. And you know, the more he gave, the more he always had. We never ran out of anything. This is one of God's promises (Proverbs 19:17 says, "He that hath pity upon the poor lendeth unto the Lord; and that which he hath given will he pay him again.") Like all God's promises, if you keep your part and do what He says, He will always keep His part.

# TEXAS RANGERS

No history of the West would be complete without including the Texas Rangers. They did more to rid the country of outlaws, and horse and cow thieves than all the other law officers in the land. They were still very active in my time. I remember several occasions when the people had to call on the Rangers for help. I knew several of them very well, as they spent lots of nights at our ranch in pursuit of men.

Two men stayed all night at the ranch driving about twenty head of real good horses. All of us boys were sure Papa would buy the whole bunch, as we always needed more horses. We got real mad at Papa for not buying the horses. The next morning after the men left, Papa said, "Don't you know those horses were stolen? No rancher ever sold his top horses." Sure enough, in about two days, here came the Rangers on their trail. The men that had stolen the horses said they were taking them to New Mexico to try to sell them. The Rangers overtook the horses about Artesia. In a few days, here came the Rangers with the horses. They never told what happened to the horse thieves, and no one ever asked them. These were all top horses taken from the Jackson Harmon Ranch down below Alpine.

There is a little rough canyon not too far south of Van Horn Well (later called Cow Thief Canyon), and some of our boys found some of the Means cattle that had the brands burned. They were sure the cattle belonged to Uncle John Means. So, they took the cattle clear back to the Means Ranch and put them in the big horse pasture and called the Rangers to come and look them over. The Rangers had the boys to kill a cow and skin her; and sure enough, on the bottom side of the hide there was the old Y-6 brand, which was the Means brand. I cannot give the names of these cow thieves, as some of these people are still alive. But, anyway, they burned an AB out of the Y-6, and the other brand was a clover leaf. But the only brand that showed beneath the hide was the old Y-6. So, the thieves were caught and there was no more brand burning in the country that I know of.

I remember another occasion that was told to me by my good friend J. B. Gillett who was with the Rangers for six years. (Two of my brother married two of his daughters.) The Rangers had trailed a Mexican from way down in Texas to the Rio Grande just below El Paso. He beat them to the river, and Col. Baylor said, "Well, boys, this is it. We cannot cross into Mexico after a man. Remember, this is an order." When the men all got to sleep except one (you may guess who he was) that one slipped away. Next morning, the man was chained to a tree. The Captain called the men up and asked who did this.

J. B. Gillett was the guilty one. He said, "I'm not going to trail a man 300 miles and let a little muddy river stop me from getting him." He didn't lose his commission. He was a Sergeant. He got his title as Captain later when he was Captain of the police department in El Paso.

Captain Gillett was one of the great men. He told me lots of stories about his life with the Rangers. He said when they were on the trail of some Indians that had raided the country and stolen everything they could get their hands on from the pioneers, they would always head for Mexico. He said the Indians were so bad to set an ambush trap that the Rangers would never enter a narrow canyon where there were boulders and brush. They would split up and go on each side of it, and sure enough, they would usually find the Indians behind the rocks, and the Rangers would come at them from the back, and the battle was on!

The Davis Mountains were full of outlaws that ran from the law in Central Texas. There were men who would brand any unbranded yearling they came across, and put their brand on him.  They also hogged the watering places and killed other people's beef and never killed one of their own.  When enough of the good people moved in, the bad moved out.   Some of them were sent to prison, some were killed, and some of them moved on further west.  As always, the law-abiding people stayed, and the heirs of the Christian people own just about all the country.  All of the outlaws come to some bad end. In my time, I have seen several men wearing big pistols and belts full of cartridges on their person and carrying a Winchester on their saddle.  I only knew three men that wore two pistols, and they were biggest cowards I ever knew.  I have never known anyone to go wrong by doing right.  It always wins out.  My dad never wore a gun, but he was respected by everyone.

At a roundup on the open range Papa was cutting (separating) his cattle from the main herd of mixed ownership.  A greenhand kept getting in the way.  Papa told him to stay out of the way, and the greenhand replied, "You go to hell!"  A cowboy reprimanded the greenhand with, "You ought not talk to that older man like that." The greenhand then said, "Old man, I told you to go to hell, but you don't have to go if you don't want to."

# CAMP COOKING

The way we cooked when we didn't have a pack mule and cooking utensils was what we called a dry camp. The first thing you did was to pick out a good big tree to camp under with lots of big limbs to hang things on....big enough to hang all the game that you killed. We carried a bucket with a wire bail on it tied about our horse's neck with the hobble we hobbled our horses with at night. In this bucket was some coffee in a sack, a cup, spoon and some sugar. We had to pack it with a rag around it so it wouldn't rattle, or it would scare our horse! After we unsaddled and staked our horses out, we built up a big fire and let it burn down to coals while we were getting ready to cook. In those days, we bought salt in small cloth sacks. We used those sacks for everything. We put salt in one, sugar in one, and so on. We would have a small sack of flour rolled up in a slicker behind our saddle to keep it dry.

The way we made our bread was to set the flour sack down and open it up and make a bowl-shaped place in the top of the sack. We would press it down with our hand until it was firm, then put in water and baking powder and lard and mix it up. When we got it made good and firm, each man would come along and pinch off a hunk big enough to make a long snake-like string of bread. Then we wrapped it around a green stick about three feet long with the end sharpened so we could stick it in the ground. We would stick that sharpened end in the ground and lean it over the coals of fire to cook the bread. When it got brown on one side, we turned it around and browned the other side.

To cook meat, we cut a long slim green stick with a fork on the end. The fork held the meat while we cooked it over the open fire, and we turned it over and over until it was cooked.

The first thing we did when we got our fire going was to take our coffee bucket and fill it with water.  We would fill up our cup and hold it in our teeth and let it pour out on our hands and wash and rinse them, and dry them on the rags we had in our bucket.  We set the rest of the water on the fire to make coffee.  We made coffee by heating the water over the fire and then putting in as much coffee as we needed to make it good and strong.  We let it boil until it looked right, then poured a cup of cold water in it and set it aside until all the grounds settled to the bottom.  That is the best coffee you ever drank!

Food always tastes better when you get smoke and ashes on it; I guess it is because you are so hungry you could eat anything.

I mentioned not having any pack mules when we made a dry camp. That meant we didn't have any beds to sleep on.  In the fall of the year up in the high country it gets cold at night.  You drag up several big dry trees—enough to burn all night.  We would take our saddle and lay it on its back so we could crawl up in the sheep skin skirts with our shoulders and back.  We would pick out a nice, soft-looking rock to lay our head on.  Of course, we left our clothes on, including our chaps.  We pulled the dry end of our saddle blanket up over us and let the wet end cover our legs.  Then we were fixed up for a good night's rest.  Ha!  That's what you think.  As soon as that wet wool blanket got hot and the steam would begin to rise, the smell would raise the dead six feet underground!  We would get up and run to the fire and warm one side while the other side froze.  So, we spent the night running to the bonfire, and turning round and round the fire.  I have seen it so cold we had to set the water bucket on the fire to melt the ice so we could make coffee.  Some of the cowboys didn't wash their faces; they didn't like to use ice for soap!

The true stories of a cowboy are much more unbelievable than any stories that some writers make up.  I know so many things that have happened to me and to others that are true, but it wouldn't do any good to write them down, as no one would believe them anyway.

A book wouldn't hold all the things I have seen happen to a bunch of cowboys and big game hunters. We were hunting up in the Black Range one time and struck a panther trail that led straight away from camp. By the time we killed her, we were too far to make it back to camp before night; we had to make one of those dry camps. We skinned the lion and laid some of the meat on the fire. We had heard how good it was from the old trappers. But when we tried to eat it, it tasted just like it smells when you skin one. I had just finished helping skin this one, and I wasn't hungry enough to eat it.

# HUNTING

I would not have time or space to write all the bear and panther races that I have been in, so I am just going to write about some of the most interesting ones. This story is about the longest bear race I ever had.

There was a stock-killing bear that was killing cattle and hogs by the dozen. He killed so many calves on the upper U Up & U Down Ranch that they had to move the cows and calves to the lower ranch. They put some two-year-old steers up there, but that didn't stop the bear....he went right on killing the two-year-old steers. We had a neighbor that had a big old white boar hog that would weigh six hundred pounds. This old killer bear ran at this big hog and locked his arms around his flanks and rode him down a steep hill for 300 yards. Of course, he bit him right behind the shoulders and cut every tendon in his back. The ground was wet, and you could see all the tracks where the old hog was pulling and the old bear's hind feet were sliding in the mud as he was skidding down the mountain. Someone found the hog killed and phoned me and Jess Fisher to come and bring our dogs. We had some really good dogs. The kill was about eight miles above the ranch where I lived at that time. The hog was killed in the head of House Log Canyon, so I called Jess to meet me there about daylight. I left the ranch at three o'clock in the morning. We met at the kill, and the old bear had been back, so the dogs left in a run straight south through Tobe Gap and over into the head of Goat Canyon before they treed.

The bear was treed in an old dead tree, and we could see him a half-mile before we got to him. We couldn't get our horses down there where the bear was treed. We got out on a bluff where we could see the bear up on the old dead tree. The blue brush was so thick you had to crawl under it. While we were on the bluff, the rock that Jess was on fell off the bluff with Jess on top of it, gun in hand. He rode that rock for twenty feet, and it never did turn over. He landed on top of it in some soft dirt and kept his feet and legs on top of the rock and wasn't pinned down. If he had been under it, I couldn't have gotten him out, as the rock was bigger than a barrel. We were 20 miles from any place I could have gotten help.

We made it on down to where the bear was treed, but just as we got near him, he came down the tree and tried to kill all of our dogs. He got after one of my dogs and ran him between my legs. My gun jammed and wouldn't fire. He blew his breath right down my throat and it sure didn't smell good. I rammed my gun barrel down his throat, but of course that didn't stop him. The dogs grabbed him by the hind legs and he turned to knock them off, and that is all that saved my life. I went under that brush on my hands and knees and got out of the fight. He left in a run down through that thick brush, and we never got a shot at him.

We had to climb back up Livermore, the biggest, highest mountain in the Davis Mountains, to get to our horses. We couldn't get our horses off anywhere, as we were going through a rock slide. My horse got his left front foot hung in a root of a fallen tree, and he couldn't pull it out. I had to get off of him, and take a big rock and break the root to get his foot out. He was so smart he didn't move until I got his foot loose. We went down the west top of Livermore for a mile, and couldn't find any place you could get a horse off.....there were too many bluffs.

We decided to go down a water chute where the water falls were steep and long. Sometimes, our horses' shoes would get red hot, the slides were so long and steep. We had the best horses in the world— you could take them any place a man could go. It was five hours from the time the bear treed the first time, until he treed the second time. We left our horses high up on the mountain so he wouldn't see us coming, but just as we got nearly close enough to shoot, he came down. The brush was so thick you couldn't see anything. We ran down to the banks of a creek. Jess went down and I went up, and sure enough, I guessed right....the bear came right under me.

I just got one glimpse of his back and I shot and broke his back. One of Jess's best dogs, an old yellow blood hound, was right under him when he fell. Although I hit him a dead shot, as he fell, he gathered her up in his arms and bit her shoulder blade all to pieces. We had to shoot him in the head and take a pole and pry his legs loose from the dog. He had crushed all the breath out of her. We had to pour water on her to bring her to life. We skinned the bear and I packed the bear hide and Jess carried his dog a half-mile straight up a steep hill to where our horses were. I carried the bear hide on my horse, and Jess carried his dog. We knew it would be impossible to go back across the mountain. We decided to go back through Goat Gap and try to make it across HO Canyon before dark, to hit an old road that hadn't been used in forty years; but we knew our horses would follow it even if it was dark. We made it to the McDaniel Ranch, and left the bear hide and the dogs there, and we started back through a brushy canyon looking for the old road. There was enough moonlight to shadow the pine trees and you could never tell what you were going to fall in, but we finally got through about midnight. When we got to the U Up and U Down beef pasture, we separated.

Jess went to his ranch, and I went to mine. I was riding along thinking about all the dangerous things that had happened to us that day, and the night was so still you could have heard a pin drop. What I didn't know was that there was an old coyote following along behind me smelling the bear blood, and he let out the loudest, most terrible yell that I ever heard. My horse jumped, and I nearly fell off. It scared me to death! I was almost to the gate going into our pasture, and had to get off to open it. I was scared and so was my horse. I got back to the ranch at one o'clock in the morning. I had left the previous morning at three. I had ridden this horse 22 hours in the roughest country in the Davis Mountains, and he came in with his head up. He was one of the best horses ever raised in West Texas. His mother was a mustang and his daddy an Arabian. He had unlimited endurance. I rode him over Livermore Mountain three times one day after a bear. It is about all some horses can do to go over it one time in a day's ride.

I hadn't been married long, and my wife and my daddy were still up when I got home from that trip. It was killing Papa because he was too old to go with me. He was the world's best hunter in his time. He told my wife, "If you ever get married again, don't marry a hunter."

We had eight dogs on this race, and there was not a dog ever came back to us. They were all at the last tree. They had been up with the meanest bear I ever saw for at least ten hours. Three of them were pure bloodhound and two were three-quarters bloodhound, and three were half-breeds. You couldn't whip them back. The only way a bear could get rid of one was to kill him. We caught a number of bear with Old Queen, the one the bear ruined her shoulder. She would still try to run on three legs.

## WILD HOG HUNTS

This hog hunt happened in Madera Canyon above the U Up and U Down Ranch. The dogs had a big maverick hog bayed up. He was about two years old and had the sharpest tusks you ever saw. I was trying to get my rope on him, and he ran at my horse and grabbed him by the front leg just under the shoulder and swung around his leg and cut all the hide and meat clear to the bone. You couldn't have cut it anymore with a butcher knife! There was plenty of grass and water right there, so after I got the blood stopped, I left the horse there for about six months until I could lead him home. But he was never any good any more, as his leg was loose. He never could control it any more, as some of the tendons were cut.

We would take a wagon along with a top on it so the hogs couldn't jump out, and haul them home in it.

We heard of some of our hogs down below our hunting lodge, so we took our old hog dog, Old Fly, and a wagon and went to find them. We got after a real wild bunch—there were five of them. Of course, we didn't know how many, but the old dog did. As fast as we would get a rope on one, he would take their trail and leave in a high run after the rest of them. When we had tied five, the old dog just laid down to rest. He had finished with the bunch. He was the best dog in the world. You could put him after anything and he would trail it up. I killed fifty-six lions with him, and he was always just as close to a lion as he could get. He kept them so busy you could slip up and kill him without him knowing you were around.

On another occasion, we were up above the ranch in the head of House Log Canyon and the dogs left out after some hogs. When they bayed them up the first time, there was an old white and black spotted sow we hadn't seen for a long time. She had nine big unmarked two-year-old pigs, all colored just like her. We had brought a wagon as far up as we could get it. So we headed them down the canyon. Every time the dogs would bay one up, we would tie him down and go on after the bunch. We had tied all of them but one; but some of the dogs were gone, too, so we went to hunt for them. We found them with the last hog, and Papa was sitting on the hog, as he never carried a rope. He was then in his seventies. He had torn his clothes in shreds and his face was bleeding where the brush had scratched him. But he didn't let the hog get away! At one time he was the fastest man in the brush that I ever saw. He grew up down in the Cedar Breaks of Texas and he knew brush.

344

The hogs kept going further and further back into the big mountains in search of food, and we didn't see some of them anymore. They went wild as any bear. We would take the hounds that we had trained to run hogs and go back in the big mountains until we found hog sign. They would tear down the whole side of a mountain eating grass and other roots they could find. When we would find a fresh trail, we were in for a fast race! Those hogs would run like a bear until the dogs stopped them. We had to shoot them and drag them out to where we could get a wagon to them.

The way you drag one is to put two ropes on him and one man goes ahead, and the other acts as a brake. You have to go straight down and straight up the hills. You can't go around the side, or your hog will roll behind a tree and you can't go. When you get in with them, you have to skin them. You can't scrape them: there isn't enough hair left on them to steam it so it will come loose.

# WILD CATTLE

The Davis Mountains have always had wild cattle in them, and all of the rough and brushy mountains of New Mexico have also. Cattle go as wild as any wild animal—wilder than deer or antelope. They will never stand and look at you unless they are in the brush where you can't see them. They can see, hear, and smell better than most wild animals. They bed down at night in a high saddle of the mountains from where they always see you first. Then they sneak down to the thickest brush and hide. They drop down on their stomach and stick their chin out on the ground with their horns and ears laid back on their neck and their eyes open big and wide. They will let you ride in five feet of them and never move. If you will stop and look real close, you can make out the shape of one. When you do, they don't get up—they bounce up.

If you are riding a horse that knows his business, you are going to have to be ready to take a beating, as he will take after her like a trained rodeo horse leaving the chute! He will go through the hole in the brush that the cow makes before it has time to close up. When you are after one of these wild cows, you hold your loop behind your leg to keep the brush from jerking it out of your hand. If you ever come to a hole in the brush ten feet wide, you have to be close enough to throw your rope. You never get but one swing of your loop.

Running wild cattle is the hardest work in the world, and the most dangerous. That's why the cowboys liked doing it. The cattle get so wild you can't round them up. You can run them into a gentle bunch of cattle and they will go right on through and never stop. The only way you can gather them is to rope them and tie them to a tree for a day or two. Then you take a set bunch of gentle cattle and untie them and try to keep them in the bunch until they get tamed down a bit. The way you tie them, you take a big stout rope about six feet

346

long and tie it around their horns with a double knot that won't get tight, then around a tree the same way, so they can go round and round the tree.

These cattle have never seen or smelled a train; and when you try to get them to the stock pens, you really have trouble! We took a bunch of them to Valentine to ship, and it took us five hours to cross the railroad to the stock pens. They didn't like the smell of the railroad track. I had to rope a big calf that belonged to one of these wild cows and lead him ahead of the herd with him a-bawling and the old cow smelling of him instead of the railroad track. When they crossed the railroad, they took off and stampeded. They tore down all the yard fences and the fences around the frijoles patches. It took us another hour to gather them up. The old big steers will lead like a horse if you know how to get them started. You give him a big jerk right toward you, then you let him get a horn on each side of your horse, and take up your slack in your rope and strike a lope. He will follow you for several miles in this way, without turning off more than two or three times. I have led them five or six miles in no time flat.

We made lots of mistakes while ranching, but the biggest mistake we ever made was in 1919 when we bought 1,000 Mexican steers from old Louis Terrazas, the biggest rancher in Mexico at that time, and turned them loose on our mountain ranch where there was lots of brush. They were already as wild as could be. There were 200 four-year-old maverick bulls. We didn't have any chute to brand them in, so we had to head and heel them and stretch them out to brand and cut them. One smart thing we did was to saw the tips of their horns while we had them down. If you want to get your horse killed, just rope a Mexican bull. You can throw him down and he bounces up and comes at you again. You don't dare rope one when you are by yourself. You have to get two ropes on him real quick, or you are in trouble. He never gives up trying to hook your horse!

We gathered on these steers for five or six years before we got the last ones packed out on pack mules. The hardest day's work I ever did in my life was about six years after we had turned those Mexican steers loose. We thought we had killed and packed out the last of them, but we hadn't. There were four of them that had been down in Madera Canyon in what the ranchers called "No Man's Land." All the ranchers on every side above and below fenced it out, as you could not get cattle out of there any way. These old steers got hungry for salt and came out to a salt lick we had on an open ridge where we rounded up the cattle to work them, the only open spot there was for miles around. My neighbor, Jess Fisher, was with me over there, and we were hunting for any cattle we had missed on the work. We saw these old big steers before they saw us. We made our way clear around them, staying out of sight in the brush. We got within shooting range of them before they saw us. We fell off our horses and started shooting. We both had Winchesters and we soon had all four of them down. I looked at Jess and he looked at me. I said, "Now what?" He said, "We will butcher them and hang them up in trees." The first thing I looked for was his brush axe he always carried, but he didn't have it.

We went to them and dragged them up under two big trees and started to butcher them. You have never seen anything as tough as a ten-year-old Mexican steer! Jess Fisher was a little man, but he was all man. He didn't know the word "can't." There was nothing he couldn't do. I have seen him load a big bear on his horse by himself. He would drag the old bear up under a big tree and throw his rope over a limb high enough to ride under. Then he would pull the bear up and ride around the tree and back under the bear and let the bear down in front of him on his horse.

Well, we were butchering those steers and got off on bear! Anyway, we went out to a red oak thicket and cut some limbs about one inch in diameter and made wedges out of them. We would cut the bones by driving our knives with a rock, then we would drive in wedges to keep our cuts open. We kept this up until we would open the brisket and the pelvis. Then we could get his guts out. We had to cut them up like you do a chicken. We cut his shoulders and hind legs off, then we cut his back in two and pulled the pieces up with a rope to the saddle horn. We would cut or break off limbs and leave enough to hook the meat on. We got them all hung up in trees the same day. The next morning, we took a wagon and hauled them in. We hung one of them up in a big oak tree between the house and the barn, and left it there for three months until we ate it all up. The meat froze solid and never did thaw. We had to saw or chop off pieces to cook. We cut all the meat off the bones of the other three steers and salted the meat down in a barrel until it was ready to hang up to dry. We cut it in big hunks as big as your fist, ran some big strings in it, and hung it up in the smoke house to dry. It was good for six months.

There was still one left down at the Bonanza Spring in the George Duncan ranch. We heard of him several times. He was an old red swayback steer, and he stayed in the brushiest country in the Davis Mountains. They never could catch him. Our good neighbor Jess Fisher that helped me butcher the four steers came over and we planned to go after "Old Swayback."

My brother Joe Evans was at our mountain ranch. So, the three of us took two pack mules and went to a little nester shack on the north end of our ranch and spent the night. Next morning, we left the pack mules there and went to Bonanza Spring to look for the old steer's tracks. Sure enough, he had watered there, and we took his trail and trailed him about three miles. He was like an old buck deer. He had a little hill that he could get on top of and see a man coming from any direction. It was in the thickest brush around. We split up—one on each side and one went over the top of the knoll. Sure enough, he was on top. He came off on the east side where Jess (the best brush hand who ever lived) was stationed. I heard the rocks a-rolling and the brush a-popping, and I ran around the hill. Believe me, it was not any trouble trailing them down the mountain!

That old horse ("Old Joe," he called him) turned over rocks half as big as a barrel. About that time I heard Jess shoot. He had run onto that old outlaw going down that steep mountain and shot him in the back of the head running full speed. The steer fell forty feet before he landed. This time we had his brush axe. We butchered and quartered him up. It was the middle of the afternoon and the pack mules were twelve miles away. So, we decided we would pack him as far as we could so we wouldn't have so far to come after him the next day with the pack mules. We put the two hind quarters on Jess's horse and led him. Joe and I each carried a front quarter in front of us. Jess walked and led his horse. We got clear inside our pasture before night. We hung the meat up and went on to camp where we had left the pack mules. That night was a cold one—it snowed and sleeted. We didn't sleep cold—we laid awake cold! The next morning we took the pack mules and went back for the meat. It was frozen solid. We were not afraid it would spoil on us. We made it back to the ranch that night with the last of the outlaws.

# HORSE AND BUGGY DAYS

If you don't think lots of things can happen to you when you grow up using horses and mules for every conveyance, just listen. I have seen 150 head of horses and mules in a rope corral at Bloys Campmeeting being roped out, bridled and harnessed to wagons, buggies and hacks and some saddled up to ride home.

I remember old Brother Bains from Alpine had a horse that had never been in a rope corral, and he kept breaking out and running off, taking other horses with him. Lee and Max Burks were already saddled up one day, so they made ready for the old horse that was having so much fun. When he broke out, they roped him and heeled and stretched him out. Then they called the preacher to come and get his horse. He had been following the horse all over the grounds with a bridle, trying to catch him!

Joe Morley lived down Cherry Canyon at what is now known as the Morley Place, and he had some mares and was trying to raise some horses. The panthers were getting all his colts. He came after Papa to bring his dogs and catch the panther. Papa was busy working cattle and couldn't go, but he let Mr. Morley have a team and hack to haul the dogs in. Night overtook him about the old flattop mountain, so he hobbled out his team and went to bed. He hadn't been down but a few minutes until the dogs left out in a run. Papa only let him have some old experienced dogs that wouldn't run anything but a bear or panther. The panther had jumped on old Pete, our old brown mule. But the mule jumped the same time the panther did, and he landed on his back. His claws tore out from in front of his hips past his tail. When this mule got well of the claw marks, he had white claw-mark scars on both hips the rest of his life. He would never get close to a big rock any more.

351

Sam Means and my brother Joe met the Slack girls at Boracho once with a buggy and team. This was the same team that Mr. Morley used—an old roan horse, and Pete, the mule. When they came up the canyon toward the house, Sam was riding backward on the roan, talking to the girls in the buggy! The Slack girls were Moss Mayfield's nieces, and they sang together as well as Sandy and Sally on Lawrence Welk's show.

I forgot to tell what happened to the panther that jumped on the mule! The dogs bayed him up and kept him until daylight. Then Mr. Morley climbed the mountain and killed him.

This roan horse I was telling you about was the ugliest horse you ever saw. His head was three feet long, with little hog eyes and great big ears. His hip bones stuck out and were a red color. He never did close his under lip (it would hold two handfuls of corn.) But he always was honest. I saw Joe run down and tree a bear, and also run a coyote to death on Old Roan, holding onto the top of the harness.

It would fill a book to try to tell all the things I remember that happened in the horse and buggy days. We hauled all our freight with wagons and mules. We would hook up four wagons, four mules to each wagon, and leave out before daylight in a high run and go 15 miles to the railroad to load up, and then back to the ranch before night. We raised our own mules and horses and broke them ourselves. We would rope these mules by the front feet and throw them down and put a halter on them. Then we let them up and led them out on a good horse with a rope tied to the saddle horn. We had a wagon tongue tied to a tree about breast high. We would wrap the rope around the tree and pull the mule's head up tight to the tree. Then we pulled the rope back to the wagon wheel and tied it. We would put the bridle and harness on him. An old mule would be hooked to the wagon and when we got the wild mule tied, we would untie the wagon tongue and take off in a high run with both wheels locked. The wild mule would soon tire. Then we would teach him to turn. We would hook the breast strap from the old mule to the halter of the wild mule. The old mules really enjoyed making the bronc mules turn. We worked the mules and rode the horses, for the most part.

We broke horses to stay in a rope corral by tying a well rope across the corner of a pen. We had one big post in the middle of the corner, and we tied the rope to the fence, then around the big post and back to the back fence on the other side. We would untie the rope from one side of the fence and run the colts in and then tie it back about breast high. We got behind them and ran them over the rope until they would not fall over the rope, but would stop when they touched the rope. You could always catch them outside, after this training, as long as they lived.

The Means and Evans families moved to San Antonio to send their children to school in the winter of 1902. We had to take our horses and buggy down there, as there were not any kind of automobiles there at that time.

The first cars we ever saw in West Texas were in 1909, and we bought two of them. The Evans family bought one and the Means family bought one. They were both bright red and shiny. They stampeded our cattle and scared our horses to death. We couldn't drive anywhere near them. Every time a horse smelled a car, he would snort and break to run. The cowboys called automobiles lots of different names....some of them not so nice! It took years to change from horses and mules to automobiles. We still use horses on the ranches, as there are just some things you cannot do in a car, such as round up cattle in rough country.

The good old days weren't all good. Some of them were very trying times. We had no doctors when you got sick, and none of the new drugs we have now. Our mothers were the doctors and nurses. They did everything: made our clothes, cooked our meals, nursed us when we were sick—everything it took to raise a family. God bless the mothers for their love and care for us!

# THE COW WORKS

Working cattle included rounding them up, cutting out the cows and calves from the cattle after they had been rounded up and thrown into one big herd. Some of the men would go change to their cutting horses while some stayed with the herd. When the first men got back on fresh horses, the others also went to change horses.

A cow work is made up of a foreman which is called the wagon boss. Next in line is the straw boss; then a bunch of cowboys that take orders from these bosses. You have heard stories of how ignorant a cowboy is. Well, let me tell you something. A cow work is the best organized group of people that have ever been thrown together. Each man is assigned a job each day, and when he learns his assignment, he will do it or kill himself trying!

Some do the roping. Some do the flanking (this means getting the cattle down and holding them until they are marked and branded.) One man is assigned to mark the ears and another to do the branding, and every man takes pride in doing his very best at the job he has been assigned.

Most of you have read books about trail herds being driven long distances, including big herds of cattle. Some of the stories were true. But most of it was hearsay, written by someone that was not along with the drive. We had indeed our share of trail driving from one ranch to another, and also to the shipping points several times each year.

Driving cattle is entirely different from what you see on TV. If our cowboys were to drive our cattle in a trot like you have seen on the screen, we would have paid those cowboys off before night and hired some real cowboys who would drive them the right way—

slowly!

You put two of your best men on each point of the cattle, men that will never turn the cattle too close and cause them to stop. You also put most of your men on each side of the herd to keep them from getting into a bunch. You never let your men go clear to the back of the drive; only the drag drivers are allowed to stay behind. When we didn't have a pasture to put them in, we had to stand guard around the cattle and horses. If we had a big herd, we would use half the men until midnight and the other half until morning. Most of the time we didn't have any watches, so we went by the stars.

The way you tell time by the stars: the handle of the Big Dipper points to the North Star, and it makes a complete circle around the North Star every night. So when it is halfway around the North Star, it is midnight and time to change guard.

I am writing these facts so some of the second and third generations will know how we did things in the early days of the West. All of the first generation has gone on to their reward, and there are only a few of us seconds left. In order that the frontier days won't be lost completely, I am writing about some of the things that happened back when the country was first settled.

I came to Van Horn in 1900 with a herd of cattle and there was no one living here except the railroad crew and the agent. There were four or five houses that the ranchers had built to stay in while they were loading out their cattle. Some of the time we had to herd the cattle 4 or 5 days before we could get a train to come pick them up. We rode all over what is now Van Horn, and we didn't see anyone. We had certain horses we stood guard on, and they always knew where the chuck wagon was. Some of the time it was so dark you could not see the ground. But if you would turn your reins loose, your horse would bring you to camp. Sometimes, it would be so dark that your horse would stick his head over the wagon before you knew you were in camp. This happened to me the first time I ever stood guard, and was I glad to get to camp!

The cattle out of our mountain ranch had never seen or smelled a train, or heard one whistle, or blow off steam, and they would run every time. They were hard to get back to the pens. I remember sometimes I would have to take them out away from the railroad and stand guard on them because we couldn't get them to the pens. One time at Kent, I herded them 3 days and nights before the Cowen boys came in with a herd and helped me pen our cattle, I have stayed in the pens shipping cattle for 4 days and nights, helping our neighbors load out. I remember one time we had to pen five herds of cattle in the shipping pens. The train came along about 4:00 in the morning, and all those cattle pushed all the east side of the pens down and took off. They were all gone, except the dead ones. We trailed them for 15 miles by the crippled ones that were left behind. It took two days to separate the different brands!

The chuck wagon cook is the most important man with the outfit. He doesn't take orders from anyone. He is his own boss. The wagon boss tells him where to make camp for the next stop, and that's all the orders he needs. He will be there and have dinner or supper ready when the boys get there without fail. If a cowboy failed to roll up his bed and bring it to the wagon, he would have to go back for it. Once of that is enough for life!

A real cowboy is a breed all his own. Some will swear, smoke, and drink. But I have never known one that didn't have a big heart. I went on the works when I was a very small boy, and the cowboys were always good to little boys. They would help you when you needed it, and I loved them for being good to me. The Means and Evans were the best cowboys I ever saw, and they didn't do any of the sinful things that I mentioned. So, it is possible to be the best at your trade, and not be a sinful man.

## THE CURCUIT RIDING PREACHER

Rev. L. R. Millican, the preacher that said the prayer for our folks when they left Central Texas to come West, within a few years came on out and began his circuit riding preaching all over West Texas. He rode horseback, while Bro. Bloys rode in a buggy on his rounds.

Bro. Lally, as we all called him, would ride any kind of horse or mule that he liked the looks of. He raised horses and mules and broke them himself. I remember one time he came by the ranch riding a bronc mule. The only way he could get off was to throw a hitch on a post to hold his head tight and keep the mule from kicking him, then he would slide down his shoulder. The next morning when Bro. Lally got ready to leave, three of us little boys went out to see him off. We loaded our nigger shooters with walnuts so we could give him a good start, and see the fun. As he went off the creek bank, we all let loose our shots, and that mule was still running and bucking when he went out of sight! Bro. Lally had his saddle bags full of Baptist literature, and that mule pitched it all out. But we boys gathered it all up and gave it to him on his next round. This was the first Baptist literature ever distributed in the West.

One time, he was at the ranch getting ready to have services. We all gathered round and he had his opening prayer, and was ready to have a song. "Will someone name a song that you like," he said. No one said a word. I thought of a good one, and suggested we sing "The Old Gray Mare Came Tearing Down the Wilderness." This almost broke up the meeting! As long as he lived, he would tell this on me to everyone, including the "high-ups."
Bro. Lally Millican was the most daring of all the men I have ever known. He was always getting into some kind of a jam with his horses and mules, and he was used to that. But when someone gave

him an automobile, that is when things really started happening. He was driving up the road to the Kelly Ranch, and there was a big ditch alongside the road. Bro. Lally began to look at it, and he said to himself, "Wouldn't it be awful if I would fall in it?" Sure enough, he fell in the ditch. But he got out (all the cars were open in those day) and he walked to the Kelly Ranch. There he got help to turn his car back over and pull it out of the ditch.

I was going to Valentine once, and here came a car just a-whizzing by me. I recognized Bro. Millican's old Dodge as he passed, and wondered what his hurry was. Sure enough, it wasn't long until I saw him leave the road and go into a ditch. He hit the bank and killed his engine, so I went on to see if I could help. When I drove up, he said, "I can't slow her down. I don't know what's the matter with her." I raised the hood and found the trouble. The spring that controls the gasoline was unhooked and the damper was wide open, giving it all the gas. I hooked the spring back and sent him on his way.

After he got too old to drive, he had one of his grandsons drive for him. They were coming down the road east of El Paso and passed too close to some bee hives. The bees got in the car with Bro. Millican and his grandson. The boy turned the wheel loose and began to fight the bees. The car left the road and hit a big tree and pushed the radiator right back through the engine. The car was still full of bees. So they jumped in an irrigation ditch to get away from the bees. Then, they had to walk back to Clint, soaking wet, to get help.

# AUTOMOBILES

The first automobiles were more or less copies from a buggy. They had let-down tops and curtains. I remember you always got wet putting up the curtains. Sometimes it would be through raining by the time you got them on.

The first one we had was a right-hand drive with the gear shift clear outside, and all the trimmings were brass. The straps that held the top forward were made of leather and had snaps to fasten them down to the front near the lamps. The lights were carbide gas lights. You had a little outfit on the fender you put the carbide in. It had some water in one can that dripped on the carbide that made the gas. You had to turn on the gas and light it with a match.

The tires were very thin and soft. They picked up every thorn in the road. The roads were deep ruts made by wagons, and were crooked as a snake. Every time the wind blew, the road would get full of thorns. We had flat tires every time we went anywhere. We learned how to patch tubes! The worst thing was having to pump them up by hand. I started from Pecos to the ranch one day and had eleven flats. All the insides of my hands were blistered from so much pumping. It took all day to go to Pecos. We would take a lunch and eat dinner on the road. And when we went to El Paso, we would have to get up before daylight and take a lunch. It would take us all day to make the trip. It took years before we could get through the sand at Plateau. We finally cut soapweed daggers and laid them across each side for the wheels to roll on so we would not stick in the sand.

In those days we used mostly Model T Fords. We had to work on them all the time we were not cranking or fixing flats. Sometimes we would have a rod bearing to replace, and we would make a new one out of a piece of saddle leather or a bacon rind. We all learned to be good mechanics. In a day's drive, 20 miles per hour was considered good time.

I wore out four Model T Fords. When our children were little, my wife would take the children up the steep hills and set them down, and come back and help me push on the car and put rocks under it so it wouldn't roll back. Some of the hills were so steep we would have to back up it, as the gasoline was gravity flow, and it wouldn't run into the engine if the hill was too steep.

I remember the first Model A Ford I bought. I came home with it, and told my wife I had bought a new car. She said, "What kind?" I told her it was a Ford. She said, "Take it back. I don't want any more Fords!" I had a hard time explaining that this Ford was a good car, and that it would pull all the hills. She said, "I will believe it when I see it." Sure enough, we went out and climbed all the hills. It was a real good ranch car. I drove it several years.

There were eight boys in our family, and we all had to learn how to drive. As we married, we had to teach our wives to drive also. We would get up too much speed sometimes and straighten out some of the crooks in the old wagon roads.

We borrowed an old steam engine from a well driller that we had to fire with wood, but it would pull. We made a drag out of some bridge timbers and railroad rails and dragged a road from Boracho to Valentine, a distance of 40 miles. It was straight most of the way. Some of that road is still in use.

We all decided to go fishing down on the head of Devil's River once. So we gathered up about forty people and ten cars of all makes and models. As we reached the camp, one car was missing. It was Uncle John M. Cowden's, so a bunch of boys went back to find him. His car had drowned out right in the middle of the river.

He had put his wife up on top of the car and got out his rod and reel and he was fishing away with water up to his armpits.  We always carried a well rope, so we tied onto his car and pulled it out.  He said, "You all go on back to camp.  I will have enough fish for supper by the time my car dries out."

When we started back out, it came a big rain, and all the side creeks were running bank full.  We didn't try to drive across them.  We tied a rope on the cars and pulled them across by hand with the engines dead to keep from getting water in the engines.

I remember the first long trip we made in automobiles was a trip to Albuquerque and Santa Fe.  We had some relatives up there we hadn't seen in several years, so we decided to go and see them.  We went through Jal, New Mexico, where my brother Ell and his wife Alice were living at the old JAL Ranch.  Of course, we stuck in the sand several times, but we had two cars, and we managed to get there finally.

We left the JAL's, headed north for Roswell.  Papa was a great believer in going in the general direction.  He didn't pay much attention to roads.  As long as they went the way he wanted to go, he used them; otherwise, he didn't let them bother him much.  We got in the middle of nowhere in the sand, and the front wheels picked up a big limb and rammed it clear through the radiator of the car that I was driving, and, of course, let all the water out of the radiator.  We did have two five-gallon cans of water along, so I took the pliers and tore out a thin part of the radiator and closed all the pipes the best I could.  I stuffed rags in the big hole and filled it up with water.  We were on an old wagon road that led to Loving.  It was crooked as a snake, and sandy as could be.

We finally reached the town of Loving.  There weren't enough people living there to fill one automobile.  But there was an old blacksmith shop that repaired wagons. I asked him if he could fix a radiator. He said, "I never saw one before." So I asked him if he had any solder. Yes, he said he did. I asked to use it, and he said, "Go ahead, if you think you can fix it." I took the radiator off and took the pliers and tore a big hole that you could run your hand through. Then I took the pliers and closed all the pipes that I could get to, and believe it or not, it held pretty good!

We started on to Roswell. The two cars we were driving were Pratt Elkhart cars. The one I was driving was a four-passenger car, and the one my brother Will was driving was a five-passenger car. We got out where we could run, and when we looked back, the other car was nowhere in sight. We went back to find them. Will's car had run a wheel off the left front. We jacked it up and found that the spindle had broken clear off. The thing that made it bad was there was not another one this side of Elkhart, Indiana. We loaded everything into the little car and finally made it to Roswell. A wrecker was sent after the car, and we ordered the necessary part.

We packed in like sardines in the little car, and went on to Albuquerque. We visited there a few days and decided to go on over to Estancia Valley where we had some more relatives. There was a hill on the way to Santa Fe that was once a mule trail, and had been made into a wagon road. It was a big steep mountain, and the bends in the road were too crooked for a car to make the turns. All of the folks got out and walked up the hill....they were afraid to stay in the car. Some of the bends, I had to back up three times to make the turns.

Papa would stay behind and put a big rock behind the wheel to keep the car from going off the mountain. We finally got up the hill, and I was a nervous wreck!! We stayed a few days with our folks at Estancia, then we went on over to Santa Fe. On the way, we came up behind a wagon with a pair of good horses hooked to it. The woman was driving and the old man was asleep up on the spring seat. When I honked the horn, those horses jumped out of their skins and the old man rolled off the wagon down the hillside and rolled clear down in a ditch 15 feet deep.

We finally got ahead of the team, and I got out and caught the bridles of the run-away horses and stopped them. The old man had to walk a quarter of a mile to catch up with his wagon. Papa said, "That's good enough for the old lazy thing....letting his wife drive while he slept!"

We headed back to Roswell to pick up the car we had left there. We got to Vaughn, and the station was out of gasoline. We didn't have near enough to make it to Roswell, but we started on anyway. We got out in the middle of nowhere and ran out of gas.

We looked and saw a sheep herder coming toward us. So I went out to meet the old Mexican in a covered wagon. Behind the wagon was a good horse saddled up. I told him we were out of gasoline. He said, "You won't find any gasoline anywhere between here and Roswell." I asked, "May I borrow your horse and go see if I can find someone on the road?" He said, "Yes, but a tourist borrowed this horse a few days ago, and he threw him off and killed him." I told him that was all right, I knew how to ride.

So I stepped on him, and I didn't give him time to buck. We left in a high run, headed toward Roswell. I hadn't gone three miles until I met a car coming and told him our trouble. He said, "I have plenty of gas. I filled up at Roswell." I told him to head down the road and I would follow. I got there at the same time he did and when I got back, that good brown horse didn't have any buck left in him.

We drew out enough gasoline to make it to Roswell, and the man in the car went on. When I got back in the car to start up, the car wouldn't move. All the bolts had fallen out of the drive shaft. It had about eight 5/16" stud bolts that held the universal joint together, and they had all worked out. I went back down the road, but didn't find a one of the bolts. There we were, sixty miles from Roswell with no drive shaft. I got under the car and started looking for some bolts that I could take out to put in the shaft. The boys had put a whistle on the muffler to show out before the girls. In putting it on, they had used three stove bolts, so I took them out. They were just the right length to go through the shaft holes. I put in three bolts and put the taps on and bradded them so they wouldn't come off and got in and started the car. It worked! We could see a big rain on the road just ahead of us. Sure enough, it poured down rain on us and the road really got muddy.

I would have to put the car in second gear and hit that mud as fast as I could to get through. All the time, I was thinking about those three little stove bolts, expecting them to strip any minute. The ground got so soft, I had to put on my mud chains. I just knew the chains would break my little bolts! But they didn't break. We made it to Roswell, and the axle we ordered was there, so we fixed the other car, and made it home without any more mishaps.

# WATER

Water on the EV Ranch has been a real problem ever since our folks settled there. They got the first well up in Panther Canyon in 1888, which was a life saver. They could not have stayed there without it. They dug two more wells there on the same stream of water, and got water enough to water the cattle. There are seventy sections of land on the EV Ranch, and we had to try and get water on other parts of the ranch.

In 1910, we drilled three wells—two of them dry—but one two miles below the ranch made less than six gallons a minute. We had to keep it running all the time. But even that was not enough. In 1912, we got another well southwest of the ranch that gave plenty of water. We piped this water three miles down the flat, but this well went dry and we had to run a pipeline from the ranch over there to it.

Then, in 1927, we drilled the second well at the little well below the ranch, and that helped out for a while. All this time, we were drilling lots of dry holes all over the ranch. Again in 1927, we got a well 630 feet deep seven miles below the ranch, but it was bad water; it ate up the tank and troughs. I had a pasture with eight sections in it and I drilled 13 dry holes on it before I got water. I pumped that well 8 months, and it went dry. All this time, we had used water witches and all kind of water hunters....still no water. All this time, I was learning something about water witching that has really paid off.

I have watered dry ranches all over the west half of Texas and most of New Mexico. I got a real big well on the EV ranch in December 1972, that will furnish water for the whole ranch. I trailed it close to the power line, so we have an electric pump on it. We ran the pipe down to the middle trough and tied into the main pipeline that goes all over half the ranch.

For some eighty years we have hunted for water at the Bloys Campmeeting. A number of wells have been drilled near the grounds. I know of four that were never equipped, and one pumped out. At first, we hauled water in barrels with a wagon and team. Then we dug a well that furnished some water. Later, we piped water from the Merrill Ranch several miles away, and it began to fail. We also at one time bought water from the Oscar Medley Ranch and piped it in.

During this time, Uncle John Means got Mrs. Knox Williams from Van Horn to witch a well, and we got a good well. We drilled another well beside it, and the two wells were sufficient for a while. But the Campmeeting grew until we needed more water. We drilled another well, but it only made 12 gallons per minute, so we didn't even equip it.

Mr. Joe Espy didn't like the idea of bringing water in just to have one week out of the year. He wanted to drill on our own land. So he told me if I would locate a place where I thought we could get water, he would pay for the drilling of the well. The Campmeeting Executive Committee agreed to equip it if the well would make 25 gallons per minute or more. I located a good well, we drilled, and got water on our own land. We took up the Medley pipeline, and ran it from the new well to the main pipelines. All the tanks were full of water at the close of the Campmeeting in 1973, and we didn't even have to pump all the time.

These are some of the great discoveries made by me in finding underground water.

# LION HUNTING

Keeping the panther from killing our cattle and deer was a job! I took over after my brothers left the ranch to start ranches of their own.

We had gotten about out of dogs. Papa was getting old and I was too busy looking after two ranches thirty miles apart. Most of it was done horseback, and I rode lots of miles between the two ranches. All this time, the panther were increasing all over the country. We got down to one old red hound we used to run hogs with. My neighbors were losing lots of stock killed by the panther and bear. I was in Valentine one day, and I saw a little blue tick female someone had lost on the river and had gone off and left her. I took her home and fed her up. When she got in shape, I bred her to our old red bloodhound and she had five pups. We raised three of them to be grown. I caught three lions with them the summer they were a year old, and then the old dog died. But those red speckled pups were natural-born lion dogs. I began to clear the ranches of lions. I caught sixteen out of John Moore's ranches, twelve out of the X-Ranch sheep pasture between Adobe and Rock House Canyons, and on and on until I had killed fifty-six lions and about twenty stock-killing bear with this pack of dogs. Then Bum Cowden gave me a registered bloodhound female and I bred her to old Fly, the only one of the dogs left. One of the pups got too hot running a lion, and someone stole the other one and took him to Louisiana to run bear with. I never did get him back.

This taught me a lesson—never run out of dogs. So every third generation of dogs, I went back to the kennels and got a pure English bloodhound to cross with my dogs. The two crosses of bloodhound and one of blue tick turned out the best big game dogs I have ever seen. It would fill a book just to tell all the bear and panther stories that I know! So, since I am writing history now, I will put those stories in another book.

But here, I am using one of the outstanding panther stories that was written by my brother Dub Evans when he and the New York doctor tied up some lion cubs and packed them in on pack mules. Here is the story just as it happened. Dub was a good hunter, and could write it up just exactly as it happened. He never stretched the truth. You can't say that about many hunters and fishermen.

Dr. Calvin of New York City reached Magdalena, New Mexico, on a Monday; and by previous arrangement was met at the Santa Fe depot at 8:30 AM by a service car driver who was to bring Dr. Calvin to the Evans Brothers Ranch that day. There was lots of snow on the road between the ranch and Magdalena, and they failed to make it out that day. They came out about halfway and the snow got so deep they turned and went back to Magdalena. Dr. Calvin phoned out and said he would make another trial the next day if he thought there was any chance to get through to the ranch. Dub Evans told him to come out as far as he could and he would come from the ranch to meet him, and that is what they did. They found lots of snow, but made it back to the ranch about 5:00 Tuesday evening. They made the necessary preparation that night to leave for a pack trip the next day, planning to camp near Jordan Canyon close to the east rim of the Middle Fork.

Dick Etheridge went with Dub and Dr. Calvin to take the pack outfit. They left early the next morning and went through the Black Mountains looking for lion sign. They camped near Green Fly tank about four o'clock that evening. The wind was blowing and it snowed hard all day, and was very disagreeable weather for riding. The next morning when they got up, they found that it had snowed two or three inches more over the eight-inch snow of the previous day, and was still snowing. Dr. Calvin was tired from the previous day's ride, so he stayed in camp with Dick, and Dub went out to look for sign.  He searched all day in the cold and wind and snow for sign, but didn't even see a cat track, but did see lots of deer.

That night back in camp, it was bitter cold—the coldest night they had ever spent out in camp.  They didn't have a thermometer with them, but back at the ranch headquarters that same night, it registered 18 below zero.

They were late getting off the next morning, but about ten minutes out of camp, they struck a cat trail.  They had only two dogs, Old Brownie and Little Brownie, and four pups.  It was just about the first hunt for these pups.  The men decided that trailing a cat would be good practice for the young dogs, so they let them stay on the trail.  It turned out that there were two cats, and luckily the dogs separated—Old Brownie and Little Brownie followed one trail down the canyon, and Short Brownie and the other three pups followed the one up the canyon.  Dub followed the dogs down the canyon and soon was able to shoot the cat and then he went back to look up the other dogs and Dr. Calvin and Dick Etheridge.  They had run their cat into a hole in the rocks, and the men decided to try to take her alive by tying her up, as Dr. Calvin wanted a live cat.  After working for a long time, they finally succeeded in snaring the cat and tying her up after pulling her out of the hole.

In the meantime, Little Brownie had gone off on another trail, so Dub followed after the dog, while Dr. Calvin and Dick returned to camp.   About a quarter of a mile north, Dub came on Little Brownie's tracks in the snow following a lion track.  He immediately put the other dogs on the trail, and unloading the dead and the live cats he was carrying on his saddle.  He followed the dogs, and soon heard them at bay.  They were barking at a lion in the top of a pinon tree, and about the time Dub reached the tree, he heard Little Brownie barking about one hundred yards farther on.  Dub soon discovered that Little Brownie had treed two lions and was running back and forth between the trees keeping them at bay, until the other dogs and the men arrived!

The men decided to shoot one of the lions and try to tie the other one up to take him back to camp. Dr. Calvin shot the one on the pine tree, and they proceeded to rope the other. First Dr. Calvin climbed the tree and tried to rope the lion. He was unsuccessful, so Dub climbed the tree; and for the first time in his life, tried to rope a lion up a tree! He succeeded in getting the rope on the lion's neck, but the lion jumped out of the tree and the rope came off, and there was the lion on the ground with the dogs. The lion hurried up another tree for safety. Dub climbed that tree and again he roped the lion, and again, the lion jumped out of the tree and pulled the rope off. The ropes were stiff and hard from the cold and the dampness, and it was very hard to draw them down about the lion's neck so they would hold. This second time the lion jumped out of the tree, Dick was successful in roping the lion and there was some quick action to keep the dogs off the lion so they could stretch him out and tie him.

They loaded the live lion across Dub's saddle in front of him, and returned to camp. Right near where they had found these two lions was a kill, a young deer, and it had been only partly eaten. They decided that there were more than two lions, and planned to return to the kill the following morning.

Sure enough, the next morning they returned to the kill, and there was sign indicating that there had been lions who returned to the kill the night before. They put the dogs on trail, and believe it or not, they discovered that there were TWO lions.

When the lions heard the dogs coming, they split up. The dogs treed the first one, and part of the dogs went on to tree the second lion. Dr. Calvin shot the second lion, and the men decided to tie up the first one and take it alive. Dick climbed the tree this time, and succeeded in tying two ropes securely about the lion's neck. Dr. Calvin took one rope and Dub the other, and they pulled that lion out of the tree. Dub said he had never seen any animal display more action than a freshly roped lion. They spring, turn, flop, and roll, striking in every direction with claws extended, he said. But by now, these men were experienced at tying up cats and lions, and they made short work of this one. They reached camp about noon and were very busy the rest of the day taking pictures and skinning the two dead lions. That afternoon, Dub went back for the cats he had left two days before, and when he saw that the cat he had left chained to a bush had freed its feet and its mouth, he decided just to kill it. He took the two dead cats back to camp and they had to skin them also.

The following day, Sunday, they packed up and headed for the ranch. They loaded the live lions on Kitty, a very dependable pack mule. After securely tying their feet and mouth again, they set them each in a Kiock (a box tied with a rope looped in each end to hang over the pack saddle.) Thus, the lions were facing toward the mule's head, tied so they could not get out, but biting and spitting at everything that moved!

Dub led the pack mule all the way home, and they reached the ranch about 5 o'clock in the afternoon, with the lions very much alive. They created no little excitement among Mrs. Evans and the children!

# A PANTHER HUNT AS I REMEMBER IT

We were working cattle out on the north pasture, and were gone until about five in the evening . While we were gone, Green Selman, our nearest neighbor, had seen a panther on top of Boracho Peak, and came to the ranch for my dogs. When he didn't find me there, he took the dogs and went back where he had seen the panther and put the dogs on his trail. They trailed the panther through all the bluffs on the mountain, and he got in the roughest place he could find and laid down on top of the highest rock he could find, where the dogs couldn't get anywhere near him. The dogs were tired, so they all laid down to rest. Mr. Selman, not knowing what this meant, called them off and started to the ranch.

When we got in, they told us he had come for the dogs and he still hadn't come in. I got a drink of water and started back to saddle up my horse to go hunt for my dogs. Lee Evans, my brother, was there, and he said, "I'll go with you." We hadn't gone but about a mile when we met Green coming in with the dogs. He told us about the race he had run with the panther all day. But he never did get a shot at the panther, and the dogs just gave out and quit. I knew why they quit—the panther was right where they quit!

When my old lead dog saw me, he forgot about being tired. He whirled around in the air and let out a long keen bark, and struck a run right back toward the peak. It was all we could do to stay up with him for nearly three miles before he stopped. He jumped up as high as he could and let out a long keen bark up a rock 50 feet high; and sure enough, the lion raised his head up. Lee shot him right between the eyes. He had to tiptoe in his stirrups to see the lion. When he shot him, he jumped straight out in the air, and landed right in between the horses, and did they jump and snort! It was dark when we got in with a tired bunch of men and dogs—and of course, the lion.

# THE GRIZZLY BEAR HUNT

We met at the Rock Pile Ranch which belonged to the Reynolds Cattle Company of Fort Worth, Texas, for most of our big bear hunts. We would have about five chuck wagons from the different ranches, and a hundred head of saddle horses, and forty or fifty hound dogs. We had one Mexican to herd the horses at night and another one to herd them by day. We always met in the fall of the year, and the weather would be cold enough to have a big bonfire. We would cut brush and pile it around the big fire for a windbreak. Then we would all get inside the big circle and tell some tall Texas stories. In most cases, the stories were new ones that happened that day about killing a bear—sometimes two or three in a day.

The most thrilling of all the hunts was when we killed the one and only Grizzly bear ever killed in Texas. In the summer of 1901, the section crew at Kent, Texas, was coming in on a hand car on the railroad. As they came by the water barrels, they saw a big bear coming from the north to get a drink out of the water barrels. He looked so big he scared them so badly, they all ran into their houses and closed the doors until the bear left and went south.

They told about the big bear. But everyone naturally thought him to be a black bear, and there wasn't anything said about it that year. But that fall the second day out, we came up on a cow that had been killed by a bear; and from the sign, it was different from anything we had ever seen. The brush was torn down and rocks turned over, and the cow had both horns broken off and her jaw pulled back and her tongue pulled out.

Most of our good bear dogs didn't bark. They just walked around stiff-legged with their bristles standing straight up. Out of forty dogs there were only four dogs that went off on the bear's trail: Papa's Old Brownie, Mr. Mayfield's Brandy, Mr. Finley's Old Drum, and one of Joe Morley's dogs (I forgot his name.) All of these were from different packs.

The men began to climb out over Livermore, and of course, the old bear crossed all of the brushy headers of Limpia Canyon. The dogs overtook him under a bluff on one of the south prongs of Limpia. John Means and Otie Finley heard the dogs barking at him. So they left their horses and climbed out on a little bluff where they could see. The old bear was right below them; and when he smelled them, he reared up on his hind feet, sniffing the air, trying to locate a smell that he had never smelled before. When he did, they both shot him right in the breast, and he bellowed like a bull. Some of the boys heard him miles away. There never was but one dog that went into him, and with one swat he broke this dog's back, jaw, and both hind legs. When he located the men, he headed straight for them, and both men emptied their guns into him, and melted him down right under the bluff they were sitting on.

One of them had a 30-30, and the other a 25-35, both small guns. After they were sure he was dead, Uncle John Means went down to look him over, and when he discovered they had killed a grizzly, he threw his hat up and said, "Ote, we have killed a grizzly!" He could tell from his size and his claws. They were long as a man's finger.

Some of the men had heard the shooting and began to gather in to the kill. They skinned him and left the head and feet on the hide. It was all a good horse could do to carry it. They did not try to come back across the mountains. They took him off to the Finley ranch and loaded him in a buckboard with a good pair of mules hooked to it, and it was dark when they got to camp by Rockpile. We were all waiting to see the hide. They unloaded it on a big rock, and it covered the whole rock.

I would like to take a picture of that rock to put in my history book.

# PIONEER PEOPLE I REMEMBER

It would be impossible to write pioneer history without using some of the names of people that made history. I will mention a few of them that I knew well, and that were our neighbors. I knew many more, but space will not permit me to tell all I remember!

One of the most interesting men I have ever known was Henry Mayfield, known to all as Old Moss. He wasn't old enough to go to the Civil War. But, he went anyway. He did lots of things he wasn't supposed to do, and I will relate a few of them.

He was one of the greatest story tellers I have ever known. When we were going to school on the ranch, we would ride 15 miles to spend the weekend with him. We would hunt rabbits and even those big lizards. We called some of them bear, and some panther, and some deer, and some antelope. He would join in the hunts with us.
In later years when he got old and needed some help to do something, he would call me to come and help him. He would make up any kind of a story just to get me over there. If it was possible to get off, I would go and help him. One time, he called me and said, "My dogs have a bear treed in the yard!" He knew I wouldn't believe him, so he called his wife to the phone to assure me that he was not lying. Sure enough, the dogs had a bear treed in the yard! He was a young bear about two years old and was crossing from one range of mountains to the other. He got thirsty and came by the tank to get a drink. The tank was about one hundred yards from the house and the dogs were loose, so when they saw him and began chasing him, he began looking for a tree. The only tree in the country was in the yard, so the bear jumped the yard fence and climbed the tree. He was still up the tree when I got there with my dogs. We got some ropes on him and pulled him down and put him in the smoke house until it got cool. Then, we let him out and gave him a good start before we put the dogs after him. They bayed him

on the side of a rough mountain, and we had a good time poking him out for another race. We had two packs of big old hounds, and they finally killed him.

Old Moss Mayfield would go to any length to play a joke on his neighbors. I remember one time he sent a Mexican fifteen miles horseback with a big hunk of meat. He wrote Papa a note and said, "I have just returned from Mexico where I killed an elk. I wanted you to have a piece of elk meat, so I sent you some." Papa smelled of it and said, "Burro meat," and took it and fed it to the dogs.

Joe Evans and Sam Means had been riding the range and they didn't have time to make it back to the Means Ranch before night. They decided to go and stay all night with Old Moss. When they got to his house, he wasn't there. But, in those days, nothing was ever locked, so they unsaddled their horses and fed them, and went in and made themselves at home. They thought Old Moss would come home soon. But he didn't. He had gone to Valentine after supplies and didn't plan to come back until the next day.

The next morning, they saddled up and started on to the ranch. They met Old Moss coming back in his old hack, so they stopped and talked a while. They told him they had spent the night at his house. "You did? What did you find to eat?" he asked. They said they made out fine. "We found some dried meat on the clothesline, so we cooked it and made some biscuits and gravy." "Dried meat! That was coyote meat I was drying for the dogs!" old Moss told them. He hit his mules with a whip and drove off.

The sun came out hot and those boys got to thinking about that coyote meat, and they began to get sick. They both just got sicker and sicker, until they just turned wrong-side-out. Of course, it was good dried beef, as dogs won't eat coyote meat, fresh or dry, but they never thought of that. They felt like killing old Moss the next time they saw him.  He got a good laugh out of that.

He was anything but a Christian man,  so everyone in the country prayed for him for forty years before he was converted.  It was a glorious day for everyone when Old Moss was converted under Dr. Truett's preaching.  He loved all of us boys, so he made a covenant with us to pray for each other every night at 9:00.  So the next year, he came to Campmeeting and told us boys, "I have got to 'fess up. One night I forgot to pray at 9:00.  I was going along in my hack with my dogs to catch a lion for one of my neighbors.  I looked at my watch, and it was after 9:00, so I stopped my team and got down on my knees and prayed for all of us."

"But," he said, "Twice this year, I had to ask the Lord for a recess. One time I was cleaning out my pen and the scraper hit a rock and threw me right up there between the mules.  I hung on until they made several rounds of the pen in a high run.  When they finally stopped, I climbed out from between them and sat down on the ground and I told those blankety-blank mules just what I thought of them!!"

"Another time, I was riding my trap line, and one of the traps had a big old coyote in it.  I got down and got me a good club and hit the old wolf a big lick on the head and tied him on my saddle and started home.  The old wolf wasn't dead.  He came to, and began to bite my horse in the flank.  The old horse bucked me off and went to the ranch.  I had to walk in.  But while I was on the ground, I had to ask the Lord for another recess to tell that old horse what I thought about him!  Do you reckon the Lord will ever forgive me for what I did?" We told him, sure, the Lord will forgive him if he would confess his sins and ask the Lord to forgive him.

You could write a book about him, and not cover all of the unusual things he did.  He lived past 90 years and was one of the greatest story tellers of all. He had had a lot of things happen to him in his lifetime and he never forgot any of them. It was the custom in those days for people to help each other. When a man got ready to build a house, he would have everything ready before he called on his neighbors to come and help him.

There were two old men who lived over in the top of the Davis Mountains. John Prude lived about three miles north of where the observatory is now, and Jim Nunn lived near the head of Cherry Canyon. As far as I know, they lived by themselves. Mr. Prude got his logs all cut and peeled and ready to start his log house. So, the first time he saw Jim Nunn, he asked him to come and help him lay his logs.

The logs had been cut and peeled a long time, so they would dry out and not be so heavy to lift when they got ready to stack them in the walls of the house. They had several of them laid in the walls when they started to lift one, and Jim Nunn raised up right slow and said, "John, I believe you had better lift this big end of the log. I hurt my back." So he walked around to the little end of the log, and when Mr. Prude reached down to get his hands under the log an old stinging scorpion stung him on the finger. Jim Nunn just fell over laughing. That scorpion had already stung him is why he wanted to change ends!! That is carrying a joke pretty far, not to dance a jig when a scorpion stings you!

Our folks landed in the center of Jeff Davis County on July 28, 1884. There were not very many people here at that time. Most of them were outlaws and cow and horse thieves. They were not good neighbors, but in 1885 and 1886, the people began to come in with their big herds of cattle and their families. I was born in 1895, so I remember all of those people. Most of them lived until I was grown, and I can tell you that they were real pioneers. They were the best people that ever lived. They believed in living and letting the other fellow live also. They would go to any length to be good neighbors. It wasn't long until the undesirables had to move on.

In those days, we knew everyone, as we had to work cattle from the Pecos River to the Rio Grande and all the people would work together. They would always throw their neighbors' cattle toward where they belonged. We also hunted big game together to keep them from killing our cattle. We got to know lots of the people hunting together. We lived near the center of the Davis Mountains, but we hunted with the men that lived on the north side of the mountains.

Some of them that I knew best, I will try and describe. You could write a book about each of them. But I will just mention a few of the outstanding things I remember about them.

We hunted a lot with four of these men that owned ranches on the north rim of the mountains. Bill Kingston would sell our cattle that got under the rim and we would sell his that topped out, as you couldn't get them back home. The country was too rough and we would send him money for the ones that we sold. That's how people trusted each other back then.

Bill Kingston looked just like Jed Clampett in the Beverly Hillbillies. I am sure Buddy Ebsen got his hat from Mr. Kingston. No one else ever had a hat that looked just like his. Every man was known by his hat after he wore it awhile. It got to looking just like the man who wore it. Bill Kingston would go to the Cattlemen's Convention at Fort Worth and he and his wife were both real hosts to everyone that came along. Soon, they began to ask people to come out and go bear hunting with him. Sure enough, one fall, about forty men took him up and began to write that they would be there to go hunting with him that fall.

Anyone else would have stopped a lot of them, but not Mr. Kingston. He borrowed horses and saddles from all his neighbors and killed some hogs and goats and beef and got ready to entertain his guests. The first morning, the dogs jumped a bear and headed up Madera Canyon. The bear began to run, and as he went over one of the lower hills of the canyon, they saw him, and all the men that were up in front began to shoot. The other men behind began to come up and ask where the bear was. Of course, the bear had gone out of sight, but it didn't bother those dude hunters. They were still shooting. When the others caught up and asked where the bear was, Mr. Kingston said, "Go to shooting. It is good shooting anywhere up the canyon!"

Mrs. Kingston was a great talker. When Bill would be telling a big story, she would say, "Wait a minute, Bill, let me talk awhile." They would go on and on, and the stories would get better and better. We kids loved to hear them both talking at the same time. She always went to the conventions with him. There were not any diners on the trains in those days. The trains had their own eating places, and they would stop the train and everyone would get off and eat. They would only give you twenty minutes to eat. Mrs. Kingston didn't like that way of eating, so she would cook up a lot of food and fill a big clothes basket full of stuff to eat. When it came time to eat, she would ask everyone on the coach where she was riding to come and eat with her, and lots of them did. She was the same type as Ma Kettle. They must have gotten a lot of the script for the show "Ma and Pa Kettle" from the Kingstons.

Mr. Bill Kingston's hunting partner was Doug Coleston who ranched in the Toyah country. They hunted a lot together. As you know, if you have ever hunted, some days just don't turn out right. They went hunting one day and they took along what we call a dude hunter—a man from the city. They got after a bear and the dogs topped over a big mountain, and by the time they got on top, the dogs were out of hearing. That country on the north side of the Davis Mountains is so rough and brushy you can't follow the dogs. They get away from you nearly every time. Anyway, they hunted for the dogs nearly all day and never did hear them again. And as in most cases in the fall of the year, the fog let down and they were lost. There were only two things they could do—either build a fire and wait until the fog lifted, or they could try to backtrack out. The ranch was in Cherry Canyon, the main canyon. They knew if they would go down one of the side canyons until they got to the main canyon, they could make it in to the ranch before night. When they reached the main canyon, they were so relieved they thought they would have a little fun out of the dude hunter. They stopped and began to argue about whether camp was up the canyon or down the canyon. One of them said the ranch was up the canyon, and the other insisted that he was turned around and that the ranch was down the canyon.

They had this man between them, so they both pulled their pistols and began to shoot over his head toward each other. They made out like they were really trying to kill each other. They would try and shoot around this fellow. He got so scared he put both his hands up and began to beg them not to kill each other. "If you boys kill each other, I will never find my way out of these mountains!" he said.

As I have mentioned before, the pioneer people were the greatest people who ever lived. I will relate some of the things that went on in the early days of the West. They knew all the holding brands and who they belonged to. They would go to any lengths to claim cattle that belonged to their neighbors, and brand the calves in the right brand and head them toward home. The Texas longhorns were entirely different from the cattle we have now. The old cows would fight for their calves to keep the varmints from killing them, and if you roped a calf to doctor it, she would get after you. If you didn't get to your horse, she would hook the pants off you. They were every color of the rainbow, and you could tell the calves, as they looked just like their mothers. I have seen an old cow with three calves with her, all unbranded—a calf, a yearling, and a two-year-old, still with their mother. You could tell from the coloring they were all hers, and no one ever questioned to whom they belonged, so they went right along with their mother.

In those days, a man's word was as good as his bond. We sold cattle for years without any forfeit or any contract. They buyers would ask how many you would have to sell and when they would be ready. I have sold thousands of cattle over the phone, sight unseen, and shaped them up myself before they left the ranch. I never had any cut back at the shipping point.

My wife's father was a real old timer. He had never done anything but ride a horse. He had been up the trail with herds of cattle. He never moved in his saddle. He could ride for hours and never move from side to side. He always said, "Ride straight like an Indian." His name was James Coats Powell. He came to this country from Coryell County with the rest of the pioneers. He ranched in the Fort Davis country and some of the Espy ranches are still named after him. He bought and sold thousands of cattle and when he bought a bunch, he would go and get them. When he sold some, he would deliver them to the buyer. I remember one time he had contracted some cattle and when he went after them they had gone up a few dollars a head. The cattle all sold by the head. We didn't know what scales were. Nothing was ever weighed. He told this man that cattle had gone up and he wanted to give him more than the contract called for! He was a great one.

One of his neighbors' houses burned down and Mr. Powell was talking to a man who said he was so sorry for the neighbor who had lost his home. Jim Powell said, "I am one hundred dollars sorry for him. How much are you?" All the cowboys loved him. He would help them out when they needed money. Most of them never paid him back. But he went right on giving money away as long as he lived. He lived to be 92 years old, and he would have made 100 if he hadn't fallen and broken his hip. That's what caused him to give up, as he couldn't get well after that.

Mr. Powell was a good big game hunter. He killed lots of bear and panther all over the country. He was one of a few that ever caught Lobo wolves with dogs. He rode so fast he would be there when the dogs overtook the wolf, and he would kill him when he turned on his dogs. You can't follow dogs any more—too many fences. In those days there were no fences to slow you down.

Jim Powell was a charter member of the famous Bloys Campmeeting and he was a regular camper for many years.

The Evans family moved to Valentine to send me and my sister Gracie to school in 1910 when I was in high school. The Finley family also moved in from their ranch and bought a house in town, as they had several young children to send to school. We were up at their house, or they were down at our house, and on the weekends, we would go to their ranch or they would go to ours. Their daughter Zora could play the piano real well and we had lots of sing-songs together. They were wonderful people and we loved them all. We were together all the time we were growing up. Mr. C. O. Finley, their father, was the man that helped John Means kill the grizzly bear. They were real close friends.

Just a few years before we were in Valentine, a man came around and put telephones in at all the ranches and gave all of us a list of rings to get our neighbors. I remember a lot of them: the Means ring was. . . (three shorts), the Evans ring was . . . - (three shorts and a long), and the Finley ring was . . . . (four shorts.) Uncle John Means got his phone, and the first one he called was Mr. Finley.

# Memories of a Ranch Wife

The Finley ranch was way up high next to the mountains and the Means ranch was down in the flat several hundred feet lower. The conversation started off, "Hello! Ote, can you hear me up there? I didn't know if you could hear me up that hill or not. I can hear you real good, as it is downhill all the way here!!"

Mr. Ote, as we called him, had hounds like everyone in those days did. One night something got into the chickens, and Mrs. Finley said to him, "Papa, something is into the chickens." She had made him a night shirt and he didn't like it. He said it was too long, so she cut it off too short. Mr. Ote got his old double barrel shotgun and started down the hill to the chicken house. He had his lantern in one hand and his gun in the other. But what he didn't know was his old hound dog was right on his heels. When he bent over to look in the chicken house, the old dog's cold nose was so close that it hit him under his short night shirt and he pulled off both barrels of his old No. 10 gauge shotgun and killed fifteen chickens.

So, he called his wife and told her to get up. "We have got fifteen chickens to pick and dress." So they worked the rest of the night dressing chickens. He called all his neighbors to come and help eat up the chickens.

He was a charter member of the Bloys Campmeeting and was treasurer for as long as he could see to write. He also was on the Executive Committee as long as he lived. I remember every time anything went wrong, he would say, "Wait a minute, boys. Let's don't do anything that would hurt anyone." He was the peacemaker of the committee.

*"Blessed are the peacemakers: for they shall be called the children of God."* (Matthew 5:9.)

I remember one time he had leased the old Circle ranch about 15

385

miles northeast of here to put some steers on. One time he was there by himself and an old cowboy came by just at noontime, and of course he asked him to eat dinner with him. They sat down to eat and Mr. Ote asked the blessing which was something new to this boy. He was on his way to Van Horn to get drunk and have a big time. He would always get drunk when he got to town. On his way to town, he got to thinking about that old man asking the blessing, and he began to realize he was a lost man. Instead of getting drunk, he went to church and was saved. He lost his taste for liquor and never drank any more. He turned out to be one of the greatest soul winners I ever knew. He was a circuit riding missionary all over New Mexico and Arizona.

# CATTLE BY THE THOUSANDS

I can remember when there were no cross fences anywhere in this country. The Southern Pacific Railroad was the south drift fence, and the Texas and Pacific Railroad was the north fence. The Means and Evans reached from Boracho to Valentine. Then the Reynolds Cattle Company reached from the south rim of the Davis Mountains to Jap Foster's on the north. They had lots of country north of the Texas and Pacific Railroad.

Jim Nunn's ranch joined the "X" Ranch and went on east to the rim of Madera Canyon, making a total of 800 sections of land all stocked with cattle, and of course, we had to go on all the works to get our cattle back. The Means, Evans and Reynolds ran a fence from Boracho to Valentine, a distance of forty miles, to divide the Means and Evans from the Reynolds. But every time it rained, the fence would wash down, and the three herds of cattle would get all mixed up several times each year. I remember some of the works when we would have round-ups so big you couldn't work them all in one day.

There had been a good rain out here at the Mexican Hill tank which is on the Hoskins ranch now. The country was all open from about the Wadell ranch to Valentine. Uncle John Means was using all of it. It was part of the Moon ranch. We threw the cattle together about 10:00 in the morning. The boss put ten men in the round-up— five on each side. They cut out the cows and calves until five o'clock before the men met in the middle. They cut on this round-up seven hours—ten of them. We didn't get all the calves out as some of them never did get with their mothers. We took the cut of cows and calves to a pasture at the little windmill and it took us three days to brand them out. We would go out and get what we thought we could brand in one day and pen them early and brand on them until night. The old-timers that were used to working big herds of cattle estimated we had six thousand cattle together.

The most calves I ever helped brand in one day was out here at Chispa where Coley Means lives now. The same thing happened. It rained out there and the cattle flocked in there from everywhere. We cut on them all day and threw the cows and calves in the horse pasture that night. It rained all night. It was in October and the calves were big and heavy. We had to wade in the mud all day. We had three men roping and three sets of flankers. Cole Means and I were flanking together. We branded 640 calves and I think they would have averaged 400 pounds each! It was the first day of the work, and our arms were sore the rest of the work.

The Means and Evans leased the old "W" ranch from the Johnson Brothers. The ranch lay east of the Pecos River from the T & P Railroad to past the state line of New Mexico. It was stocked with cattle—too many to count out, as you couldn't gather them all at one time. So, they estimated how many there were and bought them " range delivery." Range delivery means without tallying them out. We found out there were many more than the range delivery estimate. One year, we branded 6,000 calves and of course, we didn't brand them all. We had to brand them out of the round-up as there were no pens big enough to hold very many cattle. But they were small pens for horses. They were not big enough to hold the remuda we had. We caught the horses by stretching a rope around them. The way you do that is the wrangler runs the horses together and each man hands his rope to the next man until the horses are completely enclosed in a rope corral. Then the bosses begin to catch the horses as the boys call out the names of the horses they are going to ride. Each man is assigned a mount of ten horses and is given the names of horses in his mount.

The cattle were really wild sometimes and they would get away on the drive. The country was very brushy—mostly mesquite. The year after we branded the 6,000 calves, we sold all the yearlings, heifers, and steers and delivered them all at the same time. They were sold by the head and of course, some of them were not old enough to go in. They were not old enough or big enough for the buyer to take.

We had some six thousand cattle in the holding pasture at Pyote. We rounded them up and started to work on them. The pens at the pump station where we loaded them were small. We had to take them across the railroad to get to the pens, and we couldn't load very many at one time. Some of the men were cutting them out. Some were bringing them to the pens, while others were loading them on the cars. We worked hard and fast all day, and when the day was over the buyer paid us for 4,200 head of yearlings. We had to take some cows with each bunch, as you couldn't pen those wild yearlings without some cows. Then we would take the cows back and put them in the round-up. We had lots of help that day. All the Means and Evans were there and several of our neighbors helped us load out.

The reason cattle increased so fast in those days, there was no market for old cows. They were left on the range and had calves until they died of old age, and you couldn't sell just any kind of a calf. The only thing you could sell was steers from the yearlings on up to any age. This was the first time and the only time we ever sold a heifer.

All these stories I am writing are written exactly as they happened. I know, because I was a party of each and every one of them. They are not hearsay. I was there.

# BRANCHING OUT

Pioneer people continued to spread further west, so the second generation began to have cattle of their own. There wasn't enough room for the second generation. Some settled in western New Mexico where the country was just like the Indians left it. One of the ranches they bought west of Albuquerque still had some Indians left on it. Lee Evans was a man who never got discouraged when times got bad. He went to the bank and told them he was planning on buying a ranch west of Albuquerque and that he would need some money to get started. The bank asked how much he would need and he said, "Two or three hundred thousand dollars to buy a ranch and stock it with cattle." Of course the bank turned him down. "All right, I just wanted you to have the first chance to earn some interest. I will get the ranchers together and we will start our own loan company." Remember, he was in a new country as he was raised in west Texas and was a stranger there. But like his dad he did just what he told the bank he would do. He gathered a bunch of ranchers together and told them his plans. He had entertained some oil men on big game hunts and he took one of them in as a partner who had some money and could borrow a lot more, so they began to spread out. He warned those Indians that he would give them work and run their cattle if they would stay sober and quit gambling. But if they didn't, every time any of their land sold at sheriff's sale, he would buy it. Sure enough, he wound up with 400 sections of land stocked with cattle by staying on the job.

Just as he got his ranch built up, the oil people came along and leased his land for $60,000. Then they discovered uranium and gave him $40,000 lease on it. Then he began to have to pay enormous amounts of income tax. He had saved up 400 big steers to sell that same year. But of course he couldn't sell them on account of the high income tax he would have to pay. So he sent them to the feed pens in California and didn't sell them the same year.

He did so many good things with his money. He built a lodge and dug a well and fenced some land and stocked it with cattle for the old retired ministers to come to when they wore out from preaching. He also sent some fine young men through the Seminary to become preachers to take the old men's places. It didn't matter to him what denomination they were. He was also a big donor to the Boy's Ranch for their Christian training and many other good deeds too numerous to mention. I am enclosing a write-up of one of the buildings he donated which is self-explanatory.

G. W. Evans, Jr., also settled in western New Mexico at the V+T Ranch 85 miles from Magdalena. He had to take eight mules and a big heavy drag to drag a road to the ranch. The ranch reached southwest to the middle fork of the Gila River where he had a camp where they kept their horses in the winter. It later became one of the greatest hunting and fishing camps I have ever known. He still owns it and he made a hunting lodge out of it. We went there for years on our big game hunts. You could go any direction from this camp and catch a bear or a panther or kill a deer or wild turkeys. Or you could go down to the river and catch all of the mountain trout you could eat and bring some back to camp.

The bad part was the long drive to drive the cattle. It was 100 miles from the back side of the ranch to the shipping point at Magdalena. It took several days to make the drive, and it was always cold up in the high country and real hard on the cowboys to face the northers.

On one of the drives GW told the Indians he would take all the mustang horses they could have in the pens at Magdalena and when they got there they had 35 little wild horses in the pens. They were not ponies—they were real small horses. They threw them in the remuda and took them back to the ranch where the boys started breaking them. They were so small a saddle would cover one up. When they got grown they could carry a 200-pound man up and down those steep mountains. They could jump any log they could get their heads over.

He had taken a man in as a partner who was a rancher and a banker. He would lend money to the ranchers; and when times got bad, he would foreclose and the rancher would lose all he had paid on the ranch and the interest also. But Dub was about as smart as he was. He offered the old man nine different block-outs on the C-N ranch on the Augustine plains that they had bought together, and he wouldn't accept any of the propositions. So he blocked Dub off on the Montosa forest where it was so brushy you couldn't round up the cattle. You had to put the water troughs in the pens and shut the gates, and go and let the cattle in to water and then turn them in the holding pasture. But like always, the Lord takes care of his own. The Lord gave me the talent to find water, so I located eight wells for him. Then there was a bug got in those pine trees and killed thousands of them. Now you can round up the cattle. Dub bred up this herd until they were about the best cattle in that country. The cows would weigh 1200 pounds and the long yearling would weigh 700 pounds. The country was too brushy with very little water on it when he had to take it or get nothing for thirty years' work. Now it is one of the best ranches around. So this goes to prove you can't go wrong by doing right.

# THE LAST OF THE GRIZZLIES

The last of the grizzlies in the Black Range took his stand near the top of the range where the canyons head, leading southwest to the Gila River. The brush is so thick you can't see out. There is under brush and tall trees; the only way you can see is to look across the canyons, and in the fall of the year it has the most beautiful coloring—the leaves on the trees are yellow, red, and golden colors of all shades.

The ranch that uses this country is the old GOS. It is so out of the way. No one except the cowboys and the forest rangers ever ride in there. We took a pack outfit and went 30 miles back in there. Ten men in camp for ten days and we never saw a cowboy or a ranger. There were mountain trout in the creeks and deer by the hundreds. The bear and panther and wild turkeys were plentiful.

We weren't after the grizzly on this hunt, but we saw some of his sign, where he and a full-grown bull met on the side of a hill in a forest trail. Neither of them gave way to the other. The old bear knocked the bull off the trail and they tore down brush all the way down the hill. When the fight was over, the bull was dead and the grizzly was full of bull.

Up near the head of the Membres River the GOS had built a wild cow pen nine feet tall. They fixed some poles that stuck into the pen that you could push in between to get in where they put salt in, but the poles had sharp ends on them so when the cattle tried to get out, the poles would stick in their shoulders and they couldn't get out. We found where three big old stags had gone in to lick salt, and they couldn't get out. The old grizzly came along and found them in the pen. He went in and killed all three of them. He ate on them for a long time. I saw the bones of the steers. The poles didn't bother him—he just took his arms and opened them up and went in and out when he got ready.

A few years later, GW Evans, better known as Dub, decided to go after the grizzly. Several of his hunting partners went with him. They had four packs of dogs and the owners went along. One of them was our brother, Lee Evans, the one I have already written about. They took a pack outfit and went way back near the top of the Black Range where the old bear was killing cattle. They found where he had killed a cow and was still eating on her, so they went back early next morning and put the dogs after him. Out of the four packs of dogs, very few would go on after him. After miles of running him, all the men got thrown out of the race except Lee and Dub, and all the dogs had had enough of that bear except Dub's old Brownie dog. It was so rough and brushy that Dub had to leave his horse and go on foot. Every time the old dog would bay him, Dub would try and get to them; but the brush was so thick he couldn't see the bear. The bear finally took his stand in the head of a canyon that was so brushy he could see the brush move, but he couldn't get a shot at the bear. The old dog kept on barking at him to let Dub know where the bear was. The race wound up with one man and one dog, and they were playing hide-and-seek in the brush. But Dub was determined to kill him. He said when he realized they were trying to see which one would get killed, he was crawling through the brush, and there was the old bear's track on top of his, and he really got frightened. But the old dog would bark to let him know where the bear was. The old bear got so tired, he laid down and Dub could see the brush move as the bear breathed. He finally made out his form and shot. He had a big gun and he hit a vital spot, and the bear raised up and fell off down the hill, breaking the brush as he went. Dub could tell the bear was dead by the way the dog barked. He climbed up the mountain and began to give the signal shots two at a time until he got an answer from Lee, who came and helped him skin the bear. They put the hide on Lee's horse and one of them led him, and the other one walked behind and poked the horse with a limb.

He was so tired they finally had to leave the hide and come back the next day after it. I saw his hide after Dub had it mounted. It was so big it would cover a double bed like a bedspread.

These men I am writing about are all dead and gone. Lest we forget, I am jotting down some of the things that the pioneer people did that I know about. I am one of the few left, and I am 80 years old.

# JOHN Z. MEANS

I knew all the pioneer people that settled in West Texas and a lot of people in Southern New Mexico. But I am writing about the ones that I knew best, as I am not writing anything but facts. My mother's brother who came west with my folks was John Z. Means. I will try and write some of the things I remember about him.

He and my father were the closest of friends, even before Papa married John's sister, and they remained so throughout their entire lives. Uncle John was my real uncle, but many of his friends called him Uncle John. He had the greatest personality of anyone I have ever known. He was always surrounded by people listening to his stories. He was the best story teller of all people. He made friends with everyone. That's how he got his start. He lived near George Medley over on the south side of the Davis Mountains, and they became real close friends. When Mr. Medley decided to buy the Moon Ranch, he took Uncle John in as a partner. They bought the cattle "range delivery" as they were scattered over so much country, it was impossible to count them out. Sure enough, they got twice as many cattle as they paid for. This was in the early 1890's, and it was not long until Uncle John bought Mr. Medley out and also got more cattle than they estimated. This gave Uncle John a start. Then the Tally ranch came on the market and he wanted to buy it. Remember, there were no banks out here at that time. He had to have some money to pay down on the ranch. He had been trading with a man that ran the Keesey Store at Valentine. He was an old bachelor and had saved up about $2,500, and Uncle John asked him for the use of it to make a down payment on a ranch four miles north of Valentine, and the man let him have it. He also bought the cattle range delivery, as there wasn't any way of counting them out, as there were no holding pastures at that time. He bought these cattle at $6 per head and he got twice as many as he paid for. So it made them cost him about $3. The country counting both ranches reached from the Wadell Ranch to Valentine and from Wild Horse to Chispa. Remember, you couldn't sell an old cow or a heifer in those days, just steers from yearlings up. You have never seen cattle increase so fast as when you can't sell any she stuff. Anyway, in 1905, we went on the work and branded over 4,000 calves and cattle had gone up to $10 per head. In the meantime he had sold enough steers to pay the cattle out, leaving him about ten thousand cattle at $10 per head. But it wasn't but about 3 or 4 years until the State land came on the market, and it cost the ranchers a small fortune to buy it from the nesters. Some of it they never did get back.

Uncle John and my Dad always hunted together. Papa would take the dogs up the canyons, and Uncle John would top out and take a stand where he knew the bear would come out; and if he didn't tree, he would always come out where Uncle John took his stand. He would never get behind a tree—he would always sit in front so he would not have to move, which could cause the bear to smell him and go the other direction. He learned this when hunting wild turkeys down in central Texas. He said turkeys would always fly if you looked around a tree. Uncle John Means knew more about working cattle than anyone I have ever known. He could keep two or three cows and calves on the way to the cut and never strike a lope. He trained his horses to always be in the right place. When a cow looked back on one side, there he was looking her right in the face. Then she would look back on the other side, and there was the horse looking her right in the face. Then she would look at the cut and out she would go, and when we got ready to pen the cattle he would ride around and get in the gate, and he wouldn't move until all the cattle got up to the gate. Then he would just ride out and the cattle would pour into the pen. Then we could get them all in before they had time to circle the pen and come back out.

# "THE OLDTIMERS"
### By Paul Means Evans

A bunch of cowpunchers grew up in the West,

 At roping and riding, we all did our best.

We rounded up cattle from morning 'til night,

 While our mothers were praying we would all turn out right.

We pioneered Texas and New Mexico;

 We would have moved farther west, but there was no place to go.


We hunted big game all over the West.

 For horses and dogs, we had the best.

When the frost started falling and the leaves turned red,

 Look out, Mr. Bear, for you will soon be dead.

The only reason we didn't go bad,

 We had the best training that boys ever had.


When the branding was over, we rested the herds,

 Attending Campmeeting to feast on God's Word.

The ranchers had daughters all up in their teens,

 So we dressed up like dudes, and discarded our jeans.

We found what we had looked for all of our lives,

 So we fell in love and made them our wives.

# Memories of a Ranch Wife

Now we are all wrinkled and old and gray,
  But how sweet the memory of that blessed day.
There is no problem too big to bear,
  If you have a companion that's willing to share.
God gave to man the right to choose,
  If you live a clean life, you will never lose.


We have gotten too old to work cattle and hunt,
  We limp around and hurt and grunt.
We can't do the things we used to do,
  So we drag out the tables and play forty-two.
We all claim we are champs,
  We sit and play 'til we get the cramps.


It won't be long 'til we will all be due,
  But the good Lord has promised to make us anew.
Our only regret is we didn't do more
  To help people reach the other shore.

# A COWBOY'S CHRISTMAS PRAYER
## *Author Unknown*

I ain't much good at prayin', and you may not know me, Lord.

I ain't much seen in churches, where they preach the Holy Word.

But you may have observed me out here on the lonely plains,

A'looking after the cattle, feelin' thankful when it rains.


Admirin' Thy great handiwork, the miracle of grass,

Aware of Thy kind spirit in the way it comes to pass,

That hired man on horseback, and the livestock that we tend

Can look up at the stars at night and know we've got a Friend.


So here's old Christmas coming on, remindin' us again

Of Him whose comin' brought good will into the hearts of men.

A cowboy ain't no preacher, Lord, but if you'll hear my prayer,

I'll ask as good as WE have got for all men everywhere.


Don't let no hearts be bitter, Lord, don't let no child be cold.

Make easy beds for them that's sick, and them that's weak and old.

Let kindness bless the trail we ride, no matter what we're after,

And sorta keep us on Your side, in tears as well as laughter.

# Memories of a Ranch Wife

I've seen old cows a'starvin', and it ain't no happy sight:
Please don't leave no one hungry, Lord, on Thy good Christmas night
No man, no child, no woman, and no critter on four feet—
I'll aim to do my best to help You find 'em chuck to eat.

I'm just a sinful cowpoke, Lord—ain't got no business prayin'—
But still I hope you'll ketch a word or two of what I'm sayin':
We speak of "Merry Christmas", Lord, — I reckon You'll agree
There ain't no Christmas, Lord, for nobody that ain't free.

So, one more thing I'll ask You, Lord, Just help us as You can
To save some seeds of freedom for the future sons of man!

# PEACH COBBLER RECIPE

*Following is a peach cobbler recipe that I gave first to Mrs. Taylor (Helen) Norman. She loved my peach cobbler and asked for the recipe. Here is what I gave her:*

"Enough peaches to make as much pie as you will need. You can tell how much you need by the number of people you are going to feed.

Drain off the juice of the fruit into a pan the size you will need for the right amount of pie. If you don't have peaches, plums will do. Sometimes I make it out of apricots. They are good, too. If you do not have enough of one kind of fruit, mix them all together. That makes it better.

Put a hunk of butter, or more, in the juice.

Put enough flour in a pan to make the right amount of pie crust. You make pie crust just like you make biscuits, only you put in more grease. Make the crust dough stiff enough to roll out real thin. Take a saucer and cut the dough into round pieces. Put your fruit on the dough and fold over like you are making fried pies, and drop into the juice and butter warmed enough to melt the butter.

Add enough sugar and nutmeg to make it taste good. Cook it until it is the right color brown.

Serve with good, thick cow cream.

If you follow these directions CAREFULLY, you will never have a failure.

# HUNT IN DAVIS MOUNTAINS IN 1899

*Excerpt from "The Terrells, Eighty-five Years, Texas from Indians to Atom Bomb."—C. V. Terrell*
*Authorized and approved by the Texas Heritage Foundation. Printed for the author by Wilkinson Printing Co., Dallas, Texas, 1948.*

In the fall of 1899 John Means, Evans and his sons, invited my brothers, John and Preston, and me to another deer and bear hunt in the Davis Mountains. Means lived about five miles north of Valentine on the southern Pacific Railroad. We accepted the kind invitation and as agreed all of us met them at Valentine soon after daylight and in their hack they carried us to the Means ranch where we ate breakfast and began arranging to go to the Rockpile Ranch in beyond Sawtooth Mountain and at the foot of Mount Livermore, the highest peak in the southern range of the Rockies in the Davis Mountains. Means' home was known for its hospitality and he was an old-time Westerner and as fine a character as one ever meets. He was the real leader of that section as well as the leader of our hunt. His main assistant was Joe Evans, his nephew, Joe's father having married Mr. Means' sister. After breakfast Brother Preston, who was a splendid musician, especially on the piano, seeing the piano, without invitation, sat down and began to play to the delight of the two single daughters of Means, Miss Barbara and her sister, who had attended Baylor University and they both sang beautifully and played the guitar and the piano well. We all began to sing old-time songs and had a general good time. That was the first time I ever heard the song "In the God Old Summertime."

Soon everything was ready and our horses saddled. All of the Means and Evans families went with us on the hunt including all the ladies. Each of us had guns in scabbards buckled to our saddles, pistols in our belts around us, leggings to protect us while running through the catclaws and brush, spurs, and everything necessary for a good hunt. Brother Preston, who was a hardware man, was unlike Brother John and I, had never ridden a horse much. As he mounted his horse with his armament that he showed he was not used to carrying, he turned to Means and asked if he did not think he looked like Sam Bass, the noted bandit. Means' reply was, "Yes" and from that moment on Preston was called only "Sam Bass." There were at least thirty of us in the party and we arrived at the Rockpile Ranch about one o'clock in the afternoon. There was a large two-roomed house where the women slept and we slept out under the stars. The Mexican cooks had preceded us and had killed a yearling and had him drawn up with a rope and pulley to a limb up in a tree. This was in October and the mountain air was cool; no flies were about and the meat would not spoil and we ate it as we needed it.

There were several other cowmen who came and hunted with us. John T. Cowden, Sr., and his wife, of Midland, were with us. Mr. Prude who had a ranch just south of our camp came out, and so did John Holland of Alpine who brought with him an old time fiddler who added greatly to our entertainment.

The first day we started early on our bear hunt and after we struck the bear trail, we always divided, part of us following dogs after the bear and the other bunch taking a stand in the gap of a mountain where the bear would more than likely run in trying to escape from the dogs. That day I was with those who took a stand. The crowd killed the bear before he reached the gap in the mountains where we had taken a stand. We heard the shooting and soon the blowing of the horn calling the dogs all together. We knew they had the bear. We soon rode to the tree where they had killed a very large black bear. Brother Preston, not being used to riding horseback, had fallen far back behind and in our excitement we ran off and left him. After the bear was killed, we blew our horn, shot our guns, thinking he might hear us and come to us but all in vain. We returned to camp about one o'clock, ate our well prepared meal with ravenous appetites. Still uneasy about "Sam Bass" as we called Preston, we decided to organize a party to hunt him, feeling sure he was lost and unable to find the camp; but as we were getting ready to hunt him about four o'clock that afternoon, he came slowly riding in. He was utterly lost, he said, and he thought camp was one way and his horse wanted to go the other way. He said he knew his horse had more sense about the country than he did so he gave the horse his way and the horse brought him safely in. He knew he was lost and said he rolled a cigarette and got out one of his two matches to light it with but decided that if he had to stay out all night in the mountains, he would have to have a fire to keep from freezing so he threw away the cigarette and saved his two matches.

The next day we killed a large black bear that had two cubs about six months old. I had the same bad luck that day, as I was with the party that followed the dogs, and it was the party that took the stand that got the bear. Sam Bass was so sore from riding that he did not go with us that day but walked up on one of the nearby mountains to see if he could kill a deer. He said up on top of the mountain he was slowly walking and a large beautiful black-tailed buck jumped up and stood broadside looking at him about thirty yards away. He said he attempted to throw a cartridge into the barrel of the gun to shoot him and the lever hung. The deer ran off while my brother was working to get his gun unhung and he never saw him anymore. He said he knew no one would believe him and he just brought his gun to show us that it was hung and that it was not "buck-ague" that saved the life of the deer. Mr. Means took the gun, gave the lever a quick jerk, threw the cartridge into the barrel, and it was ready to shoot, and said, "Your gun was not hung; you just had the "buck-ague." The crowd all laughed and Sam Bass said, "I'll be darned!"

On the following day we left camp before daybreak. I was riding in front with Means. Old Rock, the bear dog that would not run any trail except a bear, was in our front. The other boys were to our rear holding the necked dogs back. We were not much over a mile from camp when I thought I saw a black bear in front and to our left in the distance coming down the mountain. I stopped and showed it to Means. He put his field glasses on it and replied, "Yes, it's a bear." He yelled to the boys to come on, that we saw a bear. He said, "If we ride fast, we may get to where he crosses the trail in front of us and have a sight run for him." The bear, however, beat us a little and crossed the trail about three hundred yards ahead of us. When Old Rock crossed his fresh trail in the damp frosty morning, he began to bark and turned west up the mountain. The boys turned all the dogs loose—about fifty three in all—and they immediately hit the trail and we sat on our horses and watched the bear about one-quarter of a mile in front of the dogs climbing the sloping mountain. The dogs— some of them solid red and dark and some spotted—were all doing their best to get to the bear first, and each of them was giving us the melody of his familiar bark. Evans decided we would take a stand on the other side of the mountain, and Joe Evans and Brother John follow the dogs. They overtook the bear and dogs just as they went over the mountain, the dogs being hot in the pursuit of the bear. On seeing the men on horseback, the bear attempted to climb a tree, but one of the dogs caught him by his leg and pulled him back to the ground. He turned and slapped one of the dogs against the ground and broke his back. Brother John dismounted and shot the bear in the head. He fell as if dead, and Brother John ran up to him and Joe Evans yelled to him to go back, that the bear was not dead. The bear trembled a few seconds and revived and they both shot and killed him. The wound in his head had only dazed him and the bullet did not enter his skull but glazed around it.

The next day we decided we would hunt bear south of the camp in a canyon north of Mt. Livermore. Sam Bass, having rested for two days, decided he would go with us that day. We soon struck the trail of a bear and we ran him south and around Mr. Livermore and brought him back to the canyon where we started him. The bear was thin in flesh and could climb the rugged cliffs while the dogs had to go around. My brother not being able to keep up had gone on his horse in south of the canyon and as the dogs brought the bear around the mountain, he saw Sam Bass in front of him and the dogs close behind. He climbed up a tree about two hundred yards in front of Sam Bass. As we rode over the foothill following the bear and the dogs, we saw Sam Bass, the bear, and the dogs. We stopped and Means took his field glasses and gave us the following report:

"The bear is climbing a tree. Sam Bass is galloping up toward the tree that the bear is in. He takes his gun out of the scabbard and is taking aim at the bear. He lowers the gun, puts it on the ground, goes to his horse and is taking something out of his saddle bags behind his saddle." I said, "It's his Kodak." Means said, "Yes, he is taking the bear's picture. He lays his Kodak down on the ground, picks up his gun, shoots the bear; the bear falls to the ground and the dogs all cover him."

We at once ran our horses down there and found that Sam Bass had rolled a cigarette, lighted it and was smoking, standing by the dead bear with one foot on the bear. As we rode up, Sam Bass, directing his remarks to Means, said, "If you d—-fellows could keep up, you would be able to kill a bear."

The fourth day we again went bear hunting to our west toward Sawtooth Mountain. Several of the ladies had their horses saddled and went with us. Soon we struck the trail of a bear. The bear was thin and long winded and climbed over the high cliffs that the dogs had to go around and thereby they (the dogs) lost distance. Ten of the cowboys in the party and I cut across, rode fast and took a stand in the gap in the mountain while the ladies and the others in the party followed the trail of the dogs and the bear. As both of my brothers had fortunately killed a bear on that trip, they were all so generous that they wanted me to get one also. After we had dismounted, tied our horses, and taken our stand on the cliffs overlooking the pass where we expected the bear to cross, one of the crowd suggested that they all refrain from shooting and let me have the first shot and if I did not kill him, they would. This was agreed to by all but one who was slightly deaf [Will Evans] and did not hear the agreement. Soon we saw the bear some two miles off followed by the eager barking dogs. In a few short minutes the bear started across the gap directly in front of us about two hundred yards away. The boy who was hard of hearing, not understanding our arrangements, began to shoot and as the bear did not stop, we all began to shoot at him and had ample time to empty our guns. A Mexican cook had shot two cartridges out of my gun and I did not know it so I had only three shots and the others had five each making fifty-three shots fired at that running bear, each of us claiming we hit him. But the bear never stopped nor faltered but ran out of sight to the north. We all went down where the bear had passed and we found no blood nor the slightest sign that any of the fifty-three shots had hit him, and finally he outran the dogs and was never seen by any of us again. The ladies were with Mr. Means and several of the men about a mile away had heard our cannonading. They found out that we had failed to hit the bear and when we rode up, one of the ladies stated that they heard our shooting and thought it was a Japanese and Russian battle, those countries being at war at that time.

In five days hunt we killed six bears. One day we got an old one and her two cubs about half grown. So it was not only a very successful but delightful hunt as all were out for a good time and our hosts were vying with each other to see that we were entertained.

In addition to our violin and guitar music and singing old time songs, we had a colored boy and one of Mr. Means' sons [Huling] who danced for us. They danced in unison and gave us as fine a show as one rarely sees in our modern movies. The sad part of our hunt was breaking camp telling all goodbye, as we knew that many of us would never meet again and renew our pleasant friendships.

John Means and Evans, and I think their wives, are all gone, but such noble, thoughtful, and interesting characters will long live in the memory of all who were fortunate enough to have known them, and especially those who shared their friendship on that pleasant and interesting hunt.

# PIONEER OF TEXAS CATTLEMEN PASSES AWAY

## HELPED ROUT FIRST RUSTLERS FROM BIG BEND

Fort Worth, classic of George Washington Evans, 76, as well as those of the Big Bend country and the Davis Mountain—in fact, all over Texas where the happenings of life continues in spoken, were grieved to learn of his death recently at Valentine.

Evans, according to friends who knew him, not only made a success in business, but is also quite a philosopher, a fact that his readers will know when they read of one of his many sayings—"He was alone in the wilderness, and failed 14 hours and ten days. They put up 70 gallons of honey oil, and although they didn't kill a bear, had front meat on the table every day and plenty of lard in the kitchen. Evans often told friends

### Rustler Attracted

The country began to develop, and more people came and laid out their ranches and founded their ranch. This attracted the southern cattle raisers. But Evans and Moore, leading the fight waged with cattle, for that the Davis Mountain was a renewal of bloodshed before other cattle sections. On one occasion they found 18 cattle guarded by rustlers who had burned out the brands and were returning. This two men drove the cattle to town and before daybreak they turned to their rightful owners with the exception of 18 head. Eventually the bones of the two

### Nine Children Survive.

Evans was a husband to ...
Hat Evans, who ...
American ...
with the Fort Davis ...
Congregation of the ...
charge of the service at the ...

Nine children were ...
mains of G. W. Evans ...
Evans, and ...
with Mrs. Evans ...

The others are: Mrs. Bill Co... den of near Alpine; Mrs. Grace Co... ton of Marfa; Mrs. J. W. ... L. Evans ... Evans ...

The pall-bearers were: Al... Brown ... Valentine ... J. W. Scott ...

G. W. Evans, '76, pioneer ranchman ... Davis Mountain sections, who died recen... "the friend of man."

Made in the USA
Monee, IL
18 September 2019